Organized Labor
and
American Politics
1894–1994

SUNY Series in American Labor History
Robert Asher and Amy Kesselman, Editors

Other books in this series include:

Charles Stephenson and Robert Asher eds., *Life and Labor: Dimensions of American Working-Class History*

Joyce·Shaw Peterson, *American Automobile Workers, 1900–1933*

Daniel Rosenberg, *New Orleans Dockworkers: Race, Labor, and Unionism 1892–1923*

Martin Halpern, *UAW Politics in the Cold War Era*

Michael Cassity, *Defending a Way of Life: An American Community in the Nineteenth Century*

Craig Phelan, *William Green: Biography of a Labor Leader*

Salvtore Salerno, *Red November, Black November: Culture and Community in the Industrial Workers of the World*

Richard W. Judd, *Socialist Cities: Municipal Politics and the Grass Roots of American Socialism*

Gerald Meyer, *Vito Marcantonio: Radical Politician, 1902–1954*

Howard B. Rock ed., *The New York City Artisan, 1789–1825: A Documentary History*

Robert Asher and Charles Stephenson eds., *Labor Divided: Race and Ethnicity in United States Labor Struggles, 1835–1960*

Eugene V. Dennett, *Agitprop: The Life of an American Working-Class Radical: The Autobiography of Eugene V. Dennett*

Amy Kesselman, *Fleeting Opportunities: Women Shipyard Workers in Portland and Vancouver During World War II and Reconversion*

Michael Marmo, *More Profile Than Courage: The New York City Transit Strike of 1966*

Beverly Stadum, *Poor Women and Their Families: Hard-Working Charity Cases, 1900–1930*

Elaine Leeder, *The Gentle General: Rose Resotta, Anarchist and Labor Organizer*

Perry K. Blatz, *Democratic Miners: Work and Labor Relations in the Anthracite Coal Industry, 1875–1925*

Chaig Phelan, *Divded Loyalties: The Public and Private Life of Labor Leader John Mitchell*

James R. Zetka, Jr., *Militancy, Market Dynamics, and Workplace Authority: The Struggle Over Labor Process Outcomes in the U.S. Automobile Industry 1946–1973*

Ronald L. Filippelli and Mark D. McColloch, *Cold War in the Working Class: The Rise and Decline of the United Electrical Workers*

Robert Asher and Ronald Edsforth eds., *Autowork*

Paul Buhle and Dan Georgakas eds., *The Immigrant Left in the United States*

James J. Lorence, *Organizing the Unemployed: Community and Union Activists in the Industrial Heartland*

Edited by
Kevin Boyle

Organized Labor
and
American Politics
1894–1994

The Labor-Liberal Alliance

State University of New York Press

HD 6510
.073
1998

Production by Ruth Fisher
Marketing by Nancy Farrell

Published by
State University of New York Press, Albany

For information, address State University of New York Press,
State University Plaza, Albany, NY 12246

Library of Congress Cataloging-in-Publication Data

Organized labor and American politics, 1894–1994 : The labor-liberal
alliance / edited by Kevin Boyle.
     p.   cm. — (SUNY series in American labor history)
  Includes bibliographical references and index.
  ISBN 0–7914–3951–8. — ISBN 0–7914–3952–6 (pbk.)
  1. Trade-unions—United States—Political activity—History.
2. Liberalism—United States—History. 3. United States—Politics
and government—19th century. 4. United States—Politics and
government—20th century. I. Boyle, Kevin, 1960–   . II. Series.
HD6510.073   1998
322'.2'0973—dc21   97–47472
                                                                        CIP

10 9 8 7 6 5 4 3 2 1

For
Sidney Fine

Contents

Acknowledgments ix

Introduction • *Kevin Boyle* 1

Part One: Building the Labor-Liberal Alliance

1. The Rules of the Game: Class Politics in Twentieth-
   Century America • *Richard Oestreicher* 19

2. Producerism is Consciousness of Class: Ironworkers'
   and Steelworkers' Views on Political
   Economy, 1894–1920 • *Robert Asher* 51

3. Negotiating the State: Frank Walsh and the Transformation of Labor's Political Culture in
   Progressive America • *Julie Greene* 71

4. The Failure of Minnesota Farmer-Laborism •
   Peter Rachleff 103

5. Autoworkers, Electoral Politics, and the Convergence
   of Class and Race: Detroit, 1937–1945 •
   Bruce Nelson 121

Part Two: The Labor-Liberal Alliance at Work

6. The CIO Political Strategy in Historical Perspective:
    Creating a High-Road Economy in the Post-
    war Era   •   *Stephen Amberg*   159

7. Thoughts on Defeating Right-to-Work: Reflections on
    Two Referendum Campaigns   •
    Gilbert J. Gall   195

8. Little More than Ashes: The UAW and American
    Reform in the 1960s   •   *Kevin Boyle*   217

9. Labor Law Revision and the End of the Postwar
    Labor Accord   •   *Gary M. Fink*   239

Contributors   259
Index   261

Acknowledgments

Stuart Kaufman was a driving force behind this volume. He served as co-organizer and host of the 1994 conference from which most of the essays are drawn. He presided over the two days of discussion with his customary grace and good will. And he supported the idea of publishing the papers at the conference. Stuart's sudden death last year came as a great shock. I hope that the volume will serve as one small tribute to him. He is sorely missed.

Robert Asher, the editor of the SUNY labor history series and another of the conference's organizers, has been a constant source of support. He urged me to edit the anthology, helped me to secure SUNY's backing, and, with the greatest of tact, prodded me to complete the project. I am most grateful. My thanks as well to Clay Morgan of SUNY Press; to Ronald Edsforth, the third of the conference organizers; to Robert Zieger, who read the entire manuscript with great care and insight; and to the two anonymous readers for SUNY Press. The contributors to the volume have waited far too long to see their work in print. My thanks for their patience and their hard work. My colleagues in the history department at the University of Massachusetts, Amherst, have created an ideal scholarly environment, at once friendly and intellectually challenging.

My parents, Kevin and Anne Boyle, have long inspired my work. It would be less than honest to say that Abby and Nan helped me finish the anthology. But they have done a tremendous amount to make life worth living. As always, Vicky has helped me every step of the way. I relied on her thoughtful suggestions, her computer expertise, and her careful reading of my work. More importantly, I rely on her love, which fills our home with joy.

Introduction

Most of the essays in this volume were originally presented at a conference on labor and politics at the George Meany Center, Silver Springs, Maryland, on November 14, 1994. It was a particularly propitious time and place for such a conference. Six days earlier, the Republican Party had won control of both houses of Congress for the first time since 1954. The conference bristled with talk of electoral realignments and policy shifts. None of the conference participants realized, however, just how far-reaching and swift the changes would be. No one predicted that within a year much of the welfare state would be on the brink of extinction. No one predicted that the federal government itself would be shut down for weeks at a time. No one predicted that a Democratic president would declare before a joint session of Congress that "the era of big government" was at an end. And no one predicted that the changes in Washington would trigger profound changes at the highest level of the organization then hosting us, the AFL-CIO, and therefore in the labor movement we had gathered to discuss.[1] We realized, in other words, that American politics had been altered. We did not realize then that the New Deal system, long in decline, had finally died.

The nine essays presented here mark the passing of the old order. In particular, they explore the place of organized labor in American politics from the turn of the century through the 1980s, that is, from the advent of modern American liberalism through its death throes. The volume is not a Festschrift for labor-liberalism. But neither is it a condemnation of the labor-liberal alliance. Rather, the authors probe the ambiguities of the alliance: the interests that brought la-

1

borites and liberals together and the ideological strains that divided
them; the structures that shaped the alliance and the alternatives
that labor rejected; the alliance's successes and its limits.

We are not the first scholars to undertake such analyses. Despite
claims to the contrary, labor historians never abandoned political
and institutional history. They simply altered the contours of that
history. The most dramatic changes have occurred in the historiography of the nineteenth century. In that field, a generation of historians has overturned what had been the reigning paradigm. No
longer do scholars talk of workers embodying the "spiritus capitalis-
ticus purus rectificatus." To be sure, historians continue to recognize
nineteenth-century workers' attraction to the marketplace, with its
promise of greater comfort and its potential for social mobility. But
now scholars stress the militance of many groups of workers, both
organized and unorganized, a militance fed by home-grown ideologies of class consciousness, most notably artisan republicanism. And
they trace that militance, in large part, through labor's political activities, from the workingmen's parties of the 1820s and 1830s
through the electoral activism of the Knights of Labor in the 1880s.[2]

The historiography of twentieth-century labor politics is less well-
defined. But here too the paradigm has shifted. Building on the
American exceptionalist school, an earlier generation of scholars had
argued that labor's integration into liberal reformism developed nat-
urally from working people's "job consciousness." Liberals, they said,
used the power of the federal government to give workers the economic security they sought, and workers responded by rewarding
liberals with their votes. As the republican thesis shattered the exceptionalist argument, so too did the economist interpretation collapse. In its place, labor historians have fashioned a more complex,
and often more tragic, story.[3]

Workers' nineteenth-century political ideologies were overwhelmed in the late nineteenth century, the new argument runs, by
the combined force of industrial restructuring, state and employer
repression, and ethnocultural change. Without those visions to guide
them, labor activists split in a number of directions in the closing
years of the nineteenth century. Some followed Samuel Gompers
into nonpartisanship. Others, like Eugene Debs, replaced republicanism with socialism. Still others swung to the far left, supporting
anarchism, communism, and other radical political movements. And
yet others embraced the Democratic or Republican Party, sometimes

joining the great urban machines, sometimes joining the grand progressive crusades. The divisions persisted until the 1930s and 1940s, when New Deal and wartime labor policies pulled the resurgent labor movement, particularly its vanguard industrial unions, into the Democratic Party. The demands of the Cold War then drove movement leaders to purge labor's left wing. By 1950, the American labor movement had taken on a greater political coherence than ever before, its member unions fully integrated into the Democratic Party machinery and fully committed to liberal interest group politics.[4]

The results were decidedly mixed, according to the new framework. Once given a place in the postwar liberal state, unions finally had the leverage they needed to gain economic security for their members and to promote progressive causes. The union movement's hard-won status undoubtedly benefited unionized workers, who finally were able to enjoy more fully the fruits of American capitalism. By affiliating with the Democratic Party, however, organized labor also lost its ability to articulate an alternative vision of the American political economy, a responsibility labor had shouldered since the 1820s. As labor's radical voice was stilled, class issues faded from the national agenda, replaced by the politics of race and, to a lesser extent, gender. That politics, in turn, helped to tear apart the New Deal coalition that sustained the Democratic Party's hegemony. The Republican right and its corporate allies stepped into the breach in a hesitant way in the late 1960s and 1970s, more forcefully in the 1980s. Bit by bit they chipped away at the liberal state, attacking welfare, globalizing industrial labor, redistributing wealth upward, and fatally undermining the New Deal collective bargaining system. In the process, the right reduced organized labor to a fringe movement in America, powerless to prevent the brutalities of corporate downsizing, powerless to influence public policy, powerless to reverse the national swing further and further to the right.[5]

While most historians of twentieth-century labor politics accept this general outline, some fundamental questions remain hotly debated. The most basic questions center on the analysis of agency and outcome. To what extent was organized labor's integration in the liberal order determined by structural forces—the nature of the American political system, the particulars of the New Deal bargaining regime, the nature of the working class—and to what extent by the choices labor leaders made in the first half of the century? To what extent was the labor-liberal alliance a "barren marriage," in Mike

Davis's provocative phrase, and to what extent was it fruitful, both for union members and for nonunionized workers? These broad questions raise other, more empirical, questions. Precisely what were the processes through which organized labor and liberals built their alliance? How did the alliance function in electoral campaigns and in the formation of public policy? How did different and mingled ideological commitments—producerism, socialism, and New Deal liberalism—of labor leaders, workers, and politicians intersect and interact? How did union activists and party leaders mobilize or demobilize working class voters? How did they try to shape the Democratic Party agenda? Which strategies worked and which did not?

The essays in this volume address these empirical questions and, through them, the larger questions of agency and outcome. The volume has been divided into two sections. The five essays in the first section discuss the formation of the labor-liberal alliance from the turn-of-the-century through the 1930s. Section two's four essays examine the operation and decay of the alliance from 1940 to the present. Each section begins with a broad interpretive essay that explores the contours of the period from a structural perspective. That is followed by several case studies, which build on—and at times disagree with—the opening essay. The result is eclectic and, we hope, engaging.

Richard Oestreicher opens the first section by placing the emergence of the labor-liberal alliance within a broad political and ethnocultural context. American politics does not divide along class lines, he argues, because a series of impediments prevents it from doing so. The first, and perhaps greatest, barrier is the institutional structure of public life. The winner-takes-all system of republican government creates "an inexorable logic" pushing politicians to build majority coalitions. Labor thus could not become a political entity unto itself—a labor party—since to do so would have violated "the rules of the game." Organized labor simply had to become a constituent part of a coalition. Labor's power within the major coalitions of the late nineteenth and early twentieth centuries was limited by the second barrier. Riven by racial and ethnic cleavages, the American working class often placed ethnocultural issues ahead of class concerns. Finally, the uneven benefits and costs of industrial capitalism divided workers into competing camps. Workers in thriving industries had little to bind them to those who labored in declining sectors. All told, the structural impediments to class politics were utterly overwhelming.

Then came the Great Depression and the New Deal. The economic collapse overwhelmed sectoral differences and muted ethnocultural cleavages, Oestriecher argues, as workers across the nation struggled to regain economic security. The New Dealers, led by a cadre of liberals, took advantage of this rare opening to reshape the Democratic Party's agenda. They abandoned the moralism of Progressive reform and instead offered working people economic benefits. This welded ethnic and black voters to the Democratic Party, giving the Democrats a class tinge. But it was only a tinge. The Democrats remained a coalition, as the rules of the game required. And it was an unstable coalition at that, combining southern white supremacists and northern African-Americans, Catholic conservatives and left-wing union activists. Despite these contradictions, the coalition held firm for a generation. And in that time, American politicians acted, at least mildly, in the interests of working people.

Robert Asher complicates the picture Oestreicher paints by exploring the ideological underpinnings of the labor-liberal alliance. He does so through a case study of the political views of skilled iron and steel workers in the late nineteenth and early twentieth centuries. Asher's choice of subjects is pivotal. Steel was the United States' foremost industry at the turn of the century, the symbol of national economic might. The industry also symbolized the profound class struggle that cut across late nineteenth-century America. On the shop floor, managers battled to wrench control of the production process from the industry's skilled hands and to wrench more and more labor from its unskilled workers. The battle was not limited to the shop floor, of course. It also spilled over into the streets of the steel towns, most terribly in the 1892 Homestead strike. By focusing on skilled iron and steel workers, therefore, Asher has chosen subjects who stood at the center of the "labor question" at its most contentious moment.[6]

Asher begins his essay in the wake of the Homestead strike. But his analysis goes back much further. At the turn of the century, he argues, skilled iron and steel workers continued to be united by their belief in producerism, a belief that made them inheritors of the artisan republican mantle. Producerism did not give iron and steel workers a common political program, however. Indeed, it led workers to embrace strikingly different agendas, from nonpartisanship to democratic socialism. Asher's essay thus reinforces the current view that working-class politics fragmented badly at the turn of the cen-

tury. But the fragmentation cannot be traced simply to artisan republicanism's collapse. In one key sector of the working class, at
least, the persistence of producerism contributed to the splintering
of political action.

The multiple division of labor's political agenda, ironically, laid
the groundwork for the union alliance with the liberal wing of the
Democratic Party. Julie Greene, Peter Rachleff, and Bruce Nelson
trace three very different ways the alliance developed. Greene examines the efforts of Democratic Party liberals to attract the labor
vote in the Progressive era; Rachleff shows how labor's internal divisions foreclosed the possibility of a radical, rank-and-file alternative to the Democratic Party in Depression-era Minnesota; and
Nelson traces the failed efforts of Detroit's CIO leaders to win control of that city's government in the midst of labor's great surge forward. Together, the three essays thus provide an examination of the
"pull" and "push" of alliance making from 1900 to 1940.

Greene grounds her analysis in liberals' shifting understanding of
state power in the first two decades of the twentieth century. Democratic Party leaders attempted to win working-class support during
the 1908 presidential campaign, she demonstrates, simply by adopt-
ing the political agenda of Samuel Gompers' American Federation of
Labor. But that agenda, shaped by Gomper's visceral anti-statism,
proved far too narrow to rally workers to the Democratic standard.
To win the labor vote, it was clear, the Democrats would need a much
broader vision. In the 1910s, progressive reformers—particularly
the labor lawyer Frank Walsh—gave the Democrats just what they
needed. Working both within and outside state structures, Walsh
and his fellow progressives fashioned a program that foreshadowed
much of the New Deal labor system, particularly its guarantee of collective bargaining and its legislation of working hours. Woodrow
Wilson and the Democrats adopted critical parts of the program as
their own in the 1916 campaign. And when Gompers objected to such
a sweeping agenda, the Democrats sidestepped him, instead joining
with those segments of the labor movement more open to state action on the workers' behalf. Thus did the 1916 campaign give birth to
the alliance that would reach maturity in the New Deal.[7]

This does not mean that the labor-liberal alliance of the 1930s was
predetermined in the Progressive era. Workers had the chance to pursue alternative, more radical, political paths in the depression decade,
Rachleff argues in his essay, and many sought to do so. But a series of

political conflicts undermined their efforts. Rachleff makes his case by exploring the internal dynamic of the interwar era's most successful third party, the Minnesota Farm-Labor Party (FLP). Scholars have rarely treated the FLP as a genuine alternative to New Deal liberalism. Two generations ago, Arthur Schlesinger Jr., portrayed it as a vehicle for lower class ethnics "on the make," a goal that gave them, for all their talk of sweeping social change, a "broad kinship" with New Dealers. More recently, David Brody has dismissed the FLP as an "echo" of a rural-urban radicalism that had flourished in the late nineteenth century but had been overwhelmed by "job-conscious unionism" and "farm-conscious agrarianism" in the mid-1920s.[8]

Rachleff tells a dramatically different story. In the mid-1930s, he demonstrates, radical butchermen in southern Minnesota created the Independent Union of All Workers (IUAW), a community-based union committed to a "Wobbly-flavored syndicalism." Working people in a variety of industries quickly flocked to the IUAW, seeing in it a path to empowerment. The IUAW's popular base then gave the union the leverage it needed to serve as a ginger group within the FLP, prodding it to the left. Just as the IUAW solidified its power in 1936 and 1937, however, it came under withering attack by the conventional politicians of the FLP leadership, labor leaders within the AFL and CIO, and some of the IUAW's radical founders. By decade's end, the Independent Union of All Workers had been destroyed. And so too was the radical vision it had brought to the FLP. Shortly thereafter, the Farm-Labor party merged with the Minnesota Democratic Party, whose postwar leaders would become the champions not of radical change but of mainstream liberalism.

At first glance, Bruce Nelson's essay examines a similar lost opportunity. Like Rachleff, Nelson focuses on one of the centers of 1930s labor militancy: 1937 Detroit, a city awash in a wave of sitdown strikes, a place where, in Nelson Lichtenstein's memorable words, "the world once again seem[ed] plastic and open."[9] Nelson details how Detroit's CIO leaders tried to build on the rank and file's militancy to construct an independent political base for the city's surging labor movement. They did so by running a "labor slate" in that year's municipal elections. The slate had a decidely left-wing tinge. Its members publicly committed themselves to pushing beyond New Deal reformism, which the slate's mayoral candidate criticized for not offering "a plan for a new social system." Such rhetoric seemed to match the working-class ferment in the shops and streets of Detroit. When the votes were counted in November, though, the labor slate was overwhelmed by its conservative opponents.

Nelson attributes the labor slate's defeat to many of the same factors, such as internal factionalism, that undermined the Minnesota Farm Labor Party. Nelson and Rachleff differ, however, on one pivotal point, the relationship between the rank and file and the labor movement's political possibilities in the 1930s. Rachleff sees a militant working class, unified by the IUAW, pushing labor politics to the left. Nelson sees the working class as highly fragmented, its members divided by ethnicity, race, and skill level. These differences led workers to perceive labor's political action in very different ways: some Detroit workers embraced the labor slate as the political articulation of their brand of militance; others were repelled by it. Workers' continued struggle at the point of production, moreover, alienated a massive bloc of middle-class voters, whose support the labor slate desperately needed. Unable to win middle-class allies or even to hold some of its own constituency, the labor slate could not sustain its challenge to the city's status quo. Nelson's essay therefore confirms Oestreicher's argument that ethnocultural cleavages undermined the formation of a labor party. Nelson goes further, though, showing how the divisions that cut through the Detroit working class in the late 1930s, particularly the racial divide, expanded in the early 1940s, until they threatened the very foundation of the labor-liberal alliance.

Stephen Amberg opens section two by tracing the operation of the "New Deal Order" in the years after 1940. Like Oestreicher, Amberg contends that labor politics was shaped by institutional forces. Amberg builds his analysis, however, on a more circumscribed set of forces than does Oestreicher. Instead of focusing on the constraints of republican government and ethnocultural tension, Amberg constructs his analysis around the specific political and economic structures that employers, unionists, and government officials built in the fertile decades of midcentury. The "long crises of the 1930s and 1940s," he argues, seemed to open American public life to union influence. On the shop floor, unions, major employers, and the national state forged a system of industry-level, job-control collective bargaining. And in national politics, the labor movement formalized its commitment to the Democratic Party. The leaders of more militant unions, typically those affiliated with the CIO, were not satisfied with these victories, however. They hoped to move beyond them: to give unions a role in every level of corporate decision making and to transform the Democratic Party into a truly liberal party by purging its conservative elements. They were defeated in both these efforts in the late 1940s by employer resistance and by the internal dynamics of the Democratic Party. Thus were the boundaries of postwar politics set. Organized labor's economic and political power, though substantial, would be circumscribed by the system created during the New Deal.

The system remained in place throughout the 1950s and 1960s, Amberg shows. Organized labor, particularly in oligopolistic or highly regulated industries, continued to deliver generous contracts to its members—and its members' votes to the Democrats—throughout the period. But time and again employers and party leaders turned away labor's demands for a redistribution of power. Then, in the 1970s and early 1980s, the underpinnings of the system gave way. The economy faltered badly, corporate managers turned against workplace contractualism, and a host of social issues fractured the labor-liberal alliance. These structural shifts fundamentally undermined organized labor's place in the political economy. Without even the limited power of the New Deal system behind them, workers now face lives of profound uncertainty and gnawing fear.

Gilbert Gall, Gary Fink, and I follow with three articles examining the inner workings of the system Amberg describes. Gall's essay focuses on the flip side of the postwar accord: two flashpoints of anti-labor fervor in the postwar era, "right to work" referenda in 1958 Ohio and 1978 Missouri. The campaigns came at particularly bad times for organized labor. Both 1958 and 1978 were recession years. Labor was internally divided. Major unions remained outside the AFL-CIO: in 1958, it was the Teamsters, in 1978, the United Automobile Workers (UAW). Finally, unions faced less than friendly political climates on the national level. In 1958, the U.S. Senate was in the midst of its highly visible investigation of union racketeering, and the Republican Party leadership had decided to make union "bossism" the centerpiece of its fall campaign. Twenty years later, the Carter administration, feeling the pressure of a resurgent conservatism, had begun its swing to the right. Under such circumstances, how were unions to defend themselves from conservative attacks?

The answer, Gall demonstrates, lay with the labor-liberal alliance. In each case, union activists combatted the right to work advocates by portraying the initiative as the first stage of a broader attack on the postwar liberal agenda, from low-cost housing to civil

rights. Labor then spread its message through an intensive grass-
roots campaign, which targeted African-American communities for
particular attention. The strategy worked. By conflating labor's interests and that of its liberal allies, unions were able to defeat both
initiatives. Gall thus reinforces Amberg's point that the postwar system offered working people vitally important benefits, something
those scholars promoting the new interepretation of twentieth-
century labor are often too quick to downplay.

But the benefits of the labor-liberal alliance should not be over-
drawn. The alliance also restricted labor's power in vital ways, as
Gary Fink and I discuss in our essays. We make the point through
markedly different case studies. My essay focuses on a moment of
liberal ascendancy, the Great Society, whereas Fink focuses on the
late 1970s, a period of liberal retreat. I examine the UAW's attempts
to influence policy initiatives—social welfare programs—that would
not have an immediate impact on its members. Fink details a policy
initiative, the AFL-CIO's attempts to revise the Taft-Hartley Act,
purely of interest to union members. I show that labor leaders pene-
trated deeply into the policy-making apparatus of the Johnson
White House. Fink demonstrates that labor leaders enjoyed little
power within the Carter adminstration. Despite these differences,
though, we come to similar conclusions. On the policy level, labor
could not push its liberal allies beyond the New Deal formula of
piecemeal reform and industrial pluralism.

In the particulars, Fink and I offer different reasons why this
was so. I argue that the UAW leaders' dream of using the Great Society as a vehicle for social democratic change was undermined by
the configurations of 1960s national politics. Fink shows that the
AFL-CIO's efforts at labor law reform were stymied by a vigorous
corporate counterattack on Capitol Hill. The particulars may well
be seen, however, as parts of the same dynamic. Unlike at least
some of their Progressive and New Deal predecessors, postwar liberals accepted as a given corporate officials' right to manage their
enterprises largely free of public control. By so doing, they buttressed conservatives' ability to equate unfettered capitalism with
American ideals of liberty and justice. And that, in turn, dramatically narrowed the range of policy alternatives. Fink and I thus
bring the volume back to the power of ideology. By so doing, we
highlight one of the stark differences between turn-of-the-century
labor politics and that of the postwar era. In the earlier period, la-

bor's political activism was limited by the wide variety of ideological perspectives within the movement; in the years after World War II, it was limited in part by the rigidity of mainstream liberalism. The volume therefore ends on an ambigious note. The postwar political order gave organized labor the resources it needed to protect itself and to participate in political debates. But the contours of power in the postwar era also circumscribed the debates, pushing fundamental questions about the political economy off the public agenda. That is precisely the point that the current interpretation makes. The volume also departs from the current interpretation in key ways, however. Amberg, Gall, Fink, and I all suggest that organized labor never fully accepted the limits of the postwar order. On the contrary, Amberg, Gall, and I demonstrate that at least some postwar unions continued to see themselves as champions of the forgotten American. In that sense, they never fully accepted the New Deal system. They simply could not break free from it.

Now the New Deal system itself has been broken, wiped out in the realignment of partisan loyalties and the restructuring of the American state. For a time, it appeared as if the labor movement might be swept away by those changes. Such an projection now seems too pessimistic. The labor movement is still a terribly weak force in American public life, but at least labor activists are struggling to find a new course. The papers are filled with brave talk of organizing the unorganized, with news of a new generation of activists taking the union message into working-class communities.[10] As historians, we have little to contribute to those initiatives. All we can offer is an understanding of past initiatives, of victories and losses, of promises fulfilled and promises betrayed. Labor's political future cannot be guided by such understanding, of course, but neither can it be guided without it.

South Deerfield, Mass.

NOTES

1. "Clinton Offers Challenge to Nation, Declaring 'Era of Big Government Is Over,'" *New York Times*, January 24, 1996.

2. Werner Sombart, *Why Is There No Socialism in the United States?* trans. Patricia Hocking and C. T. Husbands (White Plains, N.Y.: International Arts and Sciences Press, 1976; originally published 1906), 14. On the revolutionary roots of artisan republicanism, see Alfred Young, "George Robert Twelves Hewes: A Boston Shoemaker and the Memory of the American Revolution," *William and Mary Quarterly* 38 (1981): 561–623. The most influential discussion of artisan republicanism is Sean Wilentz, *Chants Democratic: New York City and the Rise of the Working Class, 1788–1850* (New York: Oxford University Press, 1984). Also see Wiltenz's two essays, "Against Exceptionalism: Class Consciousness and the American Labor Movement," *International Labor and Working Class History* 26 (1984), 1–24, and "The Rise of the American Working Class, 1776–1877: A Survey," in J. Carroll Moody and Alice Kessler-Harris, eds., *Perspectives on American Labor History: The Problems of Synthesis* (DeKalb, Ill.: Northern Illinois University Press, 1989), 83–151. New labor historians have produced a particularly rich literature on nineteenth-century labor politics. Many of the following studies contributed to the republican synthesis; others built on it. On antebellum political action, see Alan Dawley, *Class and Community: The Industrial Revolution in Lynn* (Cambridge, Mass.: Harvard University Press, 1976); Thomas Dublin, *Women at Work: The Transformation of Work and Community in Lowell, Massachusetts, 1826–1860* (New York: Columbia University Press, 1979), particularly chapter 7; Bruce Laurie, *Working People of Philadelphia, 1800–1850* (Philadelphia: Temple University Press, 1980); Paul Faler, *Mechanics and Manufacturers in the Early Industrial Revolution: Lynn, Massachusetts, 1780–1860* (Albany: State University of New York Press, 1981); Amy Bridges, *A City in the Republic: Antebellum New York and the Origins of Machine Politics* (Cambridge: Cambridge University Press, 1984); Steven Ross, *Workers on the Edge: Work, Leisure, and Politics in Industrializing Cincinnati* (New York: Columbia University Press, 1985); Richard Stott, *Workers in the Metropolis: Class, Ethnicity, and Youth in Antebellum New York* (Ithaca: Cornell University Press, 1990), 235–40; and, most recently, Bruce Laurie, " 'Spavined Ministers, Lying Toothpullers, and Buggering Priests': Third-Partyism and the Search for Security in the Antebellum North," in Howard Rock, Paul Gilje, and Robert Asher, eds., *American Artisans: Crafting Social Identity, 1750–1850* (Baltimore: Johns Hopkins University Press, 1995). On the civil war era see, particularly, David Montgomery, *Beyond Equality: Labor and the Radical Republicans, 1867–1872* (New York: Knopf, 1967), and Iver Bernstein, *The New York City Draft Riots: Their Significance for American Society and Politics in the Age of the Civil War* (New York: Oxford University Press, 1990); on the post–Civil War years, see among many other works, Leon Fink, *Workingmen's Democracy: The Knights of Labor and Working Class Politics* (Urbana: University of Illinois Press, 1983); Susan Levine, *Labor's True*

Woman: Carpet Weavers, Industrialization, and Labor Reform in the Gilded Age (Philadelphia: Temple University Press, 1984); Richard Oestreicher, Solidarity and Fragmentation: Working People and Class Consciousness in Detroit, 1875–1900 (Urbana: University of Illinois Press, 1986); Peter Rachleff, Black Labor in the South: Richmond, Virginia 1865–1890 (Philadelphia: Temple University Press, 1984); Eric Arnesen, Waterfront Workers in New Orleans: Race, Class, and Politics, 1863–1923 (New York: Oxford University Press, 1991); and Kim Voss, The Making of American Exceptionalism: The Knights of Labor and Class Formation in the Nineteenth Century (Ithaca: Cornell University Press, 1994). Also see Victoria Hattam, Labor Visions and State Power: The Origins of Business Unionism in the United States (Princeton: Princeton University Press, 1993), and David Montgomery, Citizen Worker: The Experience of Workers in the United States with Democracy and the Free Market during the Nineteenth Century (Cambridge: Cambridge University Press, 1993).

3. Selig Perlman, A Theory of the American Labor Movement (New York: Macmillan, 1928), is the classic statement. For applications of this view, see Marc Karson, American Labor Unions and Politics, 1900–1918 (Carbondale, Ill.: Southern Illinois University Press, 1958) and Gerald Grob, Workers and Utopia: A Study of the Ideological Conflict in the American Labor Movement, 1865–1900 (Evanston, Ill.: Northwestern University Press, 1961). This interpretation also underlies the best narrative of the 1930s labor upheaval, Irving Bernstein, Turbulent Years: A History of American Workers, 1933–1939 (Boston: Houghton Mifflin, 1969).

4. On the collapse of artisanal politics and the splintering of the labor movement's political program in the early twentieth century, see David Montgomery, The Fall of the House of Labor: The Workplace, the State, and American Labor Activism, 1865–1925 (Cambridge: Cambridge University Press, 1987). Among the best studies of labor's many political strains in the late nineteenth and early twentieth centuries are Melvyn Dubofsky, We Shall Be All: A History of the IWW (Chicago: Quadrangle Books, 1969); John H. M. Laslett, Labor and the Left: A Study of Radical Influences in the American Labor Movement, 1881–1924 (New York: Basic Books, 1970); Stuart Kaufman, Samuel Gompers and the Origins of the American Federation of Labor, 1948–1896 (Westport, Conn.: Greenwood, 1973); Nick Salvatore, Eugene V. Debs: Citizen and Socialist (Urbana: University of Illinois Press, 1982); Martin Shefter, "Trade Unions and Political Machines: The Organization and Disorganization of the American Working Class in the Late Nineteenth Century," in Ira Katznelson and Aristide Zolberg, eds., Working Class Formation: Nineteenth-Century Patterns in Western Europe and the United States (Princeton: Princeton University Press, 1986), 197–276; Michael Kazin, Barons of Labor: The San Francisco Building Trades and Union

Power in the Progressive Era (Urbana: University of Illinois Press, 1987); Arnesen, *Waterfront Workers*; Robert Zieger, *Republicans and Labor, 1919–1929* (Lexington, Ky.: University of Kentucky Press, 1969). The integration of labor and liberalism in the 1930s and 1940s is treated in a large number of works. See, in particular, Stanley Vittoz, *New Deal Labor Policy and the American Industrial Economy* (Chapel Hill: University of North Carolina Press, 1987); David Montgomery, *Workers Control in America* (Cambridge: Cambridge University Press, 1989), chapter 7; Nelson Lichtenstein, *Labor's War at Home: The CIO in World War II* (Cambridge: Cambridge University Press, 1982); Mike Davis, *Prisoners of the American Dream: Politics and Economy in the History of the U.S. Working Class* (London: Verso, 1986); Gary Gerstle, *Working Class Americanism: The Politics of Labor in a Textile City, 1914–1969* (Cambridge: Cambridge University Press, 1989); Lizabeth Cohen, *Making a New Deal: Industrial Workers in Chicago, 1919–1939* (Cambridge: Cambridge University Press, 1990); Steven Fraser, *Labor Will Rule: Sidney Hillman and the Rise of American Labor* (New York: Free Press, 1991); David Montgomery, "Labor and the Political Leadership of New Deal America," *International Review of Social History* 39 (1994): 335–60; Robert Zieger, *The CIO, 1935–1955* (Chapel Hill: University of North Carolina Press, 1995). On post-1945 events, see Steve Rosswurm, ed., *The CIO's Left-Led Unions* (New Brunswick, N.J.: Rutgers University Press, 1992); Nelson Lichtenstein, "From Corporatism to Collective Bargaining: Organized Labor and the Eclipse of Social Democracy in the Postwar Era," in Steven Fraser and Gary Gerstle, eds., *The Rise and Fall of the New Deal Order, 1930–1980* (Princeton: Princeton University Press, 1989), 122–52; Lichtenstein, *The Most Dangerous Man in Detroit: Walter Reuther and the Fate of American Labor* (New York: Basic Books, 1995); Kevin Boyle, *The UAW and the Heyday of American Liberalism, 1945–1968* (Ithaca: Cornell University Press, 1995), chapters 1–3. Some of the best work on labor-liberalism has examined the legal framework of the New Deal order. See Christopher Tomlins, *The State and the Unions: Labor Relations, Law, and the Organized Labor Movement in America, 1880–1960* (Cambridge: Cambridge University Press, 1986), and Melvyn Dubofsky, *The State and Labor in Modern America* (Chapel Hill: University of North Carolina Press, 1994). The growing literature on organized labor's racial record is also excellent. For an overview, see Michael Goldfield, "Race and the CIO: The Possibilities for Racial Egalitarianism During the 1930s and 1940s," and responses, *International Labor and Working Class History* 44 (1993): 1–63.

5. The classic overview of postwar labor politics is J. David Greenstone, *Labor in American Politics* (New York: Knopf, 1969). Also see David Brody, *Workers in Industrial America: Essays on the Twentieth Century Struggle* (New York: Oxford University Press, 1980) chapter 6; Davis, *Prisoners of the American Dream*; Alan Dawley, "Workers, Capital, and the State

in the Twentieth Century," in Moody and Kessler-Harris, eds., *Perspectives on American Labor History*, 166–182; Robert Korstad and Nelson Lichtenstein, "Opportunities Found and Lost: Labor, Radicals, and the Early Civil Rights Movement," *Journal of American History* 75 (1988): 784–811; Lichtenstein, "From Corporatism to Collective Bargaining," 140–145; Ira Katznelson, "Was the Great Society a Lost Opportunity?" in Fraser and Gerstle, eds., *New Deal Order*, 185–211; Stephen Amberg, *The Union Inspiration in American Politics: The Autoworkers and the Making of a Liberal Industrial Order* (Philadelphia: Temple University Press, 1994); Lichtenstein, *Most Dangerous Man in Detroit*, chapters 13–18; Boyle, *UAW and the Heyday of American Liberalism*.

6. Montgomery, *Fall of House of Labor*, chapter 1; David Brody, *Steelworkers in America: The Nonunion Era* (Cambridge Mass.: Harvard University Press, 1960); Nell Irvin Painter, *Standing at Armageddon: The United States, 1877–1919* (New York: W. W. Norton, 1987), 110–15.

7. In recent years, several scholars have traced the way that progressives within the labor movement and the Democratic Party nurtured the labor-liberal alliance throughout the conservative ascendancy of the 1920s. See, in particular, Fraser, *Labor Will Rule*, and Sean Savage, *Roosevelt: The Party Leader: 1932–1945* (Lexington, Ky.: University of Kentucky Press, 1991).

8. Arthur Schlesinger Jr., *The Politics of Upheaval* (Boston: Houghton Mifflin, 1960), 96–98; David Brody, "On the Failure of U.S. Radical Politics: A Farmer-Labor Analysis," *Industrial Relations* 22 (1983), 141–63.

9. Lichtenstein, *Most Dangerous Man in Detroit*, 74.

10. David Moberg, "The New Union Label," *Nation*, April 1, 1996, 11–15; "Labor Uses an Old Idea to Recruit the Young," *New York Times*, February 25, 1996.

Part One

Building
the Labor-Liberal
Alliance

Richard Oestreicher

—————————— 1 ——————————

The Rules of the Game

Class Politics in Twentieth-Century America

Introduction

Since the 1930s macroeconomics, federal policy, and electoral cleavages appear to have worked in tandem. From the late 1930s to the 1960s, Gross National Product (GNP) increased rapidly and inequality of income and wealth declined, facilitated by federal policies which were, in turn, sustained by a dominant class-based Democratic electoral majority. In each successive presidential election between 1932 and 1948, the class differences between the electoral base of the Democrats and Republicans became more pronounced. By 1948 the percentage of American working-class voters who cast ballots for the Democrats was as high as the percentage of British workers who voted for the Labor Party and higher than the percentage of French and German workers who voted for social democrats or communists.[1]

Since the early 1970s, growth rates slowed, inequality increased sharply, regressive federal policies accelerated that trend, and Republicans increasingly won national elections as explicitly class-based political appeals became less important. In nearly every presidential election since 1968, class differentiation in voting has narrowed, indeed, essentially disappearing in many elections.[2] As voting alignments have shifted, public policy has become increasingly less egalitarian. By the early 1990s, the labor movement represented about the same proportion of privately employed workers as it had at the beginning of the New Deal. Comprehensive health care coverage went down in flames. Labor law reforms, designed to safeguard the right to organize, allegedly guaranteed by the Wagner Act but effectively gutted by court and NLRB decisions, never got off the ground. Almost all social programs are chronically underfunded. The underclass grew ever larger, our cities became war zones, our infrastructure crumbled, and substantial portions of the middle-class have been pushed down to the fringes of poverty.

The contrast between the economics of the two eras is no coincidence. The social meaning of this contrast is poignantly expressed in Bruce Springsteen's song "Glory Days," in which an aging working-class baby boomer nostalgically remembers the good times of the '50s and '60s as he describes the grimmer struggle to endure the 1980s.

Most explanations for the shift between the two eras depend on three (often not mutually exclusive) lines of argument: the original sins of the New Deal,[3] the driving competitiveness of a post-industrial economy embedded in a global marketplace,[4] and the Republicans' skill at manipulating the backlash to the cultural conflicts provoked by the politics of race, gender, sexuality, immigration, and environmentalism.[5] Each of these theories is descriptively accurate, yet they are nonetheless insufficient. Original sin theorists overestimate the strength and potential of the left in the 1930s and 1940s, implicitly imbibing teleological assumptions rooted in classical Marxism. Theorists of globalization and technological change tend toward a structural determinism in which the outcome appears all but inevitable rather than the product of the actions and decisions of historical actors. Analysts of recent campaign strategies tend to train their vision on the foreground of partisan political conflict, thereby all but ignoring how the trajectory of New Deal policies and the structural pressures of a changing global economy shaped political mobilization and rhetorical strategies. All three tend to underestimate the enduring significance of the American constitutional structure and of long-term traditions in American political culture.

The evolution of twentieth-century American political economy might be better understood by historically situating discussion of the shortcomings of the New Deal, the impact of structural change, and the effects of the culture wars in two ways. First, we need to place the New Deal within a longer view of American political history. Secondly, we need to look at the range of political options available in each era and the actual political choices Americans made. In differing ways, the depression and the structural changes of post-industrial society created social crises, but concrete political actors fought for specific proposals to resolve those crises. What options did politicians, intellectuals, corporations, unions, pressure groups propose? Whose vision won? What policy decisions did Americans support? How did decisions in such areas as labor law, tax codes, fiscal and monetary policy, regulatory action, housing policy, transportation policy, welfare policy, civil rights law, or international relations shape the outcome in either period? Political choices never take place in an abstract philosophical realm where the full range of options are equally possible. Political decisions are always made in specific historical circumstance: as a struggle for power among unequal political actors, amidst the economic and social trends of their times, within a particular constitutional structure and set of political rules, embedded within powerful cultural memories and traditions. Modern American politics can best be understood by analyzing this conjuncture of circumstances, rules, and traditions.

The Redistributive Effects of the New Deal

The New Deal social contract paled in comparison to a genuine social-democratic welfare state like postwar Sweden or Britain. Health care remained private, linked to employment status, with a substantial fraction of the population excluded. Unemployment compensation and virtually all other welfare benefits remained meager and varied widely from state to state. The National Labor Relations Act, the key legislative basis for expanded unionization, excluded agricultural workers and domestics, part of a larger pattern of limiting access for people of color to the benefits of federal policy.

Despite these limitations, the New Deal social contract stimulated significant redistribution of wealth, income, and economic power. According to one study of estate tax returns, the share of national wealth held by the top 1 percent of adults declined from 31.6 percent in 1929 to 20.8 percent in 1949. In 1953 the share of the top 1 percent had creeped back up to 24.3 percent, but it held steady at around one quarter of national wealth for the next twenty years. Moreover, looking only at estate assets may understate the redistributive effects of New Deal programs since the value of Social Security entitlements are not included in the estimate of total national wealth. One study that includes a calculation of the value of future Social Security benefits estimates the share of national wealth held by the top 1 percent in 1956 as only 16.5 percent, or half the 1929 peak.[6]

While the share of national wealth held by the top 1 percent may have declined by at least a third between 1929 and 1949, their share of national income appears to have dropped even more sharply, and then remained at that level for the next three decades. The top 1 percent of income recipients received 14 percent of pre-tax national income in 1929 and 8 percent in 1949.[7] As late as 1980, their share of national income was still roughly the same as in 1949.[8] If we include the effects of progressive taxation, the wealthy's share of national income may have dropped even further.[9]

In contrast, the steepest increases in shares of national income came at the bottom. The ratio of the average income of the top fifth and the bottom fifth declined from 15.5 in 1929 to 9.0 in 1951 and 7.25 in 1969. While the position of the poor probably worsened in the early years of the Depression, their share of national income started to rise in the mid-1930s, rose sharply during World War II, and continued to rise through the late 1940s before leveling off.[10]

New Deal policies do not explain all of the egalitarian trend in income and wealth distribution from the 1930s through the 1960s. The economic impact of World War II and the favored position of the United States in the postwar economy certainly contributed. But in no other period in American history was the citizenry able to wrench as equitable a share of national bounty from the rich and powerful. New Deal policies made favorable circumstances more favorable to the entire population than they otherwise would have been. In only ten years, the Wagner Act led directly to an increase in union representation from approximately one worker in ten in 1934 (the year before the passage of the act) to more than three out of ten by 1945,[11] and strong unions forced corporations to raise wages at roughly the same rate that the economy expanded. Mean real total hourly compensation (wages plus benefits) in manufacturing tripled between 1947 and 1970 while median family money income went up 79 percent during the same years.[12] Minimum wage legislation immediately raised the incomes of millions of the poorest workers. The Social Security Act (despite the regressive nature of Social Security taxes) also raised the living standards of the elderly poor. Progressive taxation, despite all the flaws and dodges built into the system, did redistribute income. The GI Bill facilitated working-class social mobility and helped to narrow wage ratios between blue collar and professional labor by expanding the supply of the latter.[13] Federal economic policy in the era of the New Deal social contract was to the left of any other period in American history.

The Consequences of Increasing Economic Inequality since the 1970s

Over the last two decades economic inequality in the United States increased dramatically. Despite a continuing cultural predilection for egalitarian political rhetoric and cultural style, the United States now holds the dubious distinction of being the most economically unequal of all prosperous countries.[14] We have become a country with street-corner armies of beggars and motorized battalions of BMWs. This burgeoning economic inequality emerged together with a growing paralysis of public policy. For most of the last quarter century, state and federal politics have seemed gridlocked, unable to respond effectively to increasingly severe social and economic problems. Instead, ever-increasing budget deficits, coupled with a steadily declining quality of life for the majority of citizens, has produced an atmosphere of political crisis, alienation, and despair.

Perhaps the most lucid and convincing analysis of this economic trend has been expounded by former Nixon campaign staffer and conservative political analyst Kevin Phillips. In 1990, Phillips observed in his *Politics of Rich and Poor,* the top one half of one percent of American households owned nearly as much as the bottom 90 percent (27 percent of national wealth for the top 0.5 percent, 32 percent for the bottom 90 percent).[15] As he has argued more recently, disparities of income and wealth have only grown more pronounced since.[16]

Widespread popular and academic discussions of economic stagflation, the collapse of Rust Belt industries, and corporate downsizing often have had the misleading effect of implying that our social and economic problems are a function of a decline in the national economy. In fact, the country is wealthier, not poorer. While the economy grew more slowly than in the boom years of the 1950s and 1960s, growth was robust, nonetheless.

The pie is getting bigger, but most Americans are not getting a share of the extra slices. In 1993, in real dollars, the U.S. economy grew by 3 percent but the median income of American households fell by 1 percent as the well-to-do latched onto all of the increase in national income. They have done so consistently since the early 1970s. The rich have been getting richer as the rest of the population works harder just to stay even. According to economist Paul Krugman, real per capita GNP grew 39 percent between 1970 and 1990. If the 1990 national income had been divided in the same proportion as the 1970 national income the average household should have experienced a 39 percent increase in real income, but Krugman estimates the increase at only around 5 percent. Other observers argue that even a 5 percent growth in real median household income is too optimistic.[17] The real median hourly pay of individual workers actually went down sharply from $8.52 per hour in 1973 to $7.46 per hour in 1990.[18] Households managed to stay even or very slightly ahead by working more. The typical household provided more hours of labor either through multiple wage earners or longer work weeks.[19]

Prospects look even worse for the next generation. In 1990 "young families" (e.g. households with children and household head under 30) had real household incomes nearly one third lower (32 percent) than their counterparts in 1973, even though the educational levels of these household heads were higher in 1990 than in 1973.[20] Access to higher education, still one of the main paths to upward social mobility, has also grown sharply more skewed since the 1970s. Between 1979 and 1994 the proportion of children who completed college degrees increased from 31 percent to 79 percent in the most prosperous quarter of American households, while it stayed flat at 8 percent among the bottom one quarter of households. In 1979 a child from a household in the top quartile was four times more likely than a child from the bottom quartile to graduate from college. In 1994 the ratio was ten to one.[21]

The last quarter century looked tougher to the majority of Americans not because the economy ceased to grow but because the very wealthy (the top 0.5 percent of American households) seized half of all the new wealth generated by economic growth and the well-to-do (the rest of the top 20 percent) grabbed virtually all the rest.[22] If current trends continue, the prospects for the majority in the next generation look even worse.

Inadequate Explanations for the
New Deal and its Demise

Until quite recently, both to scholars and political pundits, the New Deal social contract seemed like a peculiarly American, but functionally equivalent, version of the social democratic politics that dominated most of Western Europe. Historians and political scientists who treated the New Deal this way implicitly viewed it as a natural outcome of capitalist development.[23] A crude version of the underlying logic might go like this. Capitalism exacerbates the already existing inequality of precapitalist systems by concentrating a disproportionate share of its growing wealth in the hands of industrialists and financiers. At the same time, capitalist relations of production destroy the livelihoods of agricultural smallholders and traditional craftspeople and undermine the power of agents of social control like landlords and the church. Overcoming the legacy of tradition may take several generations, but eventually the people mobilize and force democratic political reforms. Despite the influence of the concentrated wealth of great corporations, once the people force elites to grant representative government and universal suffrage, the logic of numbers is finally irresistible; there are too many workers and too few capitalists. It is only a matter of time before a political party representing the interests of working people forces capital to strike some version of the social-democratic bargain, trading guarantees of minimal individual economic security and some restrictions on the use of capital for the continued right to operate.

However, from the vantage point of the present, such a teleological explanation of the emergence of the New Deal seems puzzling, to say the least. If the combination of capitalism and democracy makes some version of the social democratic bargain inevitable, how do we explain the collapse of the New Deal coalition and the virtual abrogation of the social compromise over the last generation? Nor is the American experience unique. While the degree and nature of change has varied from country to country, social-democratic social contracts have been under attack everywhere in the world over the last generation. From an international perspective, arguments which implicitly assume that the social-democratic bargain is inherent in capitalist development seem even more problematic.

What I have called original sin theorists try to solve this contradiction by positing fatal flaws in the very construction of the New

Deal social contract, flaws so fundamental that they made its unraveling an almost inevitable function of its modes of operation. Indeed, given these flaws, most scholars who take this viewpoint question whether it is appropriate to conceive of the New Deal as a species of social democracy at all. Rather, they see a social democratic moment in the late 1930s and early 1940s when advocates of social democracy had a credible hearing in American politics. Social democrats, however, compromised away their momentum, allowing themselves to be co-opted and beaten. By 1946 any claims for meaningful social democracy in America were dead. Liberal Democratic politicians and intellectuals harbored illusions for another generation, but the dismantling of the New Deal political coalition in the 1970s was preordained by what they allowed to happen in the 1930s and 1940s. Writing about the disappointments of LBJ's Great Society, Ira Katznelson, for example, argues that "key features of partisan politics and policy-making in the 1940s . . . shaped . . . the Great Society's determinative limits. . . . The Great Society . . . is best understood in terms of a larger dynamic . . . that undercut . . . the prospects for an American social democratic politics."[24]

Among the many shortcomings of the New Deal, the two most critical to this argument were New Deal labor policy and New Deal racial policy. Despite its dramatic impact on union membership, critics contest that New Deal labor policy proved to be a Trojan horse, a Devil's Bargain. By accepting reliance on the NLRB for organizing workers and defending their rights, labor in effect transformed itself from an oppositional social movement into a coterie of governmentally licensed franchises and virtual vassals of Democratic politicians. Politicians did not deliver; the labor-Democratic merger became a "barren marriage."[25] More tragically, in the process, labor union officials and activists lost touch with working people, who came to see unions as the property of labor union and labor relations bureaucrats. Working-class traditions of struggle and self-organization eroded. When the economic climate changed in the 1970s and 1980s, and corporations began attacking previously sacrosanct union gains, neither union leaders nor most workers understood any longer how to fight back effectively.

If collaboration with the New Deal labor relations system pulled labor's teeth, liberals' acceptance of the New Deal's hands-off relationship with southern Democratic white supremacists left in place a solid political bloc opposing progressive legislation and a ticking time bomb in the heart of the Democratic coalition. As Dixie rose again in the 1960s, it brought the New Deal and the Great Society down like a house of cards. Only if there had been the political will to forcefully confront the racial ethos of southern Democrats at the peak of New Deal strength in the 1930s and early 1940s, could this outcome have been avoided.

While this analysis of the long-term effects of New Deal labor policy and of collaboration with southern racism is probably correct, the presumption that such policies resulted from a lack of political will, wisdom, or moral sensitivity among liberals and radicals seems more doubtful. Did the labor movement enthusiastically support New Deal labor policy because they suffered from paralyzing illusions or because those policies seemed so manifestly better than the labor policies of any previous regime? Could working people have won a greater measure of worker's control, codetermination of corporate investment decisions, or a more inclusive social safety net if they had forsaken NLRB procedures to go it on their own in the streets and on the shop floors? What-ifs can never be answered, but nothing in the history of the labor struggles of the previous fifty years suggests much reason that workers or unions could have done better without collaborating with Democratic politicians and the federal labor relations bureaucracy.

Likewise, did white supremacists maintain a stranglehold over the southern Democratic Party only because progressives failed to confront them on race, or because racists held politically entrenched positions and defeated efforts to budge them? The evidence here is more mixed than in the case of labor policy. Liberals knowingly accepted racially inspired exceptions and limitations in virtually every key New Deal program and agency from the Wagner Act's exclusion of agricultural and domestic workers to the FHA's consistent racial redlining of neighborhoods to liberal Democratic senators voting against a Republican antiracial discrimination amendment to a 1949 public housing bill. But the latter vote illustrated their dilemma. The Republicans proposed the amendment prohibiting racial discrimination in public housing as a tactic to defeat public housing legislation, knowing that inclusion of the amendment would swing southern Democrats against the entire bill. Liberal Illinois Senator Paul Douglas apologized to "the Negro race" when he agonizingly urged his colleagues to vote against the amendment in order to prevent defeat of "all hopes of rehousing 4 million persons."[26]

Could Democratic liberals have challenged racial segregation more forcefully in the 1930s and 1940s without risking such massive defections of voters and elected officials that they would have undermined their legislative majority? Would the country have been better off in the long run if liberals had accepted principled defeats as the political cost of raising the ante against racism? Douglas, in this case, thought not. Looking at the political landscape we can see why liberals like Douglas felt politically vulnerable. Many who did try to push the limits on racism found themselves overwhelmed by racist attack. Claude Pepper, Florida's progressive Democratic senator, for example, was deated in an orgy of red baiting and race baiting in the 1950 Florida Democratic primary as his opponents circulated propaganda with pictures of him embracing Paul Robeson. His liberal colleague in North Carolina, Frank Graham, suffered a similar fate the same year as segregationists saturated the state with leaflets urging "White People Wake Up . . . Frank Graham Favors Mingling of the Races."[27] UAW leaders and their political supporters found themselves trounced in the 1943 and 1945 Detroit mayoral campaigns by incumbent Edward Jeffries who denounced Afro-American protesters as "Negro hoodlums" and accused the NAACP of collaborating with "un-American" UAW leaders. The UAW-NAACP backed slate pulled 85 percent of the vote in Black neighborhoods, but lost heavily in those white working-class neighborhoods where UAW members were most concentrated.[28]

Ultimately, perhaps, we must ask whether the original sin critique of the New Deal is based more on political and moral assumptions about what should have happened rather than on systematic appraisal of the balance of political forces in the era. Such assumptions about what should have happened are usually implicitly rooted in classical Marxism's teleology of the expected direction of history. They fail to seriously consider the proposition advanced by David Plotke that "the main alternatives to the Democratic order were regimes well to its right. . . . the likelihood of a social democratic outcome was much smaller than that of more conservative results. . . ."[29]

If critics of the New Deal social contract fault its weakness, paradoxically, most theorists of globalization and technological change see its success as the trigger of contemporary change. Strong unions, high wage rates, high taxes necessary for the social overhead of a social contract, and a tight regulatory climate all effectively diminished domestic possibilities for corporate profit and capital accumulation. Capital sought global market places and new forms of production to escape the constraints of the social democratic bargain. "Despite appearances," writes John Holloway, "the restless movement of capital is the clearest indication of the power of the insubordination of labour."[30] Such observations, however, provide little comfort or practical tactical advice for people watching their jobs shipped overseas, their wages cut, or their workpace intensified. If original sin theorists overestimate the potential for more radical alternatives to the regime that emerged in the 1930s and 1940s, most theorists of structural change underestimate the potential political flexibility of the current world. While pressures against workers, unions, and class bargains are indeed global, the impact has been different from country to country. [31]

Finally, analysts of recent political campaign strategies, although often incisive, are too caught up in the mechanics of political campaigns to integrate their story with either historical or structural analyses. They generally see the Democratic commitment to civil rights, affirmative action, and gender equality as tactical overemphases rather than products of significant social forces. Indeed, many end their litanies of Democratic error and Republican elan by essentially asserting that Democrats can readily regain the political initiative by combining a clearer critique of free market economics with a more savvy avoidance of the contradictions of cultural politics.[32]

Historically Situating the New Deal Social Contract

Within the broadest sweep of American political history, the thirty years from the 1930s to the 1960s stand out as the only era in which either major party symbolically and programmatically defined itself clearly in class terms.[33] Looking at the thirty years of the New Deal's class bargain in this way—as an exception to a prevailing pattern in which class relations have usually not been the explicit axis of American electoral politics—forces us to look at the contrasts between the 1940s and the 1990s in a different way, to ask different questions. How have the rules of the American constitutional system and the cultural traditions of American society shaped American electoral politics? And why was the New Deal Democratic Party able to break precedent in the early 1930s and maintain a class-based political realignment for a generation thereafter?

Rules: The Effects of the American Constitutional System

The American constitutional structure, by design, is not a level playing field in which all political tendencies compete equally. The Founding Fathers, fearful of an excess of democracy, made rules that favor political elites capable of mobilizing political resources across broad geographical areas and at the multiple levels of federal, state, and local politics. These rules essentially disenfranchise any political tendency or political interest unwilling or unable to reach accommodation with the political elites who control a governing coalition.

The rules rarely change because the constitution makers made changes extremely difficult. A constitutional amendment can only be enacted by first getting two-thirds majorities of both houses of Congress and then by receiving the endorsement of majorities in three quarters of the state legislatures. Any fundamental changes in the allocation of power can be vetoed by only a few dozen politicians in the first step or a few hundred in the second: thirty-four U.S. senators or a majority of the state senators in only thirteen out of the fifty states. Proposed rules changes rarely make it through this cumbersome amendment process. The two most important changes—black enfranchisement and women's suffrage—took the bloodiest war in American history to enact in the first case and more than fifty years of dogged political agitation in the second.

The crucial constitutional features tilting the electoral playing field toward powerful elites are the apportionment of legislative seats to single-member geographic districts, the election within those districts by winner-takes-all plurality, a bicameral legislature with the senate seats allocated two to each state regardless of population, and the separation of legislative elections from the presidential election. Single-member geographically based districts, combined with the winner-takes-all plurality means that anyone who seeks power at any level of American electoral politics must be able to produce an electoral majority in a specific geographic location. A minority showing—no matter how large, even up to 49.9 percent of the vote in a district—usually yields absolutely nothing. The immediate effect is the same as if you did not vote at all.[34]

If anything less than a majority in each district is pointless, then a minority showing across many districts is equally fruitless. A labor, socialist, or other ideologically based party can draw 5, 10, 15 percent of the national vote—enough to be a major national player under different rules such as proportional representation or a parliamentary system—and come away completely empty in the United States. In 1912 the Socialists drew 6 percent of the national vote and elected no one to Congress. In contrast, a 6 percent showing by the British Labour Party in 1910 yielded forty-two parliamentary seats.

Geographically based winner-takes-all districts thus provide an inexorable logic for joining majority electoral coalitions. Class politics is a politics of mobilizing by sharpening battle lines. Coalition politics is a politics of conflict avoidance. Coalition building pressures activists and politicians to avoid conflict and controversy in order to broaden the coalition, pulling in ambivalent or lukewarm voters at the margin by assuring them you do not intend anything threatening. At the same time, the necessity of obtaining an electoral majority over a large geographic area raises the minimum threshhold of resources necessary for electoral competition. Unless you can start off big enough to look like a possible winner, even voters who are very sympathetic to your appeal will shy away, fearful that a socialist or labor vote which would otherwise go to the more approachable of the two major parties will, in effect, become a vote for the most reactionary party.

If geographically based winner-take-all districts create a structural bias in favor of cross-class political coalitions and raise the minimum entry fee for political competition, the bicameral structure of Congress and the method of electing the president magnify both tendencies. Since all legislation must pass both houses of Congress, a few dozen senators from sparsely populated rural states can veto any program even if the overwhelming majority of the electorate wants it passed. Working-class and pro-labor votes tend to be concentrated in a few populous industrial states. In 1920, eleven northern industrial states (N.Y., Ill., Pa., Ohio, N.J., Mass., Mich., Wis., Mo., Calif., Ind.) together had a majority of the American population (50.1 percent) but only 22 of 96 senators. Nevada's 77,000 people or Delaware's 223,000 had the same representation in the Senate as

New York's 10.4 million. Each vote in Nevada counted more than 100 times as much as each vote in New York. Thus working-class votes concentrated in large industrial states will be systematically undervalued. Until a series of Supreme Court decisions in the 1960s, most state legislatures exhibited similar drastic imbalances in representation between urban-industrial areas and rural areas.

Labor unions in cities like Chicago, New York City, and San Francisco often had significant local political influence. In a parliamentary system, these would have been the first strongholds of the American Labor Party. But union resources, concentrated in a relatively small number of such strongholds, never constituted a potential governing coalition in any state and were always totally inadequate for a national campaign. When the most important political objectives of unions and workers were local—such as insuring police neutrality in local union organizing—unions avoided the potential divisiveness of national party politics. In the twentieth century, as the courts began to define narrower boundaries for union activity[35] and as unions faced national and international corporations, national politics mattered more and more. Unable to contend on a national or even state level by themselves, unions and workers had to look for political allies, to join coalitions. But the support of potential political allies always carries a price. The price for unions and workers has usually been twofold: accepting party loyalty and abjuring militant tactics which strike middle-class portions of the political coalition as violent, coercive, or unresponsive to the "public interest." You could only bargain from inside the party coalition and you could not do anything which would embarrass the rest of the coalition and cost the party more votes than you could deliver. The rules of the game thus heavily favored joining into major party politics rather than independent political action. They have also meant, at various times, disciplining your own supporters to avoid their most effective tactics—sit-downs or wildcat strikes, for example—or purging your own ranks of enthusiastic organizers such as IWW's or Communists.

Finally, presidential elections add yet an additional pressure for coalition politics. The president functions like a constitutional monarch elected in a national plebiscite. A credible presidential campaign always demanded a national political base (both because of the scale of the campaign and the choice by the electoral college) and vast amounts of money. The rise of mass media further increased the price of an admission ticket to the presidential sweepstakes. Only national political parties can raise such resources, and even they are ever more dependent on large financial backers. In a parliamentary system, where the prime minister is the chosen leader of the parliamentary majority, minority parties can exert leverage by bartering their support for the parliamentary majority in exchange for key appointments or policy guarantees. The presidency in American politics, with its broad executive, appointive, and veto powers, is a much more crucial linchpin of political power than the chief executive in a parliamentary system, but under the American system you have access to presidential power only from inside the president's party.

The unique nature of the American constitutional system explains a great deal about American politics. Indeed, we may have to look no further for at least a partial answer to one of the favorite questions of American labor historians: why is there no socialist or labor party? The United States is the only industrial democracy without a significant labor or socialist party. It is also the only industrial democracy without some form of proportional or parliamentary representation.

Traditions: The Heritage of Colonialism

The constitutional bias toward cross-class political coalitions has been compounded by the heritage of colonialism which superimposed on America's class structure a racial and ethnic hierarchy borne out of conquest and enslavement. White Protestant, mainly English, Europeans seized the North American continent in centuries of warfare with native peoples and other colonialist contenders. Wealth, power, and status have ever afterward been correlated with the racial and cultural caste of the descendants of the conquerors. To be a white, Anglo-Saxon Protestant was to be of the dominant caste. To be anything else was to be of the others. Much of the deepest conflict in American politics, from the beginning of the republic to the present, has revolved around the question of who will be recognized as part of the polity, which of the others? And with what conditions?

As many political historians have empirically demonstrated, until the New Deal, the greatest partisan cleavages in American politics had been mainly ethnocultural. But ethnocultural identities were not race and status neutral. Given the broad and amorphous nature of coalition parties, both major parties have always included some members of virtually every racial and cultural group. But since their very beginnings, the Republicans have always been the party of those ethnocultural groups most closely identified with the dominant culture. The Republicans, as a consequence, have always had a greater cultural coherence than the Democrats. The Republicans defended respectable white Protestant America. Others joined if they were already militantly anti-Catholic, like the Orangemen, or if they wanted to join the club by ceasing to be what Theodore Roosevelt called "hyphenated-Americans."

The Democrats were the party of conservative white southerners and those of the outs—mainly Catholics—sufficiently acculturated to mobilize politically and look for a more hospitable political home than the Republicans. A party of southern conservatives and Catholics was always an uneasy alliance.

As the country industrialized and the ranks of potential working class voters expanded dramatically, ever greater class tensions were simmering, submerged by the cross-class character of both parties that left those voters concerned about class issues with little way to express their wishes. But beyond local enclaves of labor strength, any politicians or activists who sought to capture such sentiment and realign the parties by mobilizing around class grievances faced a daunting practical reality. In the early 1900s, close to 60 percent of the nation's industrial workers were members of subordinate racial and ethnic groups but over 40 percent were not.[36] Any party that sought to mobilize workers around a class program had to bridge the emotions and cultural contradictions of race, ethnicity, and religion. Their opponents would not only enjoy the benefits of cultural unity, but they could also hope to hold a substantial portion of that 40 percent of working-class voters who were white Protestants. Indeed, even at the greatest peak of class-mobilization in the 1940s, the Democrats never won the votes of the majority of non-southern white Protestant workers.[37] The effects of the country's racial and ethnic hierarchy thus were partisan specific. The party that wished to rally racially and culturally subordinate groups faced an overwhelming hurdle of cultural unification which the other party did not. Since the majority of workers belonged to such subordinate groups, any working-class party would face this dilemma.

Market Pressures

Finally, the anarchy of the market, a natural part of any capitalist economy, also favored cross-class coalitions and made the prospects of a more ideological, class-based politics more difficult. In a market economy with winners and losers, there will always be variations in the economic prospects and needs of different regions, industries, occupations, and individuals. Growing regions will have different public policy interests from declining regions. Industries facing tough international competition will seek different programs from industries with safe domestic markets. People who are doing relatively well will have less enthusiasm for redistributive programs than those who are doing poorly. Coalition politics is tailor made to the reality of market variations. Specific and narrow programs and concessions can be crafted to the particular interests of regions or industries at relatively modest cost to the national treasury or the national profile of the party: price supports for North Carolina tobacco or Wisconsin dairy products; a new highway, airport, or dam. The very size of the country increases the likelihood of such sectoral variations. They may often seem more pressing to working people than the broader common goals that would have to be the basis of a class appeal.

The New Deal Breakthrough

In the early 1930s, a unique set of circumstances combined with a new set of political alliance gave advocates of a more class-based politics the opportunity to partially—but only partially—overcome the structural and cultural biases which had shaped American politics up to that time. The Depression produced unprecedented suffering compounded by the psychological anxieties of a seemingly unending downward spiral from 1929 through 1933. Frugal and respectable folks found their life savings disappearing in sudden bank failures, their homes threatened with foreclosure by other banks still struggling to stay afloat, and the great factories on which they depended for employment standing idle. In these circumstances of profound distress and deep disillusionment with corporations and financial institutions, urban Democratic politicians, liberal intellectuals, and unions leaders sensed political opportunities.

FDR's first presidential victory in 1932 represented little more than a national reaction to the depression and a revulsion to the perception that Herbert Hoover and the Republicans did not care enough about people's suffering to do anything about it. When Hoover (actually a relatively activist Republican) declared that "economic depression cannot be cured by legislative action or executive pronouncement" or "no governmental action . . . can replace that God-imposed responsibility of the individual man and woman to their neighbors," he was answered by those who shouted that "Uncle Sam can help, but the man at Uncle Sam's helm will not help. He hears our cry unmoved . . ."[38]

Roosevelt drew roughly the same proportion of the vote from all classes in 1932,[39] and the Democrats offered little in either the campaigns or their first legislative ventures that could be seen as a sharp tilt toward the working class. The most important part of their first economic recovery package, the National Industrial Recovery Act (NIRA), offered a weak and unenforceable clause (section 7a) allegedly guaranteeing workers' right to bargain collectively through representatives of their own choosing, but did so without mentioning unions or establishing any mechanism to carry out the stated goal. Otherwise, the NIRA was classic coalition politics under business control. Each industry established its own code board to regulate economic behavior according to the particular needs of the industry. While theoretically the code boards included tripartite representation of business, labor, and the public, in practice, if they had any impact at all, most functioned like business trade associations. The NIRA had flopped well before the Supreme Court declared it unconsitutional in 1935. By then the Depression was already half a decade old.

The long continuation of the economic crisis pushed a substantial portion of the electorate to the left, aroused widening mass protests and increasing demands for far-reaching action. This unrest and insecurity offered both an opportunity and a threat for FDR and legions of new Democratic officeholders swept in by the Depression after years in the political wilderness. In the 1920s, outside of the South, the Democratic Party had seemed almost on the verge of extinction. Now Democratic politicians could respond to the crisis and consolidate a new political base or fail to respond and get pushed back out the electoral revolving door. They did not know quite what to do.

An alliance of three groups—urban progressive politicians, liberal intellectuals, and labor organizers—stepped into the political vacuum with a program and a vision. While they considered a range of programmatic directions including forms of national planning, regulatory action, fiscal and monetary intervention, and antimonopolism,[40] they generally shared faith in a high wage-high consumption economy with an expanded public sector, and increased public regulation of capital designed to discipline both business and labor, prevent destructive cutthroat competition, and avoid violent class warfare. Such a vision seemed both moral and practical to progressive intellectuals, activists, and politicians: moral because they believed in human equality, practical because they believed that underconsumption caused by extreme maldistribution of income had provoked the depression. Legislating this vision would demand labor laws designed to greatly strengthen but federally supervise labor unions; public works jobs and public housing projects; banking and financial regulation; and social security.

Such a program would draw the labor movement to the bosom of the Democratic Party but could be sold to farmers, homeowners, small-business people and other non-labor constituences as well. Thus Senator Robert Wagner, the sponsor of the National Labor Relations Act; Leon Keyserling, his aide, who drafted the bill; and intellectuals such as William Leiserson, future NLRB chairman who advised them,[41] did not defend the measure primarily as a defense of workers' rights as citizens. Instead, they defended unionization as an economic recovery measure as much as an end in itself. Unionization would be a mechanism for raising wage levels and hence consumption. Federal supervision would insure that unions behaved responsibly in the public interest. Likewise, while social security was desirable to remedy the insecurities of old age, it was also promoted as an antidote to underconsumption. Public works jobs would start out as emergency relief, but hopefully the accomplishments of showcase projects would overcome public scepticism about a permament expansion of the public sector.

Programmatic liberals seized the political initiative because other Democratic officeholders had no equally convincing answers for the public demand for aggressive federal action. But their programs provoked bitter controversy within the Democratic Party, and outraged conservatives of both parties began denouncing the New Deal as a catastrophic threat to liberty and as a communist plot.

Normally, given the logic of coalition politics, such opposition promotes furious backpeddling by officeholders fearful of pushing swing voters into the arms of the opposition. But in this case, just the opposite happened. From FDR on down, New Deal Democrats castigated their critics as economic royalists, malefactors of wealth, or stooges of the discredited bankers and financiers who had brought the country to ruin. In 1936 FDR sometimes sounded like a parlor Bolshevist, and he won the biggest landslide in American political history up to that time.

He could do so for two reasons: because most Democratic conservatives could not quite stomach switching parties, despite their dislike of New Deal policies, and because important new constituencies approved of New Deal policies and rhetoric so enthusiastically that they turned out in record numbers, more than counterbalancing the impact of any conservative defections. Even at as explosive a point as 1936, though, Roosevelt could not completely overcome the structural bias which drove the Democrats toward coalition building. The New Deal Democratic Party was the amalgamation of two parties: the old Democratic Party of white southerners and Catholics, and a new party of outsider constituencies—Jews, northern Blacks, and southern and eastern Europeans, mainly industrial workers. Both Democratic Parties claimed FDR's charisma and the Democratic label, although for different reasons. To the conservatives of the old Democratic Party, the New Deal was anathema. But where else should they go? Most white southerners were yellow dog Democrats—even a yellow dog or a pro-labor Yankee was better than any Republican. And Catholic conservatives discovered that the nativist smell of the Republicans still repelled most Catholic voters. When Father Charles Coughlin broke with the New Deal, he tried to pull his supporters into a third party, the Union Party, but the Union Party candidate drew less than 2 percent of the national vote in 1936. Such sachems of the old Democratic Party as Al Smith and John W. Davis tried to rally Democratic opponents of the New Deal into the Liberty League, but despite substantial financial contributions from wealthy backers, they found themselves as chiefs with no Indians.

In contrast, to the constituencies of the new Democratic Party, the majority of whom had been non-voters before the 1930s, strong unions, government jobs, and old age pensions were almost too good to be true. No politician had offered them anything really important before. Homestead, Pennsylvania, a classic mill town just up-river from Pittsburgh, had been a Republican stronghold in the 1920s. Most industrial workers there did not bother to vote. Roosevelt carried Homestead in 1936 by a five-to-one margin. A correspondent to the *Homestead Daily Messenger* explained why: ". . . never before in the history of the country, has labor been given a squarer deal." A "colored voter" for Roosevelt declared that "we are better off now than we have ever been. Mr. Roosevelt is for the worker and the poorer classes." Another Homestead voter sneeringly denounced the Republicans who "imply that Roosevelt is a tyrant and a villain because he dared to feed the hungry, clothe the naked, comfort the needy, and wipe the tears away from the eyes of those who wept."[42] Voters like these swelled presidential election turnout by more than 50 percent between 1924 and 1936 while population had increased by only 18 percent.[43]

What particularly attracted these largely ethnic working-class voters to the New Deal is that it offered these economic benefits without cultural preconditions. The pious moralism and tone of forced Americanization that had characterized most of Progressive reform was gone from New Deal liberalism. In its place were cultural symbols that suggested a much bigger American house with rooms for all, regardless of religion or birthplace or accent, and maybe even color. The glue that welded the new constituencies to the Democratic Party was made up of more than economic benefits. It was also to be found in Frank Capra films, Paul Robeson concerts, or Langston Hughes' poem, "Let America be America again (but it never was for me)."[44]

The amalgamation of new and old Democrats, a typical coalition in keeping with the American system, was an uneasy marriage for both partners. Many liberal Democrats hoped eventually to attract enough liberal Republicans to jettison the conservative baggage within their own party. Especially after 1938, conservative Democrats made common cause with Republicans in Congress to block further New Deal legislation. They were biding their time until FDR's charisma passed from the scene. But even after Roosevelt's death, to the surprise of many, the marriage seemed to hold. Truman held onto the presidency in 1948 despite defections from both the left and right wings of the Democratic Party, Eisenhower did nothing to dismantle New Deal programs, and the Democratic administrations of the 1960s seemed ready to expand the social contract further.

Undermining the New Deal Social Contract

As late as 1965 pollster Samuel Lubell could view Lyndon Johnson's 1964 landslide as not only a reassertion of the 1936 "Roosevelt coalition" but also as a decisive expansion that "shattered the coalition of Southern Democrats and Northern Republicans which first formed in 1938 to check the New Deal."[45] The 1964 election looked like a national debacle for the Republicans. Outside of the Confederacy, Goldwater carried only his home state of Arizona and that only by a 1 percent margin, but he decisively carried the heart of Dixie: Louisiana, Mississippi, Georgia, Alabama, and South Carolina. That outcome provoked Republican campaigners to reexamine their political strategy. By 1972 they had crafted a new Republican presidential majority. Nineteen sixty-four turned out to be the New Deal's last hurrah.

The initial trigger that made this new Republican majority possible was a national white backlash against the civil rights movement and other forms of African-American protest. Goldwater's 1964 victories in five Deep South states signaled that federal civil rights policy had provoked enough white southerners to renounce their historic Democratic allegiance to make the Republicans competitive in the south for the first time since Reconstruction. In the north, the massive ghetto uprisings of the late 1960s also crystalized long-simmering racial fears among core Democratic voters. Faced with an insurgent Black community, perceiving themselves threatened by lawless and criminal Black mobs, a significant fraction of northern urban (and now increasingly suburban) white Democrats began to think of themselves as white as much as Catholic, or Irish, or Polish, or working-class. Johnson's wholehearted embrace of the civil rights agenda sealed the emerging, but up to that time still incomplete, Democratic alignment of the newly-enlarged ranks of Black voters, but it also confirmed the anxieties of nervous white Democrats.

Republican strategists made a calculated decision. As late as 1960, the Republicans still claimed, as the party of Lincoln, to be the more authentic voice of racial equality. Despite Democratic gains since the 1930s, the Republicans still held onto a substantial Black vote and pointed out that the Democrats, with their Dixiecrat wing, were the home of the country's most intransigent racists. But Republican strategists decided that a concerted racial appeal to white Democrats—using publicly acceptable but easily transparent code words—held out the promise of gaining far more white voters than the number of Black voters who might be lost. This was the heart of Nixon's southern strategy or Kevin Phillips' proposals for a new Republican majority.

It worked. Republican strategists carefully crafted new rhetorical strategies designed to address white racial fears without using the overtly racist rhetoric of classic Dixiecrats, combining racially coded discussions of crime, welfare, and taxes with overlapping discontents provoked by the Vietnam War, feminism, and the gay rights movement.[46] They successfully realigned presidential politics, reducing the Democratic vote in 1968 to 43.5 percent from 61.3 percent in 1964. At the presidential level, the Democrats have never recovered. Recent concerns about the growing tide of Hispanic and Asian refugees and illegal immigrants have simply broadened and extended racial polarization. Humphrey's 1968 percentage is virtually identical to the mean of all Democratic presidential candidates from 1968 through 1992, actually a couple of tenths better than Clinton's 1992 showing.

But it did not work only because, as some political analysts seem to suggest, the Republicans cleverly manipulated cultural symbols while the Democrats squandered their natural majority by correspondingly inept campaign decisions. Republicans found it easy to look smart and Democrats found it difficult to mobilize their apparent political capital because underlying social changes since World War II had undermined the conditions which had allowed Democrats in the 1930s to partially overcome the biases against class alignments in American politics.

Among the most important of these changes were suburbanization, African-American migration, regional shifts in power, and the decline of anti-Catholicism. Together, these changes eroded the basis of party loyalty for both wings of the New Deal Democratic Party while correspondingly stimulating the shifts in Republican posture necessary to make the Republican Party a hospitable political home for disaffected ex-Democrats.

Suburbanization altered Democratic prospects in two ways. By racially remapping urban geography, suburbanization aggravated already existing racial tensions and polarization within the Democratic coalition. Federal housing and transportation policies subsidized and thus accelerated the process.[47] Secondly, as the children and grandchildren of the new immigrants moved out of urban ethnic enclaves into racially homogeneous but ethnically agnostic suburban housing tracts, they cut themselves off from the social and communal networks that had nurtured working-class consciousness. Their parents had joined the CIO at organizing meetings held at the Polish Falcons or Sons of Italy lodge, and such institutions sustained their parents' class and ethnic loyalty to the liberal wing of the Democratic Party. They spent time at the PTA or the mall. By 1967 75 percent of American union members under the age of 40 lived in suburbia.[48]

As the children of white ethnics moved out of the cities, people of color moved in. The two processes were not only intertwined, but they also functioned as mutually reinforcing trends, almost self-fulfilling prophecies. As the middle classes and well-paid unionized workers moved out of the cities, jobs followed them, and cities deteriorated, losing their economic and tax bases. As urban job opportunities disappeared, crime increased and the quality of urban life declined. The increase in Black and Hispanic population thus seemed to coincide with urban decay, confirming the prejudices of remaining white urban dwellers, adding to their incentive to flee the city.

While these interlocking migration patterns undermined the Democratic coalition, other social changes helped to make the Republicans more appealing to Catholics and southerners. The shift of population, wealth, and influence to the Sunbelt reduced the relative influence of the northern industrial states that had been the political base of most of the urban liberals who had provided the programmatic leadership for the New Deal coalition. Equally important, the traditional leadership of the Republican Party had also been located in northern and midwestern states as well. New Sunbelt elites, although just as wealthy and perhaps more conservative than eastern establishment Republicans, were less tainted with the whiff of the country club or prep school, more able to project a populist image more acceptable to conservative Democratic constituencies looking for a new political home. Similarly, the decline of anti-Catholicism removed one of the most important cultural barriers between Catholic conservatives and the Republican Party. Ironically, it was probably the election of John Kennnedy, a liberal Democrat but also the country's first Catholic president, which signaled that Protestant animosity to Catholicism was no longer a potent force in American culture. Catholics need no longer fear the Republicans.

It is a testimonial to the enduring strength of New Deal political loylaties that Democrats were able to forestall the full impact of these trends into the 1990s. At the presidential level, Republicans have dominated American politics since 1968. Democrats elected presidential candidates only after Watergate, the biggest political scandal in the nation's history, and when an eccentric Texas billionaire, Ross Perot, split the Republican ranks. Both successful Democratic candidates were Southern governors with weak ties to labor and other liberal Democratic constituencies. Democrats controlled Congress until 1994. But the unrelenting quarter-century assault on working-class income and organization suggests that this residual Democratic congressional holdover at best only slowed the dismantling of the New Deal social contract.

Conclusions

What should historians and citizens conclude from this story?

First, the inability of politicians since the 1960s to unite a majority of the American electorate around an egalitarian political economy has been a disaster for the country. Most of the wealth which has been created in the last twenty years has gone to the top 10 percent of the income and wealth pyramid, while two thirds of the population has lost ground. The majority of Americans now work more hours for less income then they did a generation ago. Two-income households are now necessary to match the living standards one paycheck once provided. The drop has been steepest for those at the bottom. The new armies of beggars on our street corners are the visible tip of the economic iceberg. The social crisis of crime, drugs, and urban deterioration is directly connected to the way partisan politics have shaped the allocation of our national resources.

Second, history matters. We cannot escape the consequences of the past, and we cannot reverse the distressing trends in our national political economy without understanding how that history has contributed to those trends.

Recognizing that history matters means understanding that the rules matter. Any analysis of American political behavior that is not grounded in an understanding of the rules will lead us astray. The tendency, for example, of some labor historians to find perfidy and treason in the hearts of anyone who accepted the rules of the game usually conflates debates about tactics with those of ideological loyalties.

Third, race matters because history matters. No advocates of class politics or economic justice will succeed in American politics unless they can find programs and rhetorical formulas which will unite diverse racial groups. But we cannot unite diverse racial groups around more egalitarian politics by simply wishing our history away as some critics of identity politics seem to be arguing.

Fourth, ideas matter. Without a vision, a set of inclusive cultural symbols, and practical legislative agenda to put that vision into practice, class politics would not have gone anywhere even in the 1930s despite the extraordinary stimulus of the depression. Mobilizing the victims—the majority of the American people—of a twenty-year Republican class war will not be an exercise in improved marketing. It will be an effort of crafting a social vision with a broad appeal, translating that appeal into specific programs and mobilizing supporters around cultural symbols of those larger objectives.

NOTES

1. Richard Oestreicher, "Urban Working-Class Political Behavior and Theories of American Electoral Politics, 1870–1940," *Journal of American History* 74 (March 1988): 1285–86.

2. Blue-collar workers, for example, split their vote 47 percent for Reagan, 46 percent for Carter, and 5 percent for Anderson in 1980; 49 percent for Bush and 50 percent for Dukakis in 1988. In 1948 the Democratic margin among blue-collar workers was nearly three to one. What has persisted, and sharply increased in recent years, is a clear correlation between household income and voting patterns: there is an almost linear relationship between household income and propensity to vote Republican in every presidential election since 1976. In most elections, however, the income level at which voting shifted from majority Democratic to majority Republican was between the 20th and 40th percentile of household income. Thus, economic inequality clearly continues to shape voting patterns but class status as defined by occupation does not. *New York Times* exit polls: *New York Times,* November 5, 1992; November 10, 1988. On the relationship between household income and voting patterns, see also Thomas Byrne Edsall, "The Changing Shape of Power: A Realignment in Public Policy," in Steve Fraser and Gary Gerstle, eds., *The Rise and Fall of the New Deal Order, 1930–1980* (Princeton: Princeton University Press, 1989), esp. 281–83.

3. Representative of this point of view are most of the authors in Fraser and Gerstle, *The Rise and Fall*. See also Mike Davis, *Prisoners of the American Dream: Politics and Economy in the History of the U.S. Working Class* (London: Verso, 1986).

4. Richard J. Barnet and Ronald E. Muller, *Global Reach: The Power of the Multinational Corporations* (New York: Simon and Schuster 1974); Richard Edwards, *Contested Terrain: The Transformation of the Workplace in the Twentieth Century* (New York: Basic Books, 1979) esp. 130–99; Robert B. Reich, *The Work of Nations: Preparing Ourselves for 21st-Century Capitalism* (New York: A. A. Knopf, 1991); Robert B. Reich, "Secession of the Successful," *The New York Times Magazine,* January 20, 1991, 16–17, 42–45; Werner Bonefeld and John Holloway, eds., *Global Capital, National State and the Politics of Money* (New York: St. Martin's, 1995); Anthony Giddens, *Beyond Left and Right: The Future of Radical Politics* (Stanford: Stanford University Press, 1994); David M. Gordon, Richard Edwards, and Michael Reich, *Segmented Work, Divided Workers: The Historical Transformation of Labor in the United States* (Cambridge: Cambridge University Press, 1982).

5. Thomas Byrne Edsall and Mary Edsall, *Chain Reaction: The Impact of Race, Rights, and Taxes on American Politics* (New York: Norton, 1991); E. J. Dionne, Jr., *They Only Look Dead: Why Progressives Will Dominate the Next Political Era* (New York: Simon and Schuster, 1996); Michael Tomsky, *Left For Dead: The Life, Death and Possible Resurrection of Progressive Politics in America* (New York: Free Press. 1996); Robert Kuttner, *The Life of the Party: Democratic Prospects in 1988 and Beyond* (New York: Viking, 1987).

6. Jeffrey G. Williamson and Peter H. Lindert, *American Inequality: A Macroeconomic History* (New York: Academic Press, 1980), 53–62. As Williamson and Lindert demonstrate by citing evidence from several studies, estimates of the distribution of wealth vary depending on the source of wealth data and assumptions about the total size of national wealth, which categories of wealth belong in the calculations, and the nature of household composition. Yet the general trend and magnitude of change is similar in all of the studies they cite. Another problem noted by critics of studies of wealth distribution (e.g., Gabriel Kolko, *Wealth and Power in America: An Analysis of Social Class and Income Distribution* (New York: Praeger, 1962)) is that none of the studies attempt to account for the systematic concealment of assets through trusts, investment in nontaxable assets, and outright fraud. Such concealment of assets from tax authorities would not effect the argument for the redistributive impact of the New Deal social contract unless it could be demonstrated that the wealthy became dramatically more adept at shielding assets from taxation after the 1930s. Since marginal tax rates rose sharply, the incentive for such shielding did increase, but it seems

hard to believe that increased effort at tax avoidance would explain all of the large changes in the distribution of income found by economic historians.

7. Williamson and Lindert, *American Inequality,* 76, 82–83. Again, the results of studies vary slightly, but all agree on the general trend.

8. Kevin Phillips, *The Politics of Rich and Poor: Wealth and the Electorate in the Reagan Aftermath* (New York: Harper Perennial, 1990) places the top 1 percent's pretax share of national income at 9 percent in 1980 (12) and the posttax share at 7 percent in 1977 (xi). Donald L. Bartlett and James B. Steele, *America: What Went Wrong?* (Kansas City: Andrews and McNeel, 1996) place the pretax 1980 share of the top 1 percent of IRS tax returns at 8 percent (6–7).

9. Williamson and Lindert, *American Inequality,* 85, for example, cite data on sharp declines in capital gains by the top 5 percent, possibly a function of changing tax policy. I nonetheless use the tentative "may" intentionally here because of the debates about the accuracy of income reporting. Williamson and Lindert attempt to quantitatively assess the issue *(American Inequality,* 86–88) and conclude that even if the wealthy concealed nearly 20 percent more of their income in the late '40s than in 1929, 60 percent of the estimated income redistribution would remain. Other scholars, however, posit the possibility of deeper levels of tax evasion by the wealthy.

10. Williamson and Lindert, *American Inequality,* 84; Phillips, *The Politics,* 12. The 1969 figure, from Phillips, is based on slightly different data and may not be completely comparable to the 1929 and 1951 figures from Williamson and Lindert. For a systematic analysis of the shrinking ratios between high- and low-income recipients from the 1930s to the 1970s, see Claudia Goldin and Robert Margo, "The Great Compression: The Wage Structure in the United States at Mid-Century," *Quarterly Journal of Economics* 107 (February 1992), 1–34.

11. U.S. Department of Commerce, *Historical Statistics of the United States: Colonial Times to 1970* (Washington, D.C.: Government Printing Office, 1975), 178, lists union membership as percentage of nonagricultural employment as 11.9 percent in 1934 and 35.5 percent in 1945.

12. *Historical Statistics,* 162–63, 297.

13. For discussion of the wage effects of the GI Bill, see Goldin and Margo, "The Great Compression," esp. 30–31.

14. Kevin Phillips, *Boiling Point: Democrats, Republicans and the Decline of Middle Class Prosperity* (New York: Random House, 1993), 8, 37.

15. Kevin Phillips, *The Politics of Rich and Poor,* 11–13, 241.

16. Phillips, *Boiling Point;* Kevin Phillips, *Arrogant Capital: Washington, Wall Street and the Frustration of American Politics* (Boston: Little Brown and Co., 1994); Kevin Phillips (speech, Kennedy School of Government conference, Cambridge, Mass., October 14, 1995).

17. James Fallows, "The Republican Promise," *The New York Review of Books* 42 (1) (January 12, 1995), 6; Paul Krugman, *Peddling Prosperity: Economic Sense and Nonsense in the Age of Diminished Expectations* (New York: W. W. Norton, 1994), 4, 125, 130–32, 136. Krugman's estimate of even modest growth in median household income depends on the downward adjustment in the consumer price index recently advocated by some economists and by the presidential commission appointed by President Clinton to study the issue. For a critique of such efforts to adjust the consumer price index downward, see Jeff Madrick, "The Cost of Living: A New Myth," *New York Review of Books* 44 (4) (March 6, 1997). For a more pessimistic interpretation of changes in household income in the '70s and '80s, see Louis Uchitelle, "U.S. Wages: Not Getting Ahead? Better Get Used to It," *New York Times,* December 16, 1990.

18. Uchitelle, "U.S. Wages."

19. The most significant study of increased work time and its consequences is Juliet B. Schor, *The Overworked American: The Unexpected Decline of Leisure* (New York: Basic Books, 1992).

20. *New York Times,* October 7, 1994; *New York Times,* April 15, 1992.

21. Karen W. Arenson, "Cuts in Tuition Assistance Put College Beyond Reach of Poorest Students," *New York Times,* January 27, 1997.

22. Krugman, *Peddling Prosperity,* 132–38; Bartlett and Steele, *America,* 6–14; Phillips, *Politics,* 8–23; Phillips, *Boiling Point,* 20–31.

23. David Greenstone, *Labor in American Politics* (New York: Knopf, 1969) explicitly makes the argument for the equivalence of the New Deal with social democracy and its roots in capitalist development, but the argument could be viewed as unstated but implicit in many classic treatments of the New Deal such as William Leuchtenberg, *Franklin Roosevelt and the New Deal, 1932–1940* (New York: Harper and Row, 1963) or Arthur M. Schlesinger, Jr., *The Age of Roosevelt, The Coming of the New Deal* (Boston: Houghton Mifflin, 1958) as well as most of the predominantly New Left scholars featured in Fraser and Gerstle, *The Rise and Fall.*

24. Ira Katznelson, "Was the Great Society a Lost Opportunity?," in Fraser and Gerstle, *The Rise and Fall.* 186–87.

25. "The Barren Marriage of American Labor and the Democratic Party," in Mike Davis, *Prisoners,* 52–102. I first heard the phrase "Devil's Bargain," used as a Faustian metaphor for New Deal labor policy, from a retired labor leader, Irving Dichter, the former secretary-treasurer of the Mine, Mill, and Smelter Workers. Others who take this perspective include Steve Fraser and Nelson Lichtenstein, both with essays in Fraser and Gerstle, *The Rise and Fall,* as well as their books on New Deal labor: Steve Fraser, *Labor Will Rule: Sidney Hillman and the Rise of American Labor* (New York: Free Press, 1991); Nelson Lichtenstein, *Labor's War At Home: The CIO in World War II* (Cambridge: Cambridge University Press, 1982).

26. Kenneth T. Jackson, *Crabgrass Frontier: The Suburbanization of the United States* (New York: Oxford University Press, 1985), 190–230, Douglas quoted on 226.

27. Samuel Lubell, *The Future of American Politics,* 3d ed. (New York: Harper and Row, 1965), 106–13.

28. August Meier and Elliott Rudwick, *Black Detroit and the Rise of the UAW* (Oxford: Oxford University Press, 1979), 202–5.

29. David Plotke, *Building a Democratic Political Order: Reshaping American Liberalism in the 1930s and 1940s* (Cambridge: Cambridge University Press, 1996) 363–64; for a similar critique of prevailing left scholarship about the New Deal order, see Kevin Boyle, "Little More Than Ashes: The UAW and American Reform in the 1960s," in this volume.

30. John Holloway, "Global Capital and the National State," in Bonefeld and Holloway, *Global Capital,* 135. See also Gordon, Edwards, and Reich, *Segmented Work,* 240–43.

31. Among insightful exceptions to this trend, see Giddens, *Beyond Left and Right,* and Charles F. Sabel, *Work and Politics: The Division of Labor in Industry* (Cambridge: Cambridge University Press, 1982). For a comparison of the American and German cases suggesting how differing political systems influenced the process differently, see Stephen Amberg, "The Contrasting Consequences of Labor-Party Alliances: Politics and Industrial Relations in the United States and Germany," (paper delivered at the Labor and Politics conference, George Meany Center, Silver Springs, Md., November 14, 1994).

32. Typical of this genre are Dionne, *They Only Look Dead,* and Tomsky, *Left for Dead.*

33. Oestreicher, "Urban Working-Class Political Behavior," 1261–64.

34. This theme and those in the following paragraphs are explored in greater detail in Oestreicher, "Urban Working-Class Political Behavior."

35. On the importance of the courts in shaping union behavior, see Karen Orren, *Belated Feudalism: Labor Law and Liberal Development in the United States* (Cambridge: Cambridge University Press, 1991); William B. Forbath, *Law and the Shaping of the American Labor Movement* (Cambridge, Mass.: Harvard University Press, 1991).

36. In 1900 immigrants and native whites of foreign parents made up 56 percent of employees in manufacturing, in 1920 51 percent. Addition of African-Americans, Asian-Americans, and Hispanics pushes the nonnative, non-WASP percentage of manufacturing workers to around 60 percent in both years. U.S. Department of Commerce and Labor, *Special Report on Occupations at the Twelfth Census* (Washington, D.C.: Government Printing Office, 1904), cxiii; U.S. Department of Commerce, Bureau of the Census, *Fourteenth Census, Population 1920: Occupations* (Washington, D.C.: Government Printing Office, 1923), 34.

37. In 1940, for example, 51 percent of non-southern white Protestant workers voted Republican. Oestreicher, "Urban Working-Class Political Behavior," 1264.

38. James L. Sundquist, *Dynamics of the Party System: Alignment and Realignment of Poltical Parties in the United States, Revised Edition* (Washington, D.C.: Brookings Institution, 1983), 200, 202–3.

39. Sundquist, *Dynamics*, 218–19.

40. Much of the scholarly literature on New Deal economic policy emphasizes the debates among policy makers between planners, antimonopolists, and Keynesians. While such debates certainly were important, for the most part, they took place within a relatively narrow ideological spectrum, all sharing some key assumptions. All, for example, assumed that the federal government would play a much more important role in regulating the economy than in the past, and even the most ardent planners assumed that the United States would remain primarily a privately owned market economy. For a useful discussion of these debates among intellectuals and policy makers, see Ellis W. Hawley, *The New Deal and the Problem of Monopoly: A Study in Economic Ambivalence* (Princeton: Princeton University Press, 1966)

41. Christopher L. Tomlins, *The State and the Unions: Labor Relations, Law, and the Organized Labor Movement in America, 1880–1960* (Cambridge: Cambridge University Press, 1985), 103–47.

42. *Homestead Daily Messenger,* October 7, 3, 13, 1936; Eric Leif Davin, "The New Deal in the Steel Valley: Class Politics in Pittsburgh and Western Pennsylvania, 1932–1960" (Ph.D. diss., in progress, University of Pittsburgh); first draft in my possession.

43. *The World Almanac* (New York: 1993), 103, 387, 470. Kristi Andersen, *The Creation of a Democratic Majority, 1928–1936* (Chicago: University of Chicago Press, 1981); Sundquist, *Dynamics of the Party System,* 229–40.

44. Langston Hughes, "Let America Be America Again," in Harvey Swados, ed., *American Writer and the Great Depression* (New York: Bobbs-Merrill, 1966), 498–501

45. Lubell, *The Future,* 1–3.

46. Probably the best analysis of these rhetorical strategies is the Edsalls' *Chain Reaction.*

47. Jackson, *Crabgrass Frontier,* chapters 11, 14.

48. Robert H. Zieger, *American Workers, American Unions, 1920–1985* (Baltimore: Johns Hopkins University Press, 1986), 138.

Robert Asher

2

Producerism is Consciousness of Class

Ironworkers' and Steelworkers' Views on Political Economy, 1894–1920

I

As E. P. Thompson has suggested, people usually define themselves as a class by identifying other classes whose interests are *in opposition* to their own.[1] Throughout the industrial world of the nineteenth century, manual workers differentiated themselves, as producers, from an amorphous group of allegedly parasitical nonproducers. Many workers in the United States shared this view, constructing a system of economic and political thought premised on their consciousness as members of the class of manual producers.

Producerism was a ubiquitous value system that had been embraced by farmers and handicraft workers all over the world since at least the middle of the seventeenth century. Producerism gave the *menu peuple* of the world a strong sense of their worth to society and of the righteousness of their attempts to organize against the economic and political elites, who were viewed as nonproducing predators whose wealth and power were amassed by robbing producers. Producerism suggested that producers had a right to a decent living (a fair day's wages, actually paid) and to personal liberty. Producers also believed they were entitled to political influence commensurate to their numbers. Harold Perkin's description of the ideal society posited by early nineteenth-century English workers reflected the influence of the producerist ethos: "Its ideal citizen was the produc-

51

tive, independent worker, and its ideal society an equalitarian one based on labour and co-operation."[2]

This essay explores the producerist ethos of one important group of workers: late nineteenth- and early twentieth-century activist skilled iron- and steelworkers. Articulate iron- and steelworkers discussed their views of political economy in the letters they wrote to the newspapers published by their union, the Amalgamated Association of Iron, Steel and Tin Workers.[3] Most of the correspondents were agents for the union newspapers, whose job it was to sell subscriptions to their union's journal and to report news about the activities of union members and local lodges. The letters clearly establish the iron- and steelworkers' dedication to producerism. They also demonstrate that producerism did not lead iron- and steelworkers as a group to embrace any particular vision of the American political economy or to follow particular tactics to construct a more just socioeconomic system. Consequently, activist iron- and steelworkers—who easily agreed on their rights, worth, and dignity as producers—diverged when they considered political strategies to advance their economic welfare. They fused their common belief in producerism and a democratic republic with advocacy of a multiplicity of political strategies. Some of the letter writers opposed any organized working class political action. Others believed that the initiative and the referendum would serve as cures for the elites' usurpation of political power. Still others advocated the election of workers to public office, lower tariffs, the Single Tax on unearned increments in land values, or partial nationalization of key industries. And some iron- and steelworkers called for the creation of a socialist sytem.

The iron- and steelworkers' commitment to producerism also led them to ignore the sexual, racial, and ethnic divisions within the working class. Although producerism defined the manual laborer by assuming that she/he was a member of a class that was exploited by nonworkers, the ideology did not consider the possibility of stratification within the class of producers. Thus the iron- and steelworkers who wrote to their newspapers did not consider the possibility that the members of one stratum of producers might exploit the workers of other stratum. While producerism, *prima face*, tended to promote the unity of manual workers, other ideologies—racism, sexism, nativism, and ethnic chauvinism—divided workers, as the essays in this volume clearly demonstrate.

Producerism therefore did not provide iron- and steelworkers the basis for common economic and political action. The ideology did, however, provide these workers with a world view that helped them order their workplace experiences. The iron and steelworkers studied here were not representative of the turn-of-the-century working class as a whole: they were too highly skilled, too thoroughly organized, too articulate, and too ideologically engaged to fill that role. As they employed a common language and as they divided over the implications of that language, iron- and steelworkers revealed many of the hopes and tensions present in the political thought of activist workers in industrializing America.

II

American labor historians have not systematically analyzed the origins of the producer ideology. My attempts to trace the European antecedents of producerism back further than late eighteenth century English artisanal radicalism have taken me to the views of Gerrard Winstanley, a radical Puritan minister who was the leading spokesman for the Diggers in the 1640s. Winstanley, who believed that God had ordained an egalitarian society of communal producers, sermonized passionately:

> No man can be rich but . . . either by his own labours, or by the labours of other men helping him. . . . If other men help him to work, then are those riches his neighbours' as well as his. . . . Rich men receive all they have from the labourer's hand, and what they give, they give away other men's labours, not their own.[4]

Few manual workers shared Winstanley's views in the sixteenth and early seventeenth centuries. That is not surprising. The urban artisans of these epochs were members of corporate communities that organically linked their lives to patrons of the higher social orders. Elites then provided economic aid and political connections that were essential to the welfare of artisanal producers, especially when they needed access to government officials. Common laborers were frequently dependent on the employment of affluent patrons. In such societies, artisans and laborers were not likely to embrace producerism, which explicitly denigrated the classes to which the artisans' and laborers' patrons and employers belonged. The breakdown of corporate communities and paternalism was a precondition to the widespread adoption and propagation of a producerist world view among artisans and common laborers.[5]

By the time of the American Revolution, producerism had become an integral part of the world view of the nation's artisans. Thomas Eaton, a New York City printer, expressed the producerist ideology in verse, proclaiming that honest workers

> a present living get,
> Through perseverance, toil and sweat,
> With carpenters and teachers too,
> And authors, printers, and a crew
> Of other useful men who wield the tool, the type, or pen,
> It fares the same—these lay the plan,
> For greatness in some other man—
> Nor do the bugs of greatness know,
> To whom they all their greatness owe,
> Or will not own the fact for they
> Alike upon the people play
> The monkey tricks of *brag* and *prate*,
> As though they did themselves create.[6]

In *The Radicalism of the American Revolution*, Gordon Wood points to the way republicans used producerist rhetoric to discredit the concept of aristocracy and the influence of notables. Attacking the luxurious, nonproductive lifestyle of aristocrats, both middle-class and lower-income republicans claimed that the honorable group in American society was the group of nonaristocratic producers. Sean Wilentz traces the divergence that occurred in the ranks of republicans beginning in the 1820s, as manual laborers increasingly rejected the consensual claim of middle class republicans that capitalists and merchants were nonaristocratic producers. This schism would intensify in the years immediately following the Civil War, as David Montgomery demonstrated in his seminal study, *Beyond Equality: Labor and the Radical Republicans, 1862–1872*.[7] But the writings of New York City machinist Thomas Skidmore marked a clear break with the notion that the new nation constituted a producer's paradise in which social processes operated harmoniously to reward fairly all those who had eschewed a life of luxury.

In *The Rights of Man to Property*, published in 1829, Skidmore hit his readers with producerist rhetoric from the start. In the third paragraph of his book, Skidmore posited that there was great inequality in the ownership of productive property and that the owners of capital "*will* live on the labor of others, and themselves perform none, or if any, a very disproportionate share, of that toil which attends them as a condition of their existence, and without the performance of which, they have no *just* right to preserve or retain that existence, even for a single hour." To remedy this inequality, Skidmore proposed that governments redistribute a great deal of land be so that all persons, upon reaching adulthood, could be given equal amounts of land and other types of capital. He also contended that the wealth each producer accumulated over a lifetime of labor would revert to the government upon the producer's death, to be part of the equal distribution to the next generation of producers.[8]

After 1865, as market capitalism and manufacturing dramatically eroded the earnings and economic independence of artisans, skilled workers and their spokesmen increasingly adopted the producerist language Skidmore had employed three decades earlier.[9] They took particular aim at the emerging class of factory owners, who allegedly were "nonproductive" manufacturers. Editors of labor newspapers led the way, employing producerist rhetoric as part of their critique of the wage system and industrial capitalism. In 1888, for instance, the editor of the Detroit *Advance and Labor Leaf*, that city's leading labor newspaper, questioned the validity of Abraham Lincoln's paradigm of social mobility, which assumed that the employed producer of today would become economically independent and would eventually employ others. The editor charged that the rich were parasites:

> We are often told that the millionaires of today were working for wages thirty or forty years ago and hence, the millionaires of thirty or forty years hence, will be the men who are now working for a dollar or two per day. These delusive statements are intended to reconcile the toiler to the condition to which monopoly is disposed to consign him. No wage earner ever has or ever can become a millionaire by honest labor. The first step

towards accumulation of a million is to cease to earn a living and go into the business of skinning others.[10]

Newspaper editors were hardly alone in voicing such sentiments. In 1902, a Colorado housewife told the state's Bureau of Labor Statistics that "we already have laws to prevent the poor from robbing the rich; we should have laws to prevent the rich from robbing the poor."[11] Those words would have had great resonance for the men who labored in the heat and dirt of the nation's iron and steel mills.

III

The iron and steel industry in the United States traced its roots to the colonial period. When manufacturers introduced steel-producing technology in the post–Civil War years, many of the workers they hired in the newly built steel mills were artisans who had been working in the iron industry (or were immigrants who had learned their skills in the English steel industry). Both American and English artisans came from a literate culture that vigorously advanced the cause of republican government and democratic republicanism (suffrage for white adult males). The skilled iron- and steelworkers who wrote to the *Amalgamated Journal* appear to have worked mostly in the finishing mills that processed iron and steel products. The fabricating mills were more dependent on skilled labor than were the blast furnaces and steel furnaces that made basic iron and steel. The large and small steel companies were more tolerant of trade unionism in the finishing mills. Although the Carnegie Corporation crushed the Amalgamated Association of Iron, Steel and Tin Workers at Homestead, Pennsylvania, in 1892 and thereafter eliminated the Amalgamated from all the basic steel mills, the nation's steel manufacturers accepted the union in its finishing mills. Only in 1910 did U.S. Steel, the industry pacesetter, move to end collective bargaining with the Amalgamated in the company's finishing mills.[12]

The newspapers printed by the unions in the iron and steel industry had developed a tradition of printing the correspondence of union members and the agents who sold the newspapers. The correspondents of the *National Labor Tribune* and the Amalgamated *Journal* frequently commented on questions of political economy. It is hard to know whether or not workers in other occupations wrote as many letters about political economy to their trade papers; it is clear that the editors of most of the other union newspapers in the United States decided against printing many letters about political economy, perhaps because they feared disagreements would weaken their unions.[13]

Those iron- and steelworkers who wrote to their papers intertwined producerism with a variety of traditions. Some combined producerism and artisanal republicanism. Old Dad Hencks, a correspondent from the Joliet, Illinois, Single Creek Lodge of the Amalgamated, wrote on April 14, 1917, of a "Republic wherein all men are on the same footing and make laws for all the people. . . ."[14] Many other steelworkers wrote to the *Journal* to celebrate the heritage of the Declaration of Independence and the American Revolution, which skilled metalworkers saw as creating a society in which men had the right to be free of tyranny. The fusion of producerism and republicanism also can be seen in the long letter on "The Problem of Today—Labor," penned in 1916 by W. J. Griffiths of Middletown, Ohio. "The Laborer's Complaint is not that BRAINS RULE," he wrote, "or that culture leads, but that conscienceless, cunning and miserly acquisitiveness are rewarded better than constructive ability or open hearted integrity. . . . Labor's Complaint is that our rulers, statesmen and many of our orators have not attempted to engraft Republican principles into our industrial system and have forgotten or denied its underlying principles . . ." Griffiths then went on to complain that the contemporary press, the clergy, political economists, and politicians were subverting the "power of the ballot," were encouraging the "oppression of the poor," and were teaching the fallacious doctrine "that production and not the equitable distribution of wealth" were the essence of civilization.[15]

While many iron- and steelworkers drew on the republican tradition to frame their producerism, others were influenced by evangelical Protestant traditions. Consider the blending of producerist ideas with Christian socialism and regenerative trade unionism[16] in the April 15, 1915, letter of Fred Charles Rising:

> The word Capitalism means to have plenty of money. Unionism means uniting of a banding together. . . . The good book says very plainly these words, "By the sweat of thy brow shalt thou eat bread" . . . yet . . . the man behind the "MONEY" does not help to carry out this scriptural command. . . . The man of money as a rule, is a very gluttonous fellow. . . . Capitalists . . .

think they are going to go straight to heaven when they die.
BUT I DOUBT IT . . . they have never once thought of the men
who are sweating away their lives in their factory. WE ORGA-
NIZE TO PROTECT AND HELP TO LIFT TO HIGHER
PLANE OF LIFE . . . TO BE ATTAINED BY THE MAJORITY
OF THE WORKING CLASS. WE STAND, I SAY, TO HELP
BETTER THE CONDITIONS OF THE MASSES. . . . UNION-
ISM IS A TONIC THAT, THE MORE YOU KNOW OF IT AND
THE MORE ONE TAKES IT INTO THEIR DAILY LIVES
AND TRIES TO LIVE UP TO ITS TEACHINGS THE MORE
THEY GET TO LIKE IT. . . . UNIONISM EDUCATES MEN
TO THE HIGHER IDEALS OF LIFE AND TO ENJOY THIS
LIFE AS HUMANS, INSTEAD OF THE CAPITALIST WAY,
LIKE SLAVES OR DOGS.

Another steelworker, L. Matt Greer of Ashland, Kentucky (in 1904),
and Wheeling, West Virginia (1914–1920), who signed his letters to
the *Journal* with the sobriquet "Hugo the Third," was an evangelical
Protestant socialist who pointed out that Christ was a manual laborer himself. "We must learn the secret of the brotherhood of man
as taught by our Lord and Savior, Jesus Christ," he said, "who
worked as a carpenter, and who picked his followers not from the
master class, but from the humble fishermen. . . ." For Greer, the
millennium meant that "all men should eat bread by the sweat of the
brow, no rich or poor, and man to live would have to work or get off
the earth, and no set of men or women riding high on flowery beds of
ease on the bowed backs of the working class." To an anonymous
evangelical steelworker in Vincennes, Indiana, the ideal society was
one that brought "every man, women and child who toils in this
country . . . together in bonds of perfect brotherhood. . . ." He had
more use for the "honest heart under a ragged shirt" than for the
"blockheaded bloat with a bank account." Men and women had a
"God-given right," he asserted, to "work and earn their living hon-
estly." Producers had to "have the right to labor and to have the
products of our labor." The "mission of Union labor" was to "give the
workers the full product of their toil. . . ."[17]

It was one thing for a steelworker to demand the *full* product of
his toil; since the early nineteenth century American workers had
embraced a labor theory of value that held that all producers should
receive the full value of the product produced by their labor, as had,

ostensibly, the archetypal artisan and yeoman farmer. It was another thing to determine the best method for building a political economy that assured workers the full value of their work. On this practical point, activist iron- and steelworkers split in a variety of directions.[18] Some of the correspondents embraced socialism as the best means of solving the injustices of the current regime, hoping that a society controlled by producers would eliminate the whole problem of apportioning the value of the laborer's work. Consider the outlook of R. D. Scrom, who in 1915 asked, "Why should we, the producers of all wealth, be the objects of charity and pity by the hypocritical rich who never produced a dollar in their lives. . . . We being the producers of everything produced why should we not produce for our own profit and enjoyment instead of producing for a wage and the bulk of the profit going to the parasitic capitalist. . . ."[19]

Many other skilled steelworkers endorsed the Single Tax—and criticized socialism—as the best path to creating a producerist economy. Single-taxers looked to a properly constructed competitive economic system as the best way to reward producers for their labor and to promote social mobility. William F. Yohe wrote from Pottstown, Pennsylvania:

> Real competition is not warlike; it is rather the emulation of the classroom, wherein even he who is last *retains all he has gained* and wherein none get allowances at the expense of others. "Competition" is the equation of values through exchange, and when free, determines unerringly just how much it is entitled to. Wages can be fairly adjusted in no other way; if there is another equitable method, Socialists have yet to point it out. The single tax on land values will bring free competition, and free competition means free men.[20]

Edward Burleigh, a Philadelphia steelworker, likewise argued that the Single Tax would "give us all the good that sincere Socialists desire without the evil which their system involves." He agreed that socialism "necessarily involves a loss of individual freedom." Socialism, he contended, would put "the means of earning a living under the control of a majority. The rule of the majority may be as imperialistic and intolerable as the rule of the few or of one." Majorities could easily trample on minority rights. "It should never be forgotten," he said, that 'the majority' is not the 'whole people.' In matters referring to government (the sole proper function of which is to preserve equal freedom), majorities should rule, since it must be either the majority or the minority; but in matters of earning a living, matters of individual action, the individual should decide. . . . In ridding ourselves of one despotism we must be careful not to subject ourselves to another."[21] Similarly, Joe Barth, a Single-Taxer from McKees Rocks, Pennsylvania, wrote in 1904[22] that working men deserved "fair living wages," that mines should be owned by the federal government, and that since socialism was "not only foreign to this country but foreign to the age," it would be better to embrace the Single Tax, which "has a broader sweep; all natural wealth should belong to the nation."[23]

While some iron- and steelworkers debated socialism and the single tax, many others expressed disillusionment with *party* politics of any form. They were skeptical of platform promises, which they saw as empty gestures. These workers believed that "reforms that are necessary in this country will come through good patriotic citizens who have the welfare of their country at heart, not through parties."[24] Joseph Hoenig, a steelworker from Lockport, New York, was fearful that workers engaged in political activity would be fired by their employers. Hoenig stressed building up the beneficial funds of the union as a precondition to effective political action. Concerned that workers were "doing nothing but voting for bosses in the factory or party bosses all over the United States," Hoenig urged workers to "vote for the initiative and referendum. That is all we want. That is the kind of socialism I want. A workingman that wants more than that wants too much. We want more, but the people will have a word to say on that. That [the initiative and referendum] will give us a government by the people, and the people will do the rest."[25] Hoenig's views echoed those of a 1894 "Populist" correspondent from Pittsburgh, who wrote to the *National Labor Tribune*, "If the bills were submitted to the people to vote on before they became laws the people would soon be qualified to know good laws from bad one. I do not think any beneficent reform will ever come until the people adopt the initiative and referendum."[26]

John McGovern, a *Journal* agent who lived in Cleveland, dealt at length with this issue in a long July 1904 letter that was directed specifically at "Hugo the Third"'s vigorous advocacy of socialism. McGovern drew on the traditional dread that the lower economic orders in the United States have had of concentrated power. He argued that *all* political power led to abusive behavior by the men who exercised it. Telling workers to be perpetual independent voters, so that they could check abusive political combinations, McGovern argued that

> The Socialist party is now a simon pure party, good in all the word implies, but let that party show signs of coming into power, politicians would be tumbling over one another getting in out of the wet, and what could "Hugo" do? After a few conventions and possibly a little money on the side, the socialistic party would become a side show again to the Democratic or Republican parties. I am of the opinion that no political institution can exist in this country that cannot or will not be controlled by money. You cannot control the independent voter as you can control an organization.

Referring to artisanal republicanism's antiprivilege tradition and the producer ethic, McGovern had a simple solution to the producer's ordeal: "Our country is a government of the people, by the people and for the people, while the economic laws that have been introduced by the fakirs in our legislative halls make one part of the citizens masters and the other part slaves. . . . I don't think that the man who will . . . represent the Socialist party at Washington at some future time will ever accomplish much as a Socialist, but as a citizen who is ready and willing to cooperate with his fellow-countrymen he will be able to give us some relief from those unjust laws that now disgraces [sic] our country. No, 'Hugo,' the independent voter is head and shoulders above the party slave."[27] A few months later, just in advance of the 1904 presidential election, McGovern made specific his understanding of political independence. He urged his fellow workers to vote for the Socialist Party of America in the upcoming presidential, congressional, and state legislative elections and then to select the "best men on the Republican or Democratic ticket to fill your county or city offices. . . ."[28]

One would expect that the differences among iron- and steelworkers would have been most pronounced during the 1912 presidential election campaign, when four dramatically different candidates vied for the White House. Unfortunately, none of the correspondents to the *Journal* commented specifically on the election, although one reference to William Howard Taft as an injunction-issuing judge was printed. The silence is easily explained: the editor of the *Journal* had adopted a nonpartisan political policy designed to prevent discord within a union whose members distributed their votes to Republican, Democratic, and Socialist Party candidates. Correspondents who were democratic socialists, such as Peter W. Kohli of Fort Wayne, Indiana, honored the paper's editorial policy but made many comments in their letters about the need for *political participation* by workers as the most effective way to end the injustices meted out to producers by capital. In July 1912, Kohli noted that iron- and steelworkers "have no friends in the public offices, and we won't have them as long as we don't get together and put them there." Contrasting political action with economic action, Kohli expostulated, "We don't want no revolution with the bullet, but we must get busy and use the ballot. You can use it this fall to a great advantage if you will. If you want it otherwise keep on striking and starving at the same time. . . . Your masters are safe behind their government's wall of protection."[29]

Kohli's orientation towards political action coincided with that of Ben I. Davis, the editor of the *Journal*. Throughout the campaign, Davis printed news notices about labor union members who ran for public office on major party tickets. He also printed columns that attacked the syndicalism favored by the Industrial Workers of the World. He welcomed the political views of socialists as long as they did not specifically endorse the Socialist Party of America. Thus readers of the *Journal* were exposed to praise for socialist ideology but never encountered the name of Eugene Victor Debs.[30]

IV

World War I and its immediate aftermath proved a watershed for politically engaged iron- and steelworkers. That is not to say that the war significantly changed activist steelworkers' perspectives. Correspondents continued to embrace their producerist and republican ideals.[31] Some hoped that, in making the "world a world democracy in practice as well as theory," the producerist ideal, enunciated by Robert Ingersol, would be attained: "The aristocracy of idleness has perished from the earth. I see a world without a slave. Man at last is free."[32] These ideals led steelworkers to view themselves as being in opposition to capitalist owners, stimulated criticism of the wartime profiteering of steel companies and other businesses, and generated class-based criticisms of National War Labor Board decisions that held down wages and forced workers to make more

wartime sacrifices than managers and owners. But these oppositional stances did not lead iron- and steelworkers to adopt a single
agenda; as in the years before the war, iron- and steelworkers continued to hold divergent views about political strategies.

In late 1918 and early 1919 many correspondents were optimistic
about the prospects for a significant increase in the powers of producers in the steel industry. But as they discussed the chances of expanding union representation in the steel industry and of achieving
a more influential position for organized labor in the postwar reconstruction, correspondents also laid bare the limits of their vision of
the working class. In particular, some steelworkers made clear that
in their view producerism did not require a steelworkers' union or a
political economy that represented the interests of "unskilled" workers. In December of 1918, an enthusiastic socialist *Journal* correspondent, P. Lamoureux of Mohawk Valley Lodge No. 11, Cohoes,
New York, raised the question of solidarity between skilled and "unskilled" steelworkers. Previously, socialist correspondents to the
Amalgamated *Journal* had talked of the need to have solidarity between union and nonunion steelworkers, a rhetorical device that deliberately skirted what they knew was a divisive issue, the place of
the unskilled and largely "new immigrant" steelworker in a union
that represented only skilled workers, the vast majority of whom
were native-born men of old Yankee and British stock and immigrants from the British Isles. Lamoureux put the case for an "equal
wage for labor in general" in terms of the interdependence of all producers, skilled and unskilled alike. He reminded skilled workers
that when economic cycles created unemployment for skilled workers, they were thrown into the casual labor market and therefore
would benefit from higher wages for unskilled workers. Lamoureux
finished his case with a flourish of producerist rhetoric: "Let us who
produce all give the best that is in us for all."[33] Lamoureux's letter
brought a rebuttal from Andrew Jensen, a fellow lodge member.
Jensen argued that "common laborers" could have "learned a trade"
but did not. By learning a trade skilled laborers increased their
"mental capacity" and became "the surgeons and doctors of industry;
without them industry would die." Economic equality between common labor and skilled labor would "cause an awful stagnation in all
industries, for nobody would bother their heads learning a trade."[34]

In the tense days of 1919 and 1920, other correspondents worked
to distinguish producerism from the "alien" doctrines of Bolshevik

socialism. Particularly instructive is the letter of A. Burdelow of the Molly Stark Lodge, Canton, Ohio, who complained in 1919 that labor was not getting a fair portion of what it produced and should share in industrial management and control of industry. "Class competition," he wrote, should "give way to class cooperation and that the lie to the survival of the fittest in industry must be killed." At the same time, Burdelow insisted that "there is no room for Bolshevism in America" and that the "lie of the class struggle must go."[35] The famous labor poet, Michael McGovern, of Youngstown, Ohio, complained on January 1, 1920, that the war had seen the "daily toil" of "workmen" enrich the "Baron's store."

> The scene is changed. The war is won,
> Our judges like to huntsmen wield
> Injunction whips o'er men who've done
> War's duty well in labor's field.

As he defended America's producers as a class, however, McGovern also warned that "American working men must not be classed with the ignorant and revolutionary Russians."[36]

Such carefully drawn distinctions carried little weight amid the hysteria of the Red Scare. By 1920 federal, state, and local government repression of unions and radical trade unionists had taken its toll on the correspondents to the *Journal*. A Reading, Pennsylvania, socialist adopted the pseudonym "XYZ",[37] while in the immediate aftermath of the Palmer Raids, "Hugo the Third" signed his letters "Jack Frost" and stopped using terms like "capitalism." Hugo also bitterly observed that the common people had stood by and allowed Christ to be crucified and now were mute as strikers and unions were being assaulted.[38] With biting irony, Joseph Murphy of Queen City Lodge No. 15, Buffalo, New York, wrote, "We fought to make the world safe for democracy. Now let's make democracy safe for the world."[39]

Despite the bitterness of the postwar backlash, iron- and steel-workers had not abandoned their hopes for a democratic, American route to a worker-controlled political economy. Proponents of third-party mobilization, for instance, continued to urge producers to vote for their interests as a class by electing workers to public office.[40] It was obvious, however, as socialist J. A. Kennerly of the Wayne Lodge No. 98 in Pittsburgh put it, that workers presently lacked enough "general and intense feeling of class consciousness" for the wage-earning class to make war on "capitalist power."[41] Since the late nineteenth century, producerism had given steelworkers a sense that they were a class apart from capitalist business-owners and managers. Republicanism had given them a proclivity for democratic politics. And most American socialists favored a democratic socialist political economy. But consensus on these basic assumptions did not automatically produce agreement on strategies for overcoming the excessive and illegitimate power of capitalist elites. Income and skill stratification among steelworkers, the divergent ethnic and racial composition of the steel industry's labor force, and a longstanding tradition of skepticism about concentrated government power prevented America's activist steelworkers from agreeing on a common strategy for transferring wealth and power from nonproducers to producers.

Perhaps because of its inablity to suggest a single agenda, perhaps because of the changes wrought by the war and its aftermath, producerism lost its place as the foremost rhetorical tool of organized labor in the years after 1920. During the next great burst of labor activism, politically active labor leaders began adding a new type of rhetoric to producerism. One example illustrates a much wider transformation. In February 1937, the Congress of Industrial Organizations forced General Motors to recognize the United Automobile Workers (UAW). Trying to build on this momentous victory to promote further organizing, CIO President John L. Lewis made a triumphant speech to a national radio audience on April 7, 1937. Lewis proclaimed the right of workers to freedom of association, demanded more representation in legislatures, and insisted that job security had to be protected through contractual rules. But Lewis' main point was that industrial and political democracy would enhance "labor's participation in the increased productivity due to industry—in order to distribute to a greater degree among our people the fruits of the genius of modern science and modern industry . . . so that more Americans, if you please, may enjoy to a higher degree a participation in these things."[42] Lewis thus articulated the same goals—democracy and a higher standard of living—as those workers who had embraced producerism had sought. But Lewis had abandoned the rhetoric that described the employer as someone who got rich solely by exploiting labor. Instead, he implicitly gave industrial management credit for successfully using science and technology to enhance production. Rather than asserting that workers had a right to the entire product of their labor, Lewis asked that workers receive a larger share of the value of the goods they produced, so that they could consume more.[43]

Producerism did not fade totally from the rhetoric of American wage earners. But democratic socialist and liberal union leaders and wage earners conscious of their membership in the class of producers were now less likely to deny the value of managerial and engineering labor. Nevertheless, wage earners and their leaders insisted that workers receive a fair share of the higher profits generated by increases in productivity that resulted from the combined efforts of manual laborers, engineers, and managers. Thus, when UAW President Walter Reuther discussed the problem of poverty at Congressional hearings in 1964, he applied classic producerist terminology: ". . . those in our economy who possess a large measure of freedom to appropriate more than their fair share of the fruits of our economy have been persistently abusing their freedom, particularly the major corporations that dominate whole industries."[44] Wage earners and labor leaders who were influenced by Keynesian economics advocated higher levels of government spending to stimulate the economy and by so doing to create the economic growth that was necessary for improvements in the welfare of producers.[45] Producerism had undergone a fundamental shift.

Like their predecessors, wage earners today are divided about the kind of political economy and political action they want. Many working people have even returned to the Jeffersonian solution of limited government, and especially limited national government power, that appealed to farmers and urban workers in the early nineteenth century. Of course, this strategy does not offer any means of providing workers with protection against the concentrated power of private sector institutions, the very problem that led late nineteenth- and early twentieth-century workers to seek to protect their interests through political action and palpable economic reform.

NOTES

1. E. P. Thompson, *The Making of the English Working Class* (New York: Pantheon, 1963).

2. Perkin also notes that "every one of these terms [used by English workers] was ambiguous." Harold Perkin, *The Origins of Modern English*

Society, 1780–1880 (London: Routledge and Kegan Paul, 1969), 231. See also the analysis on 232–35.

3. My argument is based on a reading of the *National Labor Tribune* for 1894 and the *Journal of the Amalgamated Association of Iron, Steel and Tin Workers* for 1904 and 1912–1920. It appears that activist iron- and steel-workers were more likely than their counterparts in other trades to write letters about theories of political economy and issues of union governance. I have reached this conclusion based on years of reading labor newspapers published between 1900 and 1920. This generalization does not apply to members of the IWW, who wrote a barrage of didactic letters to their newspapers. I have also closely examined *The Carpenter*, 1894–1916. Under the editorship of Peter J. McGuire, the newspaper did not publish many letters to the editor. His successor, Frank Duffy, encouraged letters, but only a scattering of the letters printed discussed political economy.

4. George H. Sabine, *The Works of Gerrard Winstanley* (Ithaca: Cornell University Press, 1941), 258, 511–12, 580–81, 595. See also Thomas C. Mendenhall, Basil D. Henning, and A. S. Foord, *Ideas and Institutions in European History, 800–1715* (New York: Holt, Rinehart and Winston, 1948), 286–87, and Christopher Hill, *The World Turned Upside Down* (New York: The Viking Press, 1972), 267.

5. See the excellent account of a corporate, paternalist community in James R. Farr, *Hands of Honor: Artisans and their World in Dijon, 1550–1650* (Ithaca: Cornell University Press, 1988).

6. Cited in Mark Alan Lause, "'Some Degree of Power': From Hired Hand to Union Craftsmen in the Preindustrial American Printing Trades, 1778–1815" (Ph.D. diss., University of Illinois at Chicago, 1985), n. 53, 275.

7. Gordon S. Wood, *The Radicalism of the American Revolution* (New York: Knopf, 1992); Sean Wilentz, *Chants Democratic: New York City and the Rise of the Working Class, 1788–1850* (New York: Oxford University Press, 1984); David Montgomery, *Beyond Equality: Labor and the Radical Republicans, 1862–1872* (New York: Knopf, 1967).

8. Thomas Skidmore, *The Rights of Man to Property: Being a Proposition to Make it Equal Among the Adults of the Present Generation: And to Provide for Its Equal Transmission to Every Individual of Each Succeeding Generation, on Arriving at the Age of Maturity* (New York: A. Ming, Jr., 1829).

9. William H. Sewell has demonstrated, in his superb study, *Work and Revolution in France: The Language of Labor from the Old Regime to 1848* (New York: Cambridge University Press, 1980), that the French Revolution played a critical role in altering conceptions of property and political sovereignty. A hierarchical system established by the fiat of a divinely authorized

monarch changed to one in which sovereignty derived from ownership of property that originated as a consequence of the transformation of nature by human labor. In this new society, productive citizens, whose labor created property, voluntarily associated with government. This change gave manual laborers the opportunity to develop a new theoretical critique of those who appeared to accumulate and control property without engaging in human labor, i.e., manual labor. By 1850 socialist thinkers in France would argue that society should be organized on a republican model in which sovereignty would reside only in "laborers of all specialties . . . a direct and universal representation of national labor" (p. 274). We need an in-depth study of the influence of the thought of French and German worker radicals on the conceptions American workers developed about political economy, i.e., producerism and republicanism. For an excellent discussion of producerist ideology and agrarian movements from 1789 to 1860, see Jeffrey M. Taylor, "The Language of Agrarianism in Manitoba, 1890–1925," *Labour/Le Travail* 23 (1989): 91–118. Taylor concludes that by the years following World War I a new generation of more prosperous farmers had abandoned the producerist world view and now sought to construct alliances with capitalists. A systematic study of the decline in producerist rhetoric in the speeches of U.S. labor leaders as the twentieth century wore on, as well as the continued influence of producerism as a grass-roots world view, would be instructive.

10. Richard Oestreicher, "Solidarity and Fragmentation: Working People and Class Consciousness in Detroit, 1877–1895," (Ph.D. Diss., Michigan State University, 1979).

11. Colorado Bureau of Labor Statistics, *Biennial Report* (1905): 104.

12. Robert Asher, "Painful Memories: The Historical Consciousness of Steelworkers and the Steel Strike of 1919," *Pennsylvania History* 45 (January 1978): 61–86, and Paul Krause, *The Battle for Homestead, 1880–1892* (Pittsburgh: University of Pittsburgh Press, 1993).

13. Examination of *The Carpenter*, 1894–1912, reveals that even under the editorship of socialist Peter J. McGuire, few rank-and-file letters that discussed political economy were printed. McGuire chose to print columns by nonunion members that discussed political economy.

14. All citations of the *Journal of the Amalgamated Iron, Steel and Tin Workers Union* will list the date only. Citations of other newspapers will give the date and name of the newspaper.

15. January 4, 1916.

16. On evangelical Protestantism's appeal to worker activists in the United States, see Herbert Gutman, *Work, Culture, and Society in Industrializing America: Essays in American Working Class and Social History* (New York: Knopf, 1976), chapter 2.

17. November 11, 1915.

18. The labor theory of value had proved malleable throughout the nineteenth century. Laborers had used the idea to justify antimonopoly legislation in the antebellum period. Both trade unionists and cooperationists had made it a mainstay of their rhetoric in the years after the Civil War.

19. January 21, 1915.

20. July 28, 1904.

21. January 28, 1904.

22. November 21, 1904.

23. Henry George's ideas appealed to many miners, but they were not as enthusiastic about protective tariffs as were many steelworkers. In 1894 a producerist miner from Colorado Spring, Colorado, told the state's Bureau of Labor Statistics, "An income tax is a very great improvement over a tariff tax. I have long considered the tariff taxes as among the most unjust used by capital to oppress labor. I would favor an income tax until such time as we can get the single tax established. . . . Private ownership of land, keeping men from using and occupying the soil, is the most prolific cause of poverty and hard times." Another miner, from Silverton, made a similar report: "The miners of this camp are most of them in favor of the single tax. . . ." Colorado Bureau of Labor Statistics, *Biennial Report* (1894): 105.

24. February 4, 1904.

25. December 29, 1904.

26. *National Labor Tribune*, October 18, 1894.

27. July 9, 1904.

28. November 3, 1904. For similar views see the letters by the Cohoes, N.Y., *Journal* agent, August 4, 1904, and by E. Perryman, Rocks Lodge No. 10, St. Louis, July 15, 1920.

29. July 4, 1912.

30. August 15, 22, and October 10, 31, 1912. Although opposed to the IWW, Davis advocated organizing unskilled workers, who otherwise would pose a danger to skilled workers when they went on strike. Ibid., August 8, 1912.

31. See J. A., Lalance Lodge No. 122, Harrisburg, Pennsylvania, January 15, 1920.

32. Howard Wogan, Lodge No. 104, Altoona, Pa., February 6, 1920.

33. December 12, 1918. See also the letter from Socialist C. Brahm of Central Lodge No. 75, Reading, Pa., December 19, 1918, that argues the case

from the perspective of a technological imperative, in language reminiscent of the 1905 Preamble to the IWW's constitution: "The machine has brought most of these would-be aristocratic unions and the individuals who compose them down to the common level and the rest will follow in due time."

34. January 1, 1919. See Lamoureux's reply, utilizing the argument developed by C. Braham in his December 19, 1918, letter, supra n. 25, that technological innovations were shortening the time period needed to train skilled labor, producing a convergence between unskilled and skilled labor. January 16, 1919.

35. February 6, 1919. See the similar letter by G. M. Bishop, Granoque Lodge No 4., October 28, 1920.

36. January 1, 1920.

37. See letters January 15, 1920; January 22, 1920, January 29, 1920.

38. September 30, 1920.

39. October 14, 1920.

40. January 15, October 28, November 4, 1920. For additional information on the political ideas of steelworkers in 1919, see Asher, op. cit.

41. February 5, 1920.

42. Address by John L. Lewis, April 7, 1937, Box 11, Henry Kraus Papers, Archives of Labor and Urban Affairs, Wayne State University, Detroit, Mich.

43. For discussions of the consumerist orientation of U.S. workers in the 1920s and thereafter, see Ronald Edsforth, *Class Conflict and Cultural Consensus: The Making of a Mass Consumer Society in Flint, Michigan* (New Brunswick, N.J.: Rutgers University Press, 1987), and Lizabeth Cohen, *Making a New Deal: Industrial Workers in Chicago, 1919–1939* (Cambridge: Cambridge University Press, 1990).

44. U.S. Congress, House, Committee on Education and Labor, *Hearings*, 88th Cong., 2d sess., 1964 (Washington, D.C.: Government Printing Office, 1964), 422–69. Cited in Kevin Boyle, *The UAW and the Heyday of American Liberalism, 1945–1968* (Ithaca: Cornell University Press, 1995), 187.

45. Ronald Edsforth, "Why Automation Didn't Shorten the Work Week: The Politics of Work Time in the Automobile Industry," in Robert Asher and Ronald Edsforth eds., *Autowork* (Albany: State University of New York Press, 1995), 155–73

Julie Greene[1]

————— **3** —————

Negotiating the State

Frank Walsh and the Transformation of Labor's Political Culture in Progressive America

A fter their defeat in the 1896 election, Democratic Party leaders such as William Jennings Bryan formulated a new goal: to recruit American workers into their coalition. If farmers alone could not bring electoral victory, surely an alliance between them and American workers would be sufficient to return the White House and dominance in Congress to the beleaguered Democrats. This new strategy made the working class central to the hopes and visions of a major party. For the next twenty years, Democratic leaders pursued their vision of farmer-labor unity, gradually building an alliance which helped reelect President Woodrow Wilson, against all odds, in 1916. Along the way, the challenge of uniting with working-class Americans raised puzzling issues for the Democrats. How exactly would they attract working-class men or women to their party? What program would appeal to them? And what groups or persons might mediate and facilitate this new coalition?

Over the last decade or more, historians and social scientists have begun focusing more attention on the state. Seeking to "bring the state back in," scholars such as Stephen Skowronek and Theda Skocpol have examined the rise of the state, its growing intervention in American life, and its impact on diverse social groups.[2] Reflecting a new institutionalist or state-centered methodology, their work has generated a more sophisticated understanding of the state and its policies. Yet this methodology also neglects important questions regarding the connections between state and society. How do social groups articulate demands and pressure the state to respond? What institutions or people negotiate with the state on their behalf and how does that mediating process evolve over time?

These questions possess particular relevance during the Progressive Era, a time when American political culture underwent a remarkable transformation. Americans debated with great fervor the proper role and function of their federal government. Facing a widespread decline in party loyalties among American voters, both major political parties experimented aggressively with ways to reach new constituencies. Thus Democratic Party leaders sought to work with groups or individuals who appeared able to lead or represent American workers. During the early Progressive Era Democrats approached this challenge by allying with the American Federation of Labor (AFL), the dominant labor institution in the United States by 1900. Yet the AFL, as a medium through which to reach the working class, presented party leaders with key weaknesses as well as strengths. Despite the personal prestige of AFL president Samuel Gompers and the nationwide network of local and state labor organizations affiliated with the AFL, its brand of trade unionism offered only one possible vision of labor politics. In a period when the question of the state grew more dominant in American reform politics, the AFL's pronounced anti-statism constituted perhaps its greatest weakness as an instrument for influencing working-class voters. This became most clear in the years after 1912, when Woodrow Wilson cast about for ways to demonstrate his commitment to political reform.

This article examines the Democratic campaign to win workers' votes during the Progressive Era, with a focus on the ways that changing notions of the state and consequent changes in political culture affected that effort. Particularly between 1912 and 1916, American political culture underwent complex changes that in turn created a new foundation for unity between the Democratic Party and working-class Americans. Perhaps the most important individual helping to shape these new efforts was radical midwestern lawyer Frank Walsh. Walsh possessed a vision of the state quite different from that held by AFL leaders. Early in 1916 Walsh dreamed aloud of a Democratic campaign pitched as "a battle between big business and the people; also 'the empire against democracy.' If Wilson would only go the whole limit on the people's side, I believe we would win a tremendous popular victory."[3] What new actors and new institutional arrangements would make such a campaign possible?

Origins of the Alliance

American workers' potential for political efficacy during the early Progressive Era rested in the American Federation of Labor. By 1900 the AFL leaders fought aggressively to consolidate their control over labor's political and economic future. Yet the AFL's relationship to the broader working class was a troubled one. Its members were predominantly skilled craft unionists. Despite important but sporadic exceptions in unions like the United Mine Workers (UMW) and the International Association of Machinists (IAM), overall the Federation's affiliated unions discriminated against female, African-American, immigrant, and unskilled workers through a variety of formal and informal measures. As a result, the AFL effectively excluded the vast majority of American workers. AFL leaders also manifested great hostility towards socialism, berating and marginalizing Socialist Party members regardless of their trade unionist credentials. Furthermore, under the leadership of Samuel Gompers, the Federation refused to work towards any but narrow trade unionist goals.[4] This presented the central dilemma for American labor politics during the early twentieth century: the dominant position held by a narrowly focused and demographically unrepresentative labor organization.

By the late nineteenth century the AFL had adopted a nonpartisan political strategy, so an alliance with the Democratic—or any other—Party did not seem likely. During the 1890s, AFL leaders developed an intense opposition to party politics of any kind, believing that what they called "party slavery" stood among the chief evils facing Americans. Although the AFL engaged in political activity, its national leaders strenuously avoided contact with the party system. Instead they worked to influence legislation by lobbying and petitioning the federal government.[5]

Two developments during the first decade of the twentieth century caused the AFL to embark upon a strenuous political effort. An unprecedented legal crisis threatened labor's future, as employers aggressively used injunctions and the Sherman Antitrust Act to break strikes and boycotts. In the most famous of these cases, the

Supreme Court held in 1908 that the Danbury, Connecticut, hatters' boycott violated the Sherman Act because the hatters had restrained interstate trade. Employers used injunctions more routinely to break strikes. William Forbath has estimated that state and federal courts issued 2,095 injunctions between 1890 and 1920. Labor's battle with the courts led the AFL to make winning anti-injunction legislation and an amendment to the Sherman Act its top political priorities during the early twentieth century.[6]

Anti-union employers also stood behind the second threat to labor stability. Beginning in 1902 the National Association of Manufacturers (NAM) and other organizations united in an open-shop drive, and within a year the membership of labor unions had begun to decline as a result. The open-shop drive battled workers and their unions in the workplace, in the courts, and in Congress. In particular, the NAM worked aggressively to strengthen its ties with conservative Republican leaders of Congress, thereby quickly reversing the AFL's early political gains.[7]

These frustrations pushed AFL leaders to attempt a more ambitious political effort and, ultimately, to transform their relationship to the party system. In 1906 and 1908 they sought to mobilize their members to vote for candidates who would support labor's political agenda. In 1906 they focused on electing trade unionists and other "friends of labor" to the House of Representatives, while trying to defeat labor's enemies. Although they failed to defeat any of the major Republican standpatters in 1906, they did elect four trade unionists to Congress. They continued to reject partisanship that year, seeking only to elect candidates who would support labor's demands, though as it happened, most of those willing to side with labor in fact belonged to the Democratic Party.[8]

In 1908 the AFL mobilization effort became more ambitious and more partisan. The AFL entered into a close partnership with the Democratic Party in hopes of electing William Jennings Bryan to the presidency. The two organizations merged their political operations to a significant degree: for example, the Democratic Party channeled money to the AFL to pay its organizers; and an AFL man made decisions at the Democrats' Labor Bureau, apparently looking to Samuel Gompers rather than Democratic leaders for approval of strategic decisions. At the same time, the AFL's mobilization effort subtly changed focus. While in 1906 AFL leaders had stressed the importance of local autonomy (encouraging local workers to use their discretion in deciding whom to support), in 1908 they stressed centralization and political discipline. Samuel Gompers needed desperately in 1908 to create an appearance of unanimous support for Bryan; to do so, organizers traveled around the country to "enforce" the AFL political program on rebellious or unenthusiastic workers at the state and local levels. Indeed, movement towards an independent labor party became less possible since Gompers attempted to suppress any movement threatening to divide trade unionists' support for the Democrats.[9]

Despite the tremendous energies thrown towards bringing workers into the Bryan camp, a Republican victory resulted. This humiliated the AFL leaders and forced them and the Democrats to question the wisdom of a nationwide alliance. Two flaws kept workers from voting for Bryan and simultaneously demonstrated the AFL's limitations as a political force. First, during this period of Republican hegemony, the Democrats and the AFL found it possible to ally without worrying much about the basis of their alliance: the key was opposition to Republicans. Beyond that, the Democrats accepted the AFL's guidance and their platform reflected the AFL's extremely narrow and anti-statist concerns. Anti-injunction legislation dominated their labor planks, complemented by such demands as the eight-hour day for federal employees (the AFL opposed eight-hour legislation for all other workers). These technical and legalistic appeals would certainly not generate enthusiasm among unorganized workers. Even among trade unionists, the Republican pitch for a strong economy and a full dinner pail generated more support than did the Democratic emphasis on injunction reform. Ironically, Bryan built his 1908 campaign on the slogan, "Shall the People Rule," demanding, for example, an income tax and direct election of senators. These issues might well have attracted broad working-class support, but Bryan stuck with Samuel Gompers's agenda and talked only about the injunction when courting workers' votes.[10]

Second, Republicans cleverly turned another AFL weakness into a major campaign issue. They charged that AFL leaders sought to "deliver the labor vote" to the Democrats, that they were, in other words, dictating to workers how they should vote. Republican newspapers and candidates across the United States jumped to adopt this line of attack.[11] The accusation stung precisely because it held some truth. The AFL had adopted a major political program and a partisan connection without any gesture towards procedures of internal democracy. In some cases, even workers who favored the Democratic Party chafed at the absence of open discussion and debate regarding political strategy and endorsements.[12] The Republican attack, in short, highlighted the AFL's limitation as a vehicle for labor politics: not only was the AFL cut off from the American working class, it could not even offer effective and uncontested political leadership to its own members.

The AFL did not try such an experiment again: rejecting strategies of mass mobilization, the federation retreated permanently from the rigors of electoral politics. Its leaders continued, however, to embrace *partisan* politics, as the period from 1910 to 1916 clearly demonstrates.

Labor and the State

To Democratic leaders, the 1908 election returns suggested that attracting working-class support required a different and more effective vehicle than the AFL. While the Democrats maintained their alliance with organized labor at the elite level, when it came to the concrete tactics of campaign politics they found another way to operate. This shift coincided with a growing disparity between the views of AFL leaders and the Democrats regarding the appropriate functions of the state. By late 1916 the Democrats had grown more willing to marshal the federal government on behalf of social justice while Samuel Gompers remained fiercely opposed to a strong state. Indeed, during these years, if anything, AFL editorials grew more extreme in their anti-statism, as more positive state visions increasingly pervaded the body politic.

These divergent views, however, did not result in alienating Samuel Gompers from the Wilson administration. Gompers himself felt he had reached the pinnacle of political influence. With the creation in 1913 of a Department of Labor and the appointment of Gompers's personal choice, ex-UMW official William B. Wilson, to head the department, the AFL finally had one of its own at the heart of the federal government. A number of other labor leaders received federal appointments, including AFL Treasurer John Lennon and AFL Vice President James O'Connell (both to the Commission on Industrial Relations) and Gompers himself (to the Council of National Defense). President Wilson also sought Gompers's opinion periodically, for example requesting his view on an appointment to the U.S. Supreme Court.[13]

Yet by early 1916 labor had little to show for its newfound political influence. President Wilson proved surprisingly recalcitrant, repeatedly waffling on or opposing bills desired by labor. He opposed the LaFollette Seamen's Act and nearly vetoed it until Andrew Furuseth and William Jennings Bryan changed his mind. More problematic was Wilson's indifference to labor's plea for exemption from the Sherman Antitrust Act. Wilson refused to give in, granting only labor's demand for jury trial in cases of criminal contempt and a statement that farm and labor unions should not be considered illegal combinations. When labor and its congressional allies protested, they won addition of a sentence stating that labor is not a commodity. Most careful observers argued at the time that this sentence would prove legalistically meaningless, and events later proved them correct. Although Gompers hailed the resulting Clayton Act as labor's "Magna Carta," it neither exempted labor from the Sherman Act nor limited the issuance of labor injunctions.[14]

A further barrier to winning labor reform during this period emerged in the AFL's anti-statism. Gompers had developed his position on the government's role during the last decade of the nineteenth century, and he maintained it consistently throughout the Progressive Era. As he stated in 1898, "Our movement stands for the wage-earners doing for themselves what they can toward working out their own salvation. But those things that they can not do for themselves the Government should do." Labor should seek only limited legislation to establish unions' right to make free use of the strike, picketing, and boycotts; to free trade unions from unfair competition with cheaper labor sources (so the AFL worked to restrict immigration and convict and child labor); and to make the government itself into a model employer.[15]

During the first decade of the twentieth century, with progressive reform blocked by standpat conservatives, Gompers rarely expressed these anti-statist ideals other than during his periodic attacks on the Socialist Party. But after 1912, when the Bull Moose, Socialist, and Democratic Parties all promoted more positive visions of the government, Gompers began more emphatically to stress the evils of state intervention. By 1912 Gompers also had to contend with energetic social reformers who proposed legislation based upon a statist vision. In 1915 he observed, "There is a strange spirit abroad in these times. The whole people is hugging the delusion that law is a panacea." He began inveighing regularly against proposals for eight-hour laws, minimum wage laws, municipal ownership, and government-sponsored health insurance. When the American Association for Labor Legislation demanded a reform such as health insurance, Gompers attacked its leaders as "barnacles" hanging on to the labor movement. How dare they presume to know what the workers need or want?[16]

The diverse reform movements against which Gompers railed and the popularity of both the Socialist and Progressive Parties combined to make questions of the state central to American political culture by the second decade of the twentieth century. President Wilson and his Democratic colleagues in the House and Senate reacted to this new political environment in ways that helped them win influential new friends. Together these changes made possible an alternative foundation for American labor politics.

President Wilson contributed powerfully to creating this new coalition through the nominations he made to the Commission on Industrial Relations (CIR). The idea for a government investigation into the causes of industrial conflict first emerged in 1910, with the bombing of the *Los Angeles Times* building providing immediate inspiration. Social reformers, labor activists, and members of the Taft administration worked together to pass the legislation that created the CIR. Ironically, Taft chose for labor's representatives on the Commission two leaders with strong loyalties to the Democratic Party, John Lennon and James O'Connell of the AFL (a third leader, Austin Garretson, represented the Order of Railway Conductors). Upon assuming the presidency, Woodrow Wilson reassessed Taft's appointments and rejected many of his choices. He accepted without change the original labor representatives (even though social reformers complained that they represented only the most narrow and conservative wing of the labor movement), but he selected different individuals to represent business and the public. These changes gave the Commission a more progressive and pro-labor agenda. Most importantly, President Wilson rejected Taft's nominee for the chairmanship (conservative Senator George Sutherland of Utah) and replaced him with a midwestern labor lawyer named Frank Walsh. Walsh's appointment radically changed the nature of the Commission and its role in American politics.[17]

An Irish-American from Kansas City, Walsh grew up in poverty and took his first wage-earning job at the age of ten. After studying law at night school, Walsh made an early name for himself by winning some dramatic cases and by successfully fighting Missouri's political bosses. Throughout his life Walsh defended workers and their unions: his more famous clients included Tom Mooney and William Z. Foster. Walsh's politics placed him in extraordinary company: a left-leaning activist with sympathies for the single tax, municipal ownership, women's suffrage, and Irish independence, he also believed devoutly in Catholicism, Woodrow Wilson, and the Democratic Party. Capable of fiery agitation on behalf of radical causes, Walsh also possessed close ties with mainstream politicians.[18]

In 1912, unable to decide whether to support Roosevelt or Wilson, Walsh met privately with the latter. Wilson convinced Walsh of his commitment to progressive reform and won his support, appointing him to head a social service bureau for the Democrats.[19] After the election, as chairman of the Commission on Industrial Relations, Walsh rocketed to nationwide fame by turning the body into a dramatic labor tribunal. Interrogating labor enemies like John D. Rockefeller Jr. and investigating such crises as the Ludlow massacre and the Lawrence textile strike, Walsh flamboyantly generated publicity and used it to crusade for social justice. Commission members travelled across the country to conduct public hearings, and consistently Walsh turned their proceedings into a brilliant political theater, one that championed oppressed workers, their unions, and even radical organizations like the IWW, while it rebuked the nefarious activities of employers.[20]

Some, like his colleague on the Commission, Florence Harriman, found Walsh biased: "He is a born agitator with a very engaging personality, and has his place, but not in the position of a judge. To me he was always the lawyer, not the judge,—always cross-examining as though capital were in the dock and always helping labor with the sympathetic spotlight." But to others Walsh emerged as one of the most popular heroes in the world of labor. Newspaper accounts of his speeches during these years provide evidence of workers' great affection for him: "The father of the workers!" cried out a supporter in New York City. A labor newspaper in Pittsburgh, Kansas, called Walsh "the most powerful influence for good among all the champions of labor."[21]

After its members had travelled across the country and talked with scores of people over nearly two years, the Commission came to an end in 1915. Walsh's assistant, Basil Manley, drafted a final report that presented in passionate detail the problems facing American workers and proposed solutions for them. Signed only by Walsh and the three labor commissioners, the final report was regarded as too sympathetic to labor by the public and business representatives and each of these factions submitted its own report. And indeed, Manley's report presented a stunning analysis of the labor question, a vision that boldly demonstrated the limitations of AFL and Democratic politics. It pinpointed four major causes of labor unrest in the United States: the unjust distribution of wealth and income; unemployment; the denial of equal justice to workers; and the denial of the right to organize and bargain collectively. As remedies, the Commission's report called for a stiff inheritance tax (it would not allow anyone to inherit more than one million dollars); a tax on owners of nonproductive land; restrictions on private detective agencies; and laws and constitutional amendments to guarantee workers' right to organize and to free them from harassment by government agencies and by employers.

Resolutely Walsh, Manley, and the labor commissioners advocated state intervention on behalf of working Americans: "The entire machinery of the Federal Government should be utilized to the greatest possible degree for the correction of such deplorable conditions as have been found to exist." As examples of the greater role the state could and should play, the report recommended expanded social services, more money to education, and the development of large construction projects run by the government as a solution to unemployment. While certainly there remained important limits to the state as envisioned by this report—it rejected what it called the German style of expansive bureaucracies, for example—this conceptualization broke firmly with decades of anti-statism as propounded by the national leaders of the AFL. With one arm it reached out to political visions of the Gilded Age labor-populist movement, and with another to state- and local-level political activists since that time.[22]

The Commission's final report thus pointed the way towards a very different political coalition within the world of labor, one no longer dominated by the AFL. Politically, its analysis of the causes of industrial unrest and its recommendations for solutions both placed the commission report closer to the Socialist than the Democratic Party. While Samuel Gompers had worked for decades to send socialists into exile, Frank Walsh and his final report promised to return them to the center of American labor politics. With its concern for issues such as social services that would not be limited to skilled craft unionists, the report's vision potentially reached beyond the privileged and exclusive boundaries of the AFL's membership. Furthermore, Walsh's report forcefully addressed the needs and problems of groups, such as female workers and tenant farmers, long ignored by the AFL. Speaking of women's employment, for example, it recommended that women receive wages equal to men and that the government encourage unionism among them.[23]

Yet in certain respects Walsh's conception of "labor" was not so different from that of Samuel Gompers. Most of the time the Commission's final report spoke not to the entire working class but to that segment affected by unionism. Repeatedly, it saw the solution to workers' problems as lying in the union movement. It failed to address the problems confronted by workers of African or Hispanic descent. The report recommended that the government use literacy tests to restrict European immigration. A special section on Chinese exclusion assessed ways to enforce the law more efficiently, suggesting, for example, special measures against individuals who smuggled Chinese workers into the country. And while the commissioners championed unionism for women, they seemed to prefer that women stay out of the work force altogether. Calling on employers to pay their male workers a family wage, the report declared, "Under no other conditions can a strong, contented, and efficient citizenship be developed." Further, the commissioners called women's labor a "direct menace to the wage and salary standards of men."[24] Thus while the Commission's final report presented a radical analysis of industrial unrest, one that attempted to examine conditions from the perspective of working people, its vision for the most part remained limited to white, male, and native-born workers.

As the commission adjourned in October 1915, Walsh and his assistants observed that their work had galvanized the country. Perhaps also realizing that their final report could stand as the centerpiece of a new political movement, Walsh decided to form the Committee on Industrial Relations in order to continue the commission's work. UMW President John White sent Walsh an unsolicited $2,000 to aid in his work, and a diverse group of reformers and trade unionists (including Agnes Nestor and Helen Marot of the Women's Trade Union League, union activists John Lennon, James O'Connell, and John Fitzpatrick, Progressive Party leader Amos Pinchot, and journalist Frederic Howe) joined forces with the new Committee.[25]

The Committee worked at a double-fisted goal: maintaining the grass-roots enthusiasm about the CIR's final report while simultaneously pushing Congress to translate its recommendations into legislation. Its members organized local support groups around the country; mobilized behind striking workers in Chicago, Youngstown, and Pittsburgh; and commissioned motion pictures. The Committee's role in strikes won it a certain notoriety, as employers denounced its activities and, in Pittsburgh, charged that Walsh "should be assassinated." Meanwhile, Basil Manley agitated for legislation to end income tax evasion by wealthy individuals and corporations.[26] These diverse activities by members of Walsh's Committee would become central to Democratic politics as President Wilson sought reelection in 1916.

During these years Americans engaged in many other social and political activities that reinforced the work carried out by Walsh and his colleagues. A congressional investigation into the political activities of the National Association of Manufacturers between 1913 and 1915 pilloried the open-shop employers for the "invisible government" they'd established in Washington, D.C. Like the CIR, this investigation created a high political drama that helped recast American political culture. At the same time, settlement house workers, professionals, and men and women active in groups like the National Child Labor Committee, the General Federation of Women's Clubs, the National Association of Colored Women, the American Association for Labor Legislation, and the National Consumers' League, worked for social justice by lobbying for legislation at the state and national levels.[27]

Meanwhile, even as Gompers raged against the "outsiders" calling for state intervention, labor activists at the local and state levels were building successful political programs that pressed the government for expanded or improved services. In city after city, workers participated in coalitions that called for intensified regulation of business and municipal ownership of utilities. Working-class demands on the state had been blocked at the national level for years by the anti-statism of their own trade union leaders. Now suddenly President Wilson, the Democrats, and progressive Republicans appeared unusually open to using state power in the interests of working people. As a result, the AFL's anti-statist agenda grew less relevant, and the AFL leaders themselves became marginalized by the changing political culture. Meanwhile, the AFL's failure to deliver the labor vote in 1908 continued to keep it strategically marginal as well.

Building the 1916 Labor Campaign

These changes in American political culture made possible a very different Democratic campaign in 1916. The AFL still had an important role to play: Gompers strongly endorsed Wilson, and this surely influenced trade union members. Yet compared to the 1908 campaign the Federation did little to ensure Wilson's reelection. In 1916 the Democratic Party stood upon its own record, which by election day involved an unabashed extension of state power on behalf of working people's rights. Samuel Gompers's agenda no longer drove the labor platform of the Democratic Party. And rather than working strategically through the AFL as they had in 1908, the Democrats now relied upon a much more diverse coalition that included the Railroad Brotherhoods, Socialists, the Women's Trade Union League, local trade unionists working for municipal reform, and the reformers clustered around Frank Walsh in the Committee on Industrial Relations.[28]

Before he could tap into this coalition, President Wilson first had to take decisive action on his own. Plotting strategy in the spring of 1916, Wilson and his advisors decided they must win over the vote of progressives who supported Roosevelt in 1912. This meant greater support for government intervention, and for labor reforms, than ever before. No longer could Wilson and his party rest with pleasing Gompers and the AFL: they already stood in Wilson's corner and, clearly, something more was needed. Now the Democrats began to focus on winning over social workers, progressives like Frank Walsh, and a broader group of working people. With this goal in mind, during the middle months of 1916, the president nominated Louis Brandeis to the U.S. Supreme Court, supported a model workmen's compensation bill, and won passage of the Keating-Owen Child Labor bill by personally pleading with senators.[29] But by far his most important step came with the railroad brotherhoods' call for a nationwide strike in the late summer.

Their struggle involved 130,000 workers on fifty-two railroads. The brotherhoods demanded an eight-hour day, with time and a half for overtime, and they refused to submit the case to arbitration.

With the Pullman boycott of 1894 a vivid memory, Wilson knew he must, in an election year, prevent the strike. In August the president proposed his solution: concession of the eight-hour day, but postponement of the issue of overtime until a special commission could study the costs of such a plan. The brotherhoods happily accepted Wilson's solution. When the employers refused, Wilson addressed Congress and called for ambitious legislation granting railroad workers the eight-hour day. Congress passed the bill, the Adamson Act, within days.[30]

Frank Walsh conferred with President Wilson at the height of the railroad crisis, and numerous newspapers attributed Wilson's decision to grant workers the eight-hour day to Walsh's influence. Certainly Walsh realized the significance of Wilson's intervention. He wrote at the time to a friend: "I am blazing with enthusiasm over the President's action in the railroad controversy. I consider it the most significant and far-reaching development in the industrial history of this nation. . . . It is a great world, and a glorious time to be in it."[31]

The Adamson Act established the basis for a campaign in which the Democrats would present themselves as the party of labor, articulating a vision of the government's responsibilities that appealed deeply to many working people. By the standards of later decades or even by those of Woodrow Wilson's contemporary, Theodore Roosevelt, who proposed a state tending towards command over society and the economy, this remained a limited vision of the government's role. Wilson converted to this view in the eleventh hour, eyeing his own reelection campaign and an impending strike that demanded urgent measures, and feeling pressure from progressives and socialists, and he most likely felt ambivalent about his own actions. His vision also remained limited to certain workers: Wilson would surely not, for example, use his governmental authority to protect the rights of African-American sharecroppers or domestic servants, or to assist the northwestern strike of Wobbly lumber workers. Yet despite its limitations, the view propounded by Wilson and the Democrats signalled a significant change in national-level politics. In the 1912 campaign Wilson had stressed his opposition to government "paternalism" that would make workers unequal to other citizens. Such rhetoric disappeared entirely in 1916. Buttressed on the one hand by their recent legislative triumphs (the Adamson Act, the workmen's compensation act, and the child labor law) and on the other by Frank Walsh and his work with the Commission on Industrial Relations, the Democrats and Wilson could demonstrate their willingness, under certain circumstances, to employ the government on behalf of workers' struggles for social justice. This went well beyond the state Samuel Gompers envisioned: one capable only of interfering negatively with workers' rights and hence one fundamentally distrusted by its citizens.

The Adamson Act thus demonstrated how far the AFL had slipped out of the mainstream of labor politics. The Federation had neither worked for nor supported the most important labor reform of the Progressive Era. Samuel Gompers continued to oppose legislation on the question of hours. As he wrote in the *American Federationist* in March 1916, eight-hour legislation only added "another obstacle to the achievement of a real, general eight-hour day" because it forced workers to struggle through political as well as economic channels.[32] But facing new realities of state intervention on behalf of the eight-hour day, Gompers grew oddly quiet on the entire question. Throughout the 1916 campaign, Gompers strongly supported Wilson and neglected to discuss their disagreement over issues like the Adamson Act or immigration restriction. Instead the AFL chief focused on the victory represented by the Clayton Antitrust Act. As in 1908, the injunction dominated the AFL's political universe.

Frank Walsh, meanwhile, campaigned nationwide on behalf of Wilson, filling the gap created by the AFL's inactivity. Over the years Walsh had developed enviable ties to labor activists positioned across the political spectrum, yet his approach to politics contrasted sharply to that of conservatives like Gompers. Walsh appreciated the advantages of state intervention on workers' behalf, and though friendly with the conservative bloc that dominated the AFL as well as with the predominantly Republican leaders of the railroad brotherhoods, Walsh's strongest alliances remained with activists in progressive unions like the United Mine Workers. Furthermore, while Gompers had labored for years to define the "labor movement" in a way that excluded the Socialists, Walsh's vision embraced them and the IWW as well. Many Socialists rewarded Walsh's labors with unusual personal affection. Even Eugene Debs, campaigning for Congress in Indiana in 1916, asked Walsh to come and speak in his favor. As a local Socialist activist wrote on Debs's behalf, "We believe you can do more than anybody else to send Debs to Congress. . . . While you may not be a Socialist, yet, we know that you served this country perhaps as much or more than any other man . . ." Walsh's correspondents over the years included such radical leaders as Emma Goldman, Joseph Ettor, Elizabeth Gurley Flynn, and Arthur LeSueur.[33]

Walsh agreed to conduct an extensive speaking tour—nearly three weeks long—for the Democratic National Committee, but he insisted on carrying out his mission in an independent way. George West, his assistant on the CIR, travelled in advance of Walsh to arrange matters with local union activists. West remained independent of Democratic politicians and ensured, wherever he went, that Walsh would "speak alone and [be allowed] to handle subject in your own way . . ." Behind the scenes most of the work involved in planning Walsh's tour was carried out by Kacy Adams, the publicity director for the United Mine Workers, and by local union activists (especially those associated with the UMW) in towns across the country. When Walsh finally set off on his journey, William Harvey and two other men from the Democratic National Committee accompanied him to assist in all matters, but Walsh paid his own expenses.[34]

Walsh's tour began in New York state and stretched as far west as Kansas City, but he focused on mining districts in Ohio, Indiana, Michigan, and West Virginia. Sending the Democrats a list of local UMW leaders to contact in each location, Kacy Adams explained Walsh's appeal: the miners, he said, "are strong for Walsh; in fact he is their ideal in public life, and you will find that they will do everything possible to make his meetings a success." In addition to his popularity with labor crowds, Walsh could also, the Democrats believed, draw Socialists over to Wilson. Begging the Democratic National Committee (DNC) to send Walsh out to Kansas, a local politician wrote that the 15,000 miners in his region were mostly "red card" men, and "Frank P. Walsh is the only man in the world who can swing this Socialist vote to Wilson . . ."[35]

In his speeches and writings, Walsh created the sort of labor program that, more successfully than the AFL agenda in 1908, could win many American workers over to the Democratic Party. Walsh's labor program discussed the issues raised in the official report of the CIR, stressing for example the evils of an unjust distribution of wealth. To this he added a ringing celebration of Wilson's action in the railroad crisis, telling workers that the president "freed more slaves than Lincoln did"! Placing Wilson's presidency in the broadest possible terms, Walsh declared that 1916 would mark the end of "industrial despotism" which allowed "a few men to exercise autocratic control over the lives . . . [of] millions of producers." When Teddy Roosevelt criticized the eight-hour bill, Walsh attacked him: Roosevelt, he said, had become "the political gunman of the exploiting interests" hired by them to "break the force of the nation's eight-hour movement."[36]

Across the country, observers saw workingmen rallying behind President Wilson's reelection campaign. In Wilkes-Barre, Pennsylvania, a town considered strongly loyal to Theodore Roosevelt, workers turned the cold shoulder when the ex-president visited. Some five thousand gathered to march in protest against his attacks on President Wilson and the eight-hour day, but the mayor forbade their parade. In Toledo, historically a safe town for the Republicans, party leaders feared mass defections to the Democrats. The Republicans sent scores of field workers out to proselytize among workingmen. Yet their attempt to organize a meeting among railroad workers, with the star speaker a Brotherhood of Locomotive Engineers member who denounced the Adamson Act, failed miserably. A crowd of brotherhood men charged the stage, silenced the speaker, and then led all but a handful of the audience members out to another hall, where they passed resolutions praising the president and his eight-hour legislation. And perhaps even more worrisome to Republican managers was the fact that unorganized workers likewise appeared supportive of the president. At the large factories, Democratic sentiment spread quickly. When Republican candidate Charles Evans Hughes visited a Toledo auto factory, the owner introduced him as "our candidate." The warm welcome did not prevent workers there from heckling Hughes "unmercifully."[37]

In industrial states like Indiana and Illinois, the votes of organized AFL workers had for years been drifting towards the Democratic Party, but railroad employees and nonunion workers in mass production had remained predominantly Republican in their political sympathies. Thus Republican campaign managers focused their efforts on preventing defections among these latter two groups of workers. They enjoyed little success, especially among railroad workers. Rank-and-file railroad workers hailed the president as, for example, in New York City when one hundred of them surrounded his private car at Grand Central Station. The president came out to greet the men, listening to them call out: "Vote for Wilson, scratching Hughes; join the union, pay your dues!" Another yelled, "Three cheers for the man who's for the eight-hour day!" Railroad unions matched the energetic support provided President Wilson by their rank-and-file members, giving him unprecedented institutional assistance. The Order of Railroad Telegraphers assigned at least fourteen organizers to Wilson's campaign. Meanwhile the railroad brotherhoods entered into campaign politics for the first time, appealing to each member to support President Wilson. In the magazine of the Locomotive Firemen and Engineers, a leading editorial declared: "We have absolutely no doubt that Mr. Hughes owes his nomination to Wall Street, to the powers of wealth and special privilege, to the big employing interest—in short, to the master class— and that these interests are spending enormous sums of money in an effort to elect him President of the United States."[38]

In states like Illinois where women could now vote, Republicans found it difficult to predict the outcome. Straw polls generated remarkably diverse results, from a Republican effort that predicted 85 percent of the vote going to Hughes, to an independent poll that estimated only 40 percent for the Republican candidate. All sides seemed to agree, however, that *working-class* women would vote overwhelmingly for President Wilson. In Chicago the Women's Trade Union League (WTUL) was better organized than any other women's group, and its members favored Wilson by 85 percent. WTUL members like Agnes Nestor stood at the forefront of those Chicago activists who formed a Working Women's Independent Woodrow Wilson League in September. Thus with female as well as male workers the eight-hour issue seemed to be exerting an influence, though the peace issue clearly also helped Wilson win women's votes.[39]

Thus in 1916 the Democrats created a campaign that focused on problems faced by working people and offered solutions to those problems. A remarkable coalition came together to make the campaign possible: Frank Walsh stood as its star attraction, but joining him were the AFL, the railroad brotherhoods, the WTUL, and prominent labor representatives like John Lennon and William B. Wilson. The president's action on the railroad crisis, especially when added to previous gains such as the child labor act, made it clear that victory could come only by winning unprecedented support from workers.

From all around the country came reports that businessmen felt enraged by Wilson's new politics. As a North Carolinian wrote to Josephus Daniels, "I am certainly receiving 'A Frost' from most of the bankers and cotton mill men. They are mad about the child labor law and the 8 hour law. Something ought to be done to straighten these matters out with these people." In the eyes of southern businessmen, Wilson "made an absolute surrender to organized labor." Consequently, the Democrats found it more difficult than usual to raise money for their campaign. Yet, for every alienated employer, dozens of workers appeared ready to support Wilson. These circumstances encouraged the Democrats to focus with greater intensity on the labor vote. William McAdoo, one of the president's leading advisors, worried aloud to his chief about the loss of business support and concluded, "we should pay especial attention to labor throughout the rest of the campaign. . . . it is from that element that we can most certainly draw a large support." Party leaders thus devoted more money (approximately $35,000) to labor mobilization than to any other aspect of the campaign.[40]

How did the Democrats and their supporters define this elusive labor vote? Strategists did reach out to the working class more inclusively than in 1908, for example, and in this way they pointed towards Democratic campaigns of future decades. Both in its substance and style, the Democratic campaign appealed to unorganized male and female workers, unionized female workers, and tenant farmers. Many of the themes propounded by Walsh and the Democrats could appeal to unorganized as well as organized workers, and speakers regularly visited nonunion factories. The Democrats also made a determined effort to win the votes of Socialists and progressives who favored positive state action. This suggested a significant transformation of Democratic strategy since the heyday of Samuel Gompers, who had carefully and deliberately portrayed Socialists as the pariahs of the labor movement.

But despite these changes, Democratic Party strategy certainly did not speak to the entire working class. Still dominated by ideas of white supremacy, the Democratic Party lacked the ability to launch a campaign that would appeal to African Americans or other nonwhite workers. Like Samuel Gompers had before them, Democratic strategists in 1916 centered their labor campaign on the union movement. Frank Walsh worked carefully with activists from the UMW and other unions wherever he toured, and he and the Democrats targeted unionized industries, regions, and factories when deciding where to focus their campaign. The party's effectiveness remained clearest among white, male, trade unionists. Recruiting the "labor vote" meant, first and foremost, the vote of union workers. As Colonel Edward House described the campaign in his diary, "It is true we have organized wealth against us, and in such an aggregate as never before. On the other hand, we are pitting organized labor against it, and the fight is not an unfair one."[41]

Many other factors helped strengthen the Democrats' cause among working-class voters. Republican candidate Hughes, speaking poorly and breaking a picket line in California, contributed a great deal to Wilson's victory. The belief that Hughes would take the country into war strengthened Wilson's appeal for many working people. And America's war-fueled prosperity proved a bounty to Wilson's reelection campaign, undercutting Republican efforts to portray the Democrats as the party of depression.[42]

As the campaign wound down, most observers felt uncertain about which candidate would win. Eastern returns came in first, bringing victory to Hughes. Only when western returns arrived, early the next morning, did it become clear that Wilson had won his reelection battle. Wilson won with 9,129,606 popular and 277 electoral votes to Hughes's 8,538,221 popular and 254 electoral votes. Hughes won the entire east and middle west except for New Hampshire and Ohio. Wilson swept the south and west except for Minnesota, Iowa, South Dakota, Oregon, and West Virginia. Finally Wilson achieved what Bryan and others had attempted since 1896: to unite the south and west. To many, this finally freed the party from bowing to eastern plutocrats. Others, like Frank Walsh's confidante Rabbi Stephen Wise, put a different and western spin on the victory: "To think that we can have a great forward-looking party and free that Party from the racial and social Toryism of the South and the industrial and economic reactionism of the East!"[43]

Yet this triumph also transcended region. To win, Wilson had created a new coalition, one that realized a dream articulated by William Jennings Bryan: to unite farmers and workers together with those struggling towards social justice. The Democrats' campaign successfully polarized the electorate into left and right and brought many workers rallying to their side. A Washington state trade unionist wrote to Gompers in exultation at Wilson's victory, saying: "We were never so united before." Throughout the campaign polls predicted that workers would back Wilson. A poll of union officials by the *Literary Digest* in September found that of 457 who responded, 332 said their members supported Wilson. Forty-seven officials stated that their members would support the Socialist candidate Allan Benson, and a mere forty-three predicted support for Hughes.[44]

These predictions apparently were on the mark. Analysis of voting returns in twenty-two industrial counties across the United States reveals a striking pattern of support for Woodrow Wilson: in every case they gave Wilson a higher percentage of the vote than they had in 1912, and often by a very wide margin. Lucas County, Ohio, with Toledo as its major city, gave Wilson 24 percent more of its vote than in 1912; the vote for Wilson in Wayne County (Detroit), Michigan, rose by 19 percent; and in Los Angeles County it rose by 10 percent. In addition, Wilson's campaign dramatically intensified a trend begun a decade earlier, whereby trade unionists gradually shifted their loyalties to the Democratic Party. Eighteen out of these twenty-two counties gave Wilson more votes in 1916 than they had given any Democratic presidential candidate thus far during the twentieth century. Only in 1900 had the counties encompassing Chicago; New York; and Scranton and Williamsport, Pennsylvania, given the same or a larger percentage of their vote to the Democratic candidate.[45]

Especially in New Hampshire, Ohio, California, Washington, Idaho, and New Mexico, workers' votes seem to have gone largely to Wilson and contributed to his victory. The Ohio victory is particularly instructive for understanding trade unionists' reactions to the Wilson campaign. Frank Walsh, Woodrow Wilson, and Charles Hughes all campaigned energetically in this state. Historically voting Republican, Ohio gave Wilson a margin of some 90,000. Except for Cincinnati, with its large German-American population, every industrial city in the state went to Wilson.[46]

Socialists also supported Wilson in large numbers. Estimates of the numbers that defected from their party to vote Democratic range from 250,000 to 300,000. Particularly in the Rocky Mountain states, the midwest, and New York state, Wilson made important gains among Socialists. In every one of the twenty-two industrial counties examined above, the Socialist vote went down, often by a high percentage. For example, in 1912, Socialists won 12 percent of the vote in each of three counties: San Francisco County; Mahoning County (Youngstown), Ohio; and Cook County (Chicago). In 1916 the Socialist vote in each of these three counties dropped to 4 percent or lower. The president's support for labor and his administration's role in keeping the United States out of war persuaded many Socialists to support him.[47] Miners' leader John Walker of Illinois, for example, joined better-known Socialists such as Mother Jones and Max Eastman in strongly supporting Wilson in the 1916 campaign. Ultimately Walker's support for Wilson led to his expulsion from the Socialist Party. To Walker, Wilson deserved support both because of his commitment to peace and, more importantly, because of what he had done for labor. In particular, Walker cited the Adamson Act. He explained to a friend his position on eight-hours legislation: "I have always favored the getting of progress by whatever means it was easiest to get it, and . . . getting it by a legislative process was not only the easiest way, but was the most enlightened civilized way. . . ."[48]

Conclusion

Rarely had workers and their interests been so central to a presidential campaign as they were in 1916. Arthur Link first pointed out the parallels between the 1916 presidential election and those of 1896 and 1936: in no other political battles during that forty-year period, he argues, did the United States see such a clearcut political alignment. Wilson, allied with progressives in the labor movement and social justice camps, effectively polarized the electorate into right and left. And Frank Walsh's vision for the campaign had been realized. He had hoped it might become, as he confided to a friend, "a battle between big business and the people. . . ." Now in November, with the election won, Walsh could proclaim: "I am the happiest man in America over the Wilson victory." [49]

While the AFL remained a central part of the Democratic coalition in 1916, and would continue in such a role during the war years to come, perhaps the most interesting aspect of the presidential campaign lay in the contributions made by people outside of labor's dominant institution. To observers with an eye for the future, these contributions might have suggested the future contours of American politics. Labor issues remained central to the campaign, but in a way that transcended the outlook of Samuel Gompers and his pure and simple allies. The keys to Wilson's successful coalition had included a progressive program that spoke broadly to the needs and interests of working people, rather than focusing only on legalistic problems, and that accepted the need for state intervention; an inclusive strategy that reached out to Socialists as much as to moderate and conservative workers and that relied also on ties between labor activists and social justice progressives; and leadership offered by people, such as Frank Walsh, who stood out-side of the AFL.

Only by taking action much broader than the AFL ever sup-ported—using government intervention to achieve the eight-hour day for one group of workers—did Wilson and the Democratic Party succeed in uniting working people to such an extent. His effort made the president a popular hero for American workers in a way which superseded any presidential candidate up to that time, foreshadow-ing the impact Franklin Roosevelt would have on workers during the 1930s. Yet there remained important limitations to this first alliance between the Democratic Party and labor. As we have seen, even if the Democrats reached out more inclusively to workers than they previously had, they still centered their strategies on the union movement. A great many working people remained untouched by the political tactics of Woodrow Wilson and Frank Walsh. Democratic politicians rarely if ever focused on the political needs and problems of female, African-American, and immigrant workers. Even for many native-born white workers, most notably those from Germany and Ireland, the global politics of World War I made them resist sup-porting Woodrow Wilson. Anything resembling a "class vote" for the Democratic Party (or even, for that matter, a fully unified trade union vote) remained decades away, requiring significant economic, social, demographic, and ideological transformations before they could be realized.

Yet the 1916 campaign proved important because it ended the AFL's political dominance and introduced into the heart of American politics a more positive vision of the state's role. In the immediate af-termath of the election, as the United States entered the Great War, these changes forced the AFL to choose between two undesirable op-tions: its leaders could watch as groups and individuals outside its purview continued to shape American labor politics, or they could abandon some of their own traditional opposition to an interven-tionist state. Under Samuel Gompers's leadership, the AFL chose the second option. After decades of anti-statism, America's dominant trade union movement collaborated closely with government bu-reaucracies to support the nation's effort during the First World War. Numerous labor leaders, from Samuel Gompers to John Walker, served enthusiastically on government boards during the war. The AFL established the American Alliance for Labor and Democracy, funding it with money received from the federal government, to oppose pacifist and antiwar groups and individuals within the labor movement. Finally the AFL worked with the government to suppress the IWW in western industries like lumber and mining.[50]

During the war Frank Walsh served as co-chairman, with William Howard Taft, of the National War Labor Board. This position gave Walsh a chance to implement the recommendations put forward by the final report of the Commission on Industrial Relations. Under his leadership the NWLB encouraged employers to support unionization and specifically forbade them to interfere with unionization efforts; while in practice enforcement remained problematic, the membership of trade unions grew dramatically during the war years.[51]

Conditions changed immediately upon the cessation of military hostilities, however. Amidst tense confrontation between workers and employers and an atmosphere of antiradical hysteria (which the AFL itself helped generate through its attacks on the IWW), the federal government with its bedridden chief executive failed to defend even the most modest conception of working-class rights. The government quickly dismantled its wartime bureaucracies and turned deaf to labor's requests for assistance. Instead, its most visible action in 1919 became the raids launched by presidential hopeful A. Mitchell Palmer. Meanwhile, employers mobilized to construct a new open-shop drive, known as the "American Plan," one more widespread and more devastating than that of nearly twenty years before. The government provided little protection, and the nation's courts grew more determined to buttress the employers' actions with antilabor decisions of their own. As a result, membership in AFL unions drastically declined, from a high of four million in 1920 to fewer than three million by 1924.[52]

Under these circumstances the alliance between labor and the Democrats quickly dissolved. By 1920 Frank Walsh, always a bellwether, coldly turned away from the Democratic Party and refused to support its candidate for the presidency. Angrily Walsh declared in a widely reprinted article: "The next election will not be a political contest, it will be a coroner's jury on the corpse of the Democratic party."[53] AFL leaders tried to sustain their alliance with the Democrats, but their efforts grew increasingly feeble. While they urged support for the Democrats in the 1920 elections, and lamented at the Republican victory that November, by 1924 even AFL leaders could no longer justify supporting the Democratic Party. Instead the AFL officially endorsed independent presidential candidate Robert

LaFollette in 1924, breaking its tie to the Democrats for the first time in sixteen years. Knowing LaFollette would lose, and divided among themselves over whom to support, AFL leaders did little beyond issuing their endorsement. They maintained an extremely low and awkward profile during the campaign.[54]

Thus a promising labor-Democratic alliance came to a shabby end. It would have to be re-created a decade later under dramatically different circumstances. Indeed, the 1930s labor movement diverged from its predecessor in crucial ways. The labor vote, in the sense of a united bloc of workers, would become a force in American politics in ways Gompers could hardly have imagined. With the rise of the Congress of Industrial Organizations and the shaping influence of the Communist Party, organized labor at last reached beyond the native-born white workers who dominated the skilled crafts. By the end of World War II, trade unionism included a larger and more diverse proportion of American workers than ever before. This suggests a final important contrast between the labor politics of 1916 and that of 1936. Although appeals to labor and workers' votes became central to both campaigns, organized labor played a different role in each case. In 1936 workers and their unions exerted a dynamic political influence, and the Democratic Party reacted to their innovations. In 1916, on the other hand, Democratic Party leaders and activists like Frank Walsh emerged as the political innovators, dragging the AFL reluctantly behind them.

--- NOTES ---

1. This article originated in my larger study of the AFL, titled *Pure and Simple Politics: The American Federation of Labor and Political Mobilization, 1881 to 1917* (New York: Cambridge University Press, 1998). For their suggestions and advice on this essay, I am very grateful to Kevin Boyle, Melvyn Dubofsky, Leon Fink, Dana Frank, James Maffie, Richard Schneirov, Shelton Stromquist, and the anonymous readers for SUNY Press.

2. Stephen Skowronek, *Building a New American State* (New York: Cambridge University Press, 1982); Theda Skocpol, *Protecting Soldiers and Mothers: The Political Origins of Social Policy in the U.S.* (Cambridge, Mass.: Harvard University Press, 1992). For a work of labor history in-

formed by this school, see Melvyn Dubofsky, *The State and Labor in Modern America* (Chapel Hill: University of North Carolina Press, 1994).

3. Frank Walsh to Basil Manley, June 26, 1916, Frank Walsh Papers, New York Public Library.

4. For background on the social and political history of the working class, see two essays by David Brody: "The American Worker in the Progressive Era: A Comprehensive Analysis," in his *Workers in Industrial America: Essays on the 20ᵗʰ Century Struggle*, 2d ed. (New York: Oxford University Press, 1993), 3–47; and "The Course of American Labor Politics," in his *In Labor's Cause: Main Themes on the History of the American Worker* (New York: Oxford University Press, 1993), 43–81. For further information on the AFL, consult Louis Lorwin, *The American Federation of Labor: History, Policies, and Prospects* (Washington, D.C.: Brookings Institution, 1933); Philip Taft, *The A.F.L. in the Time of Gompers* (New York: Harper and Row, 1957); and Louis Reed, *The Labor Philosophy of Samuel Gompers* (Port Washington, N.Y.: Kennikat Press, 1966).

5. Greene, *Pure and Simple Politics*, chapter 2. For a representative statement by Samuel Gompers on these issues see his editorial, "The A.F. of L. and Political Action," *American Federationist* (hereafter cited as *AF*) 5 (June 1898), 73–74.

6. Greene, *Pure and Simple Politics*, chapters 4 and 5; Arnold Paul, *Conservative Crisis and the Rule of Law: Attitudes of Bar and Bench, 1887–1895* (Ithaca: Cornell University Press, 1960); Felix Frankfurter and Nathan Greene, *The Labor Injunction* (New York: Macmillan, 1930); Christopher Tomlins, *The State and the Unions: Labor Relations, Law, and the Organized Labor Movement in America, 1880–1960* (Cambridge: Cambridge University Press, 1985); William Forbath, "The Shaping of the American Labor Movement," *Harvard Law Review* 102 (April 1989), 1151–52, 1249–50.

7. Julie Greene, "Dinner-Pail Politics: Employers, Workers, and Political Organization during the Progressive Era," in Eric Arnesen, Julie Greene, and Bruce Laurie, eds., *Labor's Histories: Class, Politics, and the Working-Class Experience* (Urbana: University of Illinois Press, forthcoming); see also Philip Foner, *History of the Labor Movement in the United States*, vol. 3, and *The Policies and Practices of the American Federation of Labor, 1900–1909* (New York: International Publishers, 1964); Robert Wiebe, *Businessmen and Reform: A Study of the Progressive Movement* (Cambridge, Mass.: Harvard University Press, 1962); William C. Pratt, "The Omaha Business Men's Association and the Open Shop, 1903–1909," *Nebraska History* 70 (Summer 1989), 172–83; and Thomas A. Klug, "Employers' Strategies in the Detroit Labor Market, 1900–1929," in Nelson Lichtenstein and Steven Meyer, eds., *On the Line: Essays in the History of Auto Work* (Urbana: University of Illinois Press, 1988), 42–72.

8. Julie Greene, *Pure and Simple Politics*, chapter 4.

9. For the AFL's official political position in 1908, see Gompers, "Both Parties Have Spoken: Choose Between Them," *AF* 15 (August 1908), 598–606; on financial arrangements between the two organizations, see Gompers to Norman Mack, August 28, 1908, American Federation of Labor Records: The Samuel Gompers Era (Microfilming Corporation of America, 1979) (hereafter cited as AFL Records); Frank Morrison to M. Grant Hamilton, October 4, 1908, Frank Morrison Letterbooks, Perkins Library, Duke University. On the AFL's role at the Democrats' Labor Bureau, see Frank Morrison to M. Grant Hamilton, September 16, 1908, Morrison Letterbooks. And on Gompers's effort to suppress independent movements, see Greene, *Pure and Simple Politics*, chapter 6.

10. Hamilton to Morrison, July 25, 1908; Hamilton to Gompers, September 22, 1908; John Lennon to Gompers, November 4, 1908; all in AFL Records.

11. See, for example, *Danville* (Ill.) *Commercial-News*, September 8, 1908; M. Grant Hamilton to Frank Morrison, July 25, 1908, AFL Records.

12. William D. Mahon to Gompers, May 12, 1908; Gompers to the AFL Executive Council, April 15, 1908; J. Harvey Lynch to Gompers, April 18, 1908; all in AFL Records.

13. Greene, *Pure and Simple Politics*, chapters 7 and 8; Gompers to William B. Wilson, July 13, 1916, AFL Records; Internal memo written by R. Lee Guard, July 14, 1916, AFL Records; Gompers to Woodrow Wilson, December 16, 1912, Woodrow Wilson Papers, 2d ser., Library of Congress; Newton D. Baker to Gompers, October 30, 1916, AFL Records. For other views on the relationship between labor and the Democrats during Wilson's Presidency, see Melvyn Dubofsky, "Abortive Reform: The Wilson Administration and Organized Labor, 1913–1920," in James E. Cronin and Carmen Sirianni, eds., *Work, Community, and Power: The Experience of Labor in Europe and America, 1900–1925* (Philadelphia: Temple University Press, 1983), 197–220; Dallas Lee Jones, "The Wilson Administration and Organized Labor, 1912–1919," Ph.D. Diss., Cornell University, 1954; and John S. Smith, "Organized Labor and Government in the Wilson Era, 1913–1921: Some Conclusions," *Labor History* 3 (Fall 1962), 265–86.

14. Stanley Kutler, "Labor, the Clayton Act, and the Supreme Court," *Labor History* 19 (Winter 1962), 19–38; Dallas L. Jones, "The Enigma of the Clayton Act," *Industrial and Labor Relations Review* 10 (January 1957), 201–21; Arthur Link, *Wilson: The New Freedom* (Princeton: Princeton University Press, 1956).

15. Gompers, "Eight Hour Constitutional Amendment," *AF* 5 (June 1898), 110–13; Reed, *The Labor Philosophy of Samuel Gompers*; Fred Green-

baum, "The Social Ideas of Samuel Gompers," _Labor History_ 7 (Winter 1966), 35–61.

16. Gompers, "Self-Help is the Best Help," _AF_ 22 (February 1915), 113–15; Gompers, "Municipal Ownership and Organized Labor," _AF_ 23 (February 1916); Gompers, "Labor vs. Its Barnacles," _AF_ 23 (April 1916), 268–74.

17. Dubofsky, "Abortive Reform," 204–5; James Weinstein, _The Corporate Ideal in the Liberal State, 1900–1918_ (Boston: Beacon Press, 1968), 172–213; and Graham Adams Jr., _Age of Industrial Violence, 1910–1915_ (New York: Columbia University Press, 1966).

18. This portrait of Walsh is drawn from his papers, held at the New York Public Library, and especially from Ralph Sucher, "Biographical Sketch of Frank P. Walsh," Walsh Papers.

19. Mrs. J. Borden Harriman, _From Pinafores to Politics_ (New York: Henry Holt and Co., 1923), 131; Sucher, "Biographical Sketch of Frank P. Walsh," Walsh Papers.

20. On the commission, the definitive source is Adams, _Age of Industrial Violence;_ see also John Commons, _Myself_ (New York: Macmillan, 1934), 167–68; U.S. Commission on Industrial Relations, _Final Report and Testimony Submitted to Congress by the Commission on Industrial Relations_, Senate Document No. 415, 1st Sess. (Washington: Government Printing Office, 1916); and David Montgomery, _The Fall of the House of Labor: The Workplace, the State, and American Labor Activism, 1865–1925_ (New York: Cambridge University Press, 1987), 361.

21. Harriman, _From Pinafores to Politics_, 136; New York _Call_, 5 July 1916, Personal Scrapbooks, Walsh Papers; _Pittsburgh_ (Kans.) _Workers' Chronicle_, June 30, 1916, Personal Scrapbooks, Walsh Papers.

22. U.S. Commission on Industrial Relations, _Final Report and Testimony_, 18–19.

23. U.S. Commission on Industrial Relations, _Final Report and Testimony_, 71–73; _Schenectady Citizen_, October 20, 1916, Personal Scrapbooks, Walsh Papers.

24. U.S. Commission on Industrial Relations, _Final Report and Testimony_, 68, 71–72. Frank Walsh formally dissented from the provision of the report that demanded literacy tests for immigrants.

25. John White to Frank Walsh, November 16, 1915, Frank Walsh Papers, New York Public Library; "A Follow-Up Committee on Industrial Relations," _Survey_ 35 (November 13, 1915), 155; Graham Adams, _Age of Industrial Violence_, 220.

26. See Joseph McCartin, "'No Haven of Ideas': Frank P. Walsh, the Struggle for Industrial Democracy, and the Unravelling of Progressivism, 1913–1920," unpublished manuscript in author's possession; on Manley and income tax evasion, see S. T. Hughes for the Newspaper Enterprise Association to President Wilson, May 19, 1916, Woodrow Wilson Papers.

27. On the investigations into the NAM, see Robert Hunter, *Labor in Politics* (Chicago: Socialist Party of America, 1915). On efforts to expand the state's role, see Theda Skocpol, *Protecting Soldiers and Mothers*; Kathryn Kish Sklar, "The Historical Foundations of Women's Power in the Creation of the American Welfare State, 1830–1930," in Seth Koven and Sonya Michel, eds., *Mothers of a New World: Maternalist Politics and the Origins of the Welfare State* (New York: Routledge, 1993); Molly Ladd-Taylor, *Mother–Work: Women, Child Welfare, and the State, 1890–1930* (Urbana: University of Illinois Press, 1994).

28. Historians have commonly seen the 1916 campaign as a moment of unprecedented closeness between the AFL and the Democratic Party. In a recent study, for example, David Sarasohn comments that in 1916 the AFL "functioned almost as an arm of the Democratic effort . . ." Although organized labor continued to be important in the Democrats' calculations, in terms of actual campaign work, cooperation between the two peaked in 1908. For contrasting views see, Sarasohn, *The Party of Reform: Democrats in the Progressive Era* (Jackson, Miss.: University Press of Mississippi, 1989), 206, 237; Harold Livesay, *Samuel Gompers and Organized Labor in America* (Boston: Little, Brown, and Co., 1978), 170; and Gwendolyn Mink, *Old Labor and New Immigrants in American Political Development: Union, Party, and State, 1875–1920* (Ithaca: Cornell University Press, 1986), 204, 256.

29. Sarasohn, *The Party of Reform*; Arthur Link, *Wilson: Campaigns for Progressivism and Peace, 1916–1917* (Princeton: Princeton University Press, 1965).

30. Arthur Link, *Woodrow Wilson and the Progressive Era, 1910–1917* (New York: Harper and Row, 1954); Greene, *Pure and Simple Politics*, chapter 8.

31. For newspaper accounts that Walsh was behind the Adamson Act, see the *Boston Journal*, August 24, 1916; and the *New York Sun*, August 22, 1916, Personal Scrapbooks, Walsh Papers. The headline of the latter article reads: "WILSON HEEDS WALSH'S PLAN." For Walsh's appraisal, see Frank Walsh to Daniel Kiefer, August 30, 1916, Walsh Papers.

32. Gompers, "Regulation by Law! Law!! Law!!!" *AF* 23 (March 1916), 191–94. Luke Grant, a labor journalist who supported Hughes rather than

Wilson in 1916, was one of many who noted Gompers's awkwardness regarding the Adamson Act. Since Gompers had worked so hard against hours legislation, Grant wrote to a friend, "It amuses me now to see him so ardently supporting Wilson who did . . . the very thing against which Sam has so often declaimed. Doesn't that bear out what I say, that we are all partisan in spite of ourselves?" Luke Grant to John Walker, September 28, 1916, John Walker Papers, University of Illinois.

33. Noble Wilson to Walsh, September 30, 1916, Walsh Papers. On Walsh's efforts in the 1916 campaign, see also Joseph McCartin, *Labor's Great War: The Struggle for Industrial Democracy and the Origins of Modern American Labor Relations, 1912–1921* (Chapel Hill: University of North Carolina Press, forthcoming).

34. *New York Times*, "Wilson Will Greet Volunteers Today," October 16, 1916, Personal Scrapbooks, Walsh Papers; George West to Walsh, October 2, 1916, Walsh Papers; Walsh to Dante Barton, October 3, 1916, Walsh Papers.

35. Walsh Itinerary, n.d., Walsh Papers; Kacy Adams to W.P. Harvey, October 6, 1916, Walsh Papers; no signature to Democratic National Headquarters, October 17, 1916, Walsh Papers.

36. Boston *Herald*, October 16, 1916; *Los Angeles Record*, September 9, 1916; *Schenectady Gazette*, October 17, 1916: all in Walsh Papers.

37. "Reports to Wilson Predict Landslide", *New York Times*, October 23, 1916, 3; "Toledo Labor Vote United For Wilson: Eight-Hour Law Turns the Scale to Democrats in Normally Republican County" *New York Times*, October 19, 1916, 5.

38. "8-Hr Law Aids Wilson in Illinois," *New York Times*, October 25, 1916, 6; "Railroad Men Cheer Wilson," *New York Times*, October 19, 1916, 1, 3: H. B. Perham, President, Order of Railroad Telegraphers, St. Louis, to Gompers, October 26, 1916, reel 81, AFL Records; "Railway Unions Ask Votes for Wilson," *New York Times*, October 27, 1916, 2; "Wants Hughes Defeated," *New York Times*, November 2, 1916, 6. Perham sent his organizers to work in Pennsylvania, Oklahoma, Maryland, New York, Indiana, Ohio, and Colorado.

39. "Eight-Hour Law Aids Wilson in Illinois," *New York Times*, October 25, 1916, 6; and see the *Washington Trade Unionist*, September 22, 1916, 3.

40. A. W. McLean to Josephus Daniels, September 13, 1916, Josephus Daniels Papers; McLean to Henry Morgenthau, September 25, 1916, Josephus Daniels Papers; Charles Adair to Democratic National Committee, Chicago, November 2, 1916, Thomas Walsh Papers; William Blackman to Thomas Walsh, August 24, 1916, Thomas Walsh Papers; Senator Thomas Gore to Henry Hollis, October 4, 1916, Thomas Walsh Papers; William McAdoo to Pres-

ident Wilson, September 24, 1916, William McAdoo Papers. All collections cited in this note are at the Library of Congress, Manuscripts Division.

41. See William Harvey to Walsh, October 11, 1916, Walsh Papers; Basil Manley to Fred Howe, June 22, 1916, Walsh Papers. For an example of Frank Walsh addressing the problems of agricultural workers, see *The Rebel*, July 1, 1916, Personal Scrapbooks, Walsh Papers. The House quote comes from Sarasohn, *The Party of Reform*, 217.

42. See Arthur Link, *Wilson: Campaigns for Progressivism and Peace*, (Princeton: Princeton University Press, 1965), 45–47, 106–10; Grant Hamilton, "Labor Would be Ignored," *Washington Trade Unionist*, November 3, 1916, 1; see also on labor and militarism, Grant Hamilton, "Issue is Clearly Defined," *Washington Trade Unionist*, October 27, 1916, 1. While the peace issue was undoubtedly important, my reading of the evidence concurs with scholars such as David Sarasohn, who see labor and social justice issues as more influential in the 1916 campaign. See Sarasohn, *The Party of Reform*, chapter 7 and especially p. 212. On the war prosperity, see Gilbert C. Fite and Jim E. Reese, *An Economic History of the United States*, 3d ed. (Boston: Houghton Mifflin, 1973), 444–47.

43. Arthur S. Link and William M. Leary Jr., "Election of 1916," in Arthur M. Schlesinger Jr., ed., *The Coming to Power: Critical Presidential Elections in American History* (New York: Chelsea House Publications, 1971), 320–21; Stephen Wise to Frank Walsh, November 15, 1916, Walsh Papers.

44. C. O. Young, Portland, Ore., to Gompers, November 9, 1916, reel 81, AFL Records; Sarasohn, *The Party of Reform*, 216; S. D. Lovell, *The Presidential Election of 1916* (Carbondale, Ill.: Southern Illinois University Press, 1980), 165.

45. Voting data comes from the Inter-University Consortium for Political and Social Research, Ann Arbor Michigan, Data File 8611, principal investigators Jerome Clubb, William Flanigan, and Nancy Zingale. The counties examined were Los Angeles and San Francisco Counties, Calif.; Pueblo County, Colo.; Fairfield and New Haven Counties, Conn.; Cook County (dominated by Chicago) and Vermilion County (Danville), Ill.; Marion County (Indianapolis), Ind.; Knox County (Rockland), Maine; Essex County (Lawrence), Mass.; Wayne County (Detroit), Mich.; Jackson County (Kansas City), Mo.; Douglas County (Omaha), Nebr.; Atlantic County (Atlantic City), N.J.; New York County and Kings County (Brooklyn), N.Y.; Cuyahoga County (Cleveland), Lucas County (Toledo), and Mahoning County (Youngstown), Ohio; and Allegheny County (Pittsburgh), Lackawanna County (Scranton), and Lycoming County (Williamsport), Penn. For more on voting results in these counties between 1904 and 1916, see Greene, *Pure and Simple Politics*.

46. See Arthur Link and William M. Leary, "Election of 1916," 320; and Sarasohn, *The Party of Reform*, 227. S. D. Lovell's findings reinforce my own. Examining the eight states and counties with the largest number of wage earners, all of them in the northeastern region, Lovell found that in every case Wilson's vote increased in 1916 over the votes Democrats had received since 1904, and in most cases the increase was quite dramatic. Lovell also demonstrated that in nearly every case a Democratic vote this high would not be seen again until the 1928 or 1932 elections. S. D. Lovell, *The Presidential Election of 1916*, 168–69, 177.

47. County-level voting statistics come from the ICPSR, *op cit*. See also Sarasohn, *The Party of Reform*, 220–21; Montgomery, *The Fall of the House of Labor*, 365; "Through the Editor's Eyes," *Pearson's Magazine* 37 (January 1917), 92; Arthur Link, *Wilson: Campaigns for Progressivism and Peace*, 162.

48. John Walker to Luke Grant, September 30, 1916, Walker Papers; Walker to L. L. Jackson, November 6, 1916, Walker Papers; Walker to Adolph Germer, September 28, 1916, Walker Papers.

49. Arthur Link, *Wilson: Campaigns for Progressivism and Peace*, 124; Frank Walsh to Basil Manley, June 26, 1916, Walsh Papers; Walsh to Dr. Wise, November 12, 1916, Walsh Papers.

50. On these developments see Philip Taft, *The A.F. of L. in the Time of Gompers*; Frank L. Grubbs, *The Struggle for Labor Loyalty: Gompers, The A.F. of L., and the Pacifists, 1917–1920* (Durham, N.C.: Duke University Press, 1968); Melvyn Dubofsky, *We Shall Be All: A History of the Industrial Workers of the World* (New York: Quadrangle Books, 1969), chapter 16.

51. The best source on the NWLB is Joseph A. McCartin, *Labor's Great War*.

52. Bernard Mandel, *Samuel Gompers: A Biography* (Yellow Springs, Ohio: Antioch Press, 1963), 505. For additional background on these events, consult Montgomery, *The Fall of the House of Labor*.

53. Harold Charles Bradley, "Frank P. Walsh and Postwar America," Ph.D. diss., St. Louis University, 1966, 205–6.

54. No author, "Read! Think! Choose! The Democratic and Republican Platforms," *American Federationist* 27 (August 1920), 729–43; Samuel Gompers, "'Normalcy' vs. Progress," *AF* 27 (October 1920), 913–18; Gompers, "Reaction in the Saddle," *AF* 27 (December 1920), 1081–86; Gompers, "We Are in to Win," *AF* 31 (September 1924), 741–43; Gompers, "Why Labor Should Support La Follette and Wheeler," *AF* 31 (October 1924), 808–9; Bernard Mandel, *Samuel Gompers*, 517–23.

Peter Rachleff

———————————— 4 ————————————

The Failure of Minnesota Farmer-Laborism

The Minnesota Farmer-Labor Party (FLP) was the most successful state-level example of the labor movement's involvement in
third-party politics during the Great Depression, if not in all of
American history. It elected two governors, two United States senators, half a dozen congressmen, and dozens of state legislators and
local officials. It also succeeded in passing some of the most progressive state legislation enacted anywhere in the country during the
1930s. In its heyday, it provided support for farmers facing mortgage
foreclosures, workers engaged in struggles to win union recognition
and contracts, and the unemployed in their efforts to support themselves and their families. Indeed, it would be a misnomer to call the
FLP Minnesota's "third" party since, during the years of its existence
(1918–1944), it consistently outdistanced the Democratic Party, and
often the Republicans.[1]

Yet, ultimately, the FLP failed as an independent expression of
workers' political interests. In the mid-1930s, it became embroiled in
conflicts with militant labor unions, such as the Minneapolis Teamsters and the Hormel Packinghouse workers. It also failed to realize
efforts by party activists to launch a nationwide third party in
1935–36. In 1938, it lost its grip on state government and was unable to prevent the passage of a labor relations law that served as a
precursor to the postwar federal Taft-Hartley Act. In 1944, it gave up
its own organization and identity to merge with the Democratic
Party and to form the Democratic Farmer-Labor Party (DFL). By
1948, Hubert Humphrey and his allies had purged remaining radical elements from the DFL and captured its leadership.[2]

In this essay, I will explore contingent explanations for the failure of the Farmer-Labor Party, internal to the party itself and the wider labor movement. I will focus on three sets of problems: internal hierarchy within the FLP; conflict between the American Federation of Labor (AFL) and the Congress of Industrial Organizations (CIO); and sectarian conflict between left-wing organizations, particularly the Communist Party (CP) and the Trotskyist-oriented Socialist Workers Party (SWP). In order to explore these dynamics, I will focus on the Independent Union of All Workers (IUAW), which began in the Austin, Minnesota, Hormel plant in the summer of 1933, spread across Austin's workplaces, and brought a model of community-wide unionism to thirteen midwestern cities and towns until it dissolved itself in 1937 in order to merge piecemeal with AFL and CIO national unions.[3]

The FLP behaved all too much like a traditional political party. Its officeholders often held themselves apart from, even above, the party's grass-roots organizations. They played fast and loose with party platforms, used patronage to build personal machines, and rewarded friends outside the ranks of the farmer-labor movement. Constituency organizations—Farmer-Labor Association clubs, Farmer-Labor Party precinct caucuses, and local unions—had little success holding the party's victorious candidates accountable to them. These problems gnawed at the FLP's fabric, leaving an undertone of mistrust and discontent even—or even more so—when the party was winning elections.[4]

Floyd Olson's administration—typically considered the high point of Farmer-Laborism—was also the high point of these problems. Olson held the governor's seat from 1930 to 1936, and he was even mentioned as a potential national third party candidate for president in 1936. His death from stomach cancer that year prematurely ended his meteoric career. It also left him on a pedestal, constructed equally by a sculptor who placed his statue on the green outside the state capitol and by a number of biographers, who have lionized him as the most charismatic leader in Minnesota's history.[5]

Olson helped to shape this image himself. He traded effectively on his roots as the son of Scandinavian immigrants who had grown up in the ethnically-mixed neighborhood of Minneapolis' near north side. He even claimed to have joined the Industrial Workers of the World (IWW) in 1912, after having dropped out of the University of Minnesota and ridden the rails to the Pacific Northwest. While governor, Olson frequently adopted a radical posture, criticizing capitalism and urging the creation of a system "based on need."[6]

But the reality of Olson's career and political practice was at some distance from this image. In 1918, a Republican governor who was actively repressing the labor movement appointed him Hennepin County district attorney, and, when he ran for reelection, after the establishment of the Farmer-Labor Party, it was on the Democratic ticket. After he joined the FLP in 1924, he became known for his back-room efforts to moderate the party's program, as well as for turning his back on liquor and gambling activities in Hennepin County. In 1930, when he gained the FLP nomination for governor, he was instrumental in expunging such radical notions as "public ownership" from the party's platform. During the campaign, he organized his own "All Party Volunteer Committee," which included Republicans, Democrats, and independents as well as Farmer-Laborites. And, after his victory, he maintained this independent organization under his own control and used his patronage powers to build his personal following.[7]

Olson's activities while in office seemed designed to satisfy all sides. Though his public stance for a moratorium on farm mortgage foreclosures gained nationwide attention, his administration addressed this issue through the development of a mediation program between banks and borrowers that led to the renegotation of loans and helped defuse angry farm movements. In the summer of 1933, he mediated a temporary settlement in the Hormel strike, ending the first sit-down strike of the Great Depression years. During the Minneapolis truckers' strike of 1934, he directed the national guard to raid the headquarters of both the union and the Citizens Alliance. The national guard also took control of the streets away from the strikers, which allowed an increasing number of nonunion trucks to operate and weakened the union's hand. As the labor movement grew in size and strength, Olson came under increasing criticism from activists within it. Their expressed concerns ranged from his actions in office to his ever-closer friendship with prominent anti-union businessmen like Charley Ward and Richard C. Lilly.[8]

These criticisms, raised not only by labor activists but also by such veteran farm activists as A. C. Townley, received powerful articulation in the summer of 1935, when Walter Liggett, an independent journalist and publisher whose credentials, like Townley's, went back to the pre–World War I North Dakota Non-Partisan

League, published a scathing pamphlet entitled *Floyd B. Olson: Radical or Racketeer?* Liggett had recently collaborated with militant elements within the resurgent labor movement, serving as editor of the short-lived *Austin American*, a paper controlled by the Independent Union of All Workers. This gave even more weight to his accusations that Olson had assumed a radical demeanor only when it had no practical bearing, that he had taken financial aid from unsavory interests in order to further his own career, and that he had thrown considerable state-controlled business their way.[9]

Liggett understood that the mid-1930s presented a historical opportunity that came along all too rarely, an opportunity which could be blunted by radical poseurs. "If the insurging [sic] progressive and radical movements of the Corn Belt and Northwest can merge without falling under the control of Floyd B. Olson and his ilk," he wrote, "the American people will soon have a third party which has grown from our own soil, and which expresses the needs and desires of a large segment of the country." He continued:

> But, if professional politicians, while pretending radicalism, snatch control as Floyd Olson has snatched control of the Farmer-Labor Party of Minnesota, the country will simply see another such betrayal as of the Populists in 1896 or the Bull Moose in 1916.[10]

Liggett's pamphlet got him attention of a different sort than he might have desired. Olson's powerful backers and allies sought to deflect Liggett's criticisms by smearing him as a right-wing scandalmonger and a self-interested blackmailer. Later that summer, Liggett was indicted on a morals charge, together with Frank Ellis, the controversial militant leader of the IUAW. This charge certainly undermined both men's credibility in the eyes of the public. Though Liggett was acquitted, Ellis was convicted and sentenced to a long prison term. Two years later, Ellis would be exonerated and pardoned when one of the witnesses recanted her testimony. But a week after Ellis' acquittal, Liggett was murdered, machine-gunned in front of his wife and daughter in a Minneapolis alley. Who was behind this murder, and the frame-up that predated it, remains a mystery.[11]

These events contributed to the disorganization of the internal opposition to the direction of the Farmer-Labor Party. Olson and his "All Party Committee" strengthened their control over the FLP, even as they pulled back from national discussions of a third-party challenge to Roosevelt in 1936. They were also able to insure a smooth transition of power within the FLP when Olson fell ill and died in 1936. As the reins of power became more tightly grasped and as the FLP became tied more tightly to the national Democratic Party in 1936–1938, grass-roots enthusiasm and activism waned in Minnesota.[12]

The momentum of Minnesota's labor movement was further disrupted by internal schisms, one between the AFL and the newly emerging CIO and another between Communists and Trotskyists. The state's two most militant unions—Teamsters Local 574 in Minneapolis and the Independent Union of All Workers in Austin—had played important roles transcending such divisions. Beginning in 1933 and 1934, both unions incorporated activists of diverse political stripes, promoted the unionization of the unorganized beyond their own parameters, placed the highest priority on the expansion and militancy of the labor movement as a whole, and kept pressure on the Farmer-Labor Party itself. But by 1936–1937, conflict between the AFL and the CIO and between Communist and Trotskyist factions within unions began to exact a toll on both of these important unions. I will explore how these dynamics developed within the Independent Union of All Workers.[13]

The depression conditions of the 1930s—irregular work, low wages, abusive foremen, dirty and dangerous conditions—made packinghouse workers eager to organize, particularly if they sensed that they had an opportunity to succeed. Workers who had already been drawn to some expression of labor radicalism—including socialism, communism, Trotskyism, and militant syndicalism—often stepped forward first, initiated workplace actions, and experimented with organization. In these ideologies and the organizations which promoted them, workers found an explanation of their situation, a strategy for changing that situation, and a network of activists ready to work together. In 1933, 1934, and 1935, these activists collaborated effectively with each other, paying less attention to ideological or sectarian differences among themselves and more attention to their shared goals of building broad, militant unions.[14]

Frank Ellis, a feisty ex-Wobbly, played the key role in holding these forces together. He not only shaped the IUAW's structure and its emphasis on democracy and solidarity but also imprinted its very character with his combative personality. In his late forties, Ellis' labor "vita" included the 1904 meatpacking strike in St. Joseph, Missouri; free-speech fights from Omaha to Seattle; the IWW's famous battles in Centralia and Everett, Washington; a seat on the IWW's executive board in the early 1920s; and a lengthy list of arrests, including an indictment for "criminal syndicalism." A skilled "boomer" butcher (i.e., a man who moved from job to job, finding it easy to get hired because of his skills), Ellis had worked in packing plants all across the midwest before coming to Hormel in 1928. A contemporary recalled him as an inspirational organizer who "managed to capture workers' restlessness." He would "set a group of workers on edge for a few weeks, get them to do some thinking." Often, his first contacts were with workers who had already been drawn to some form of labor radicalism, be it socialism, communism, Trotskyism, or a more syndicalist militancy. In the Hormel plant, in other Austin workplaces, and in packinghouses and factories in cities and towns in Minnesota, Iowa, Wisconsin, and the Dakotas, workers responded to Ellis and these activists.[15]

In the spring of 1933, Ellis began meeting with a group of young hog-kill workers. Mostly Austin natives, they were angered by deteriorating working conditions, the tyranny exercised by foremen, and their "second-class" status in the community. They had already connected themselves to Ray Dunne and Carl Skoglund, two Minneapolis Trotskyists with a widespread reputation for being organizational strategists, who would soon emerge as the architects of Teamsters Local 574. The hog-kill gang would provide the IUAW with much of its dynamism, and they would be elected to a number of key union offices.[16]

Trotskyism provided these young men with a network of contacts around the upper midwest, and it also linked them to other activists within the Hormel plant, such as Joe Voorhees and Carl Nilson. Both of these men, in their late 20s or early 30s, had had professional careers disrupted by the depression. From a "very respectable family," Voorhees had attempted to follow his father's footsteps into teaching, but he had lost his job when his rural school had been forced to close. A husky young man with a growing family, Voorhees moved to Austin and found a job on the loading dock at Hormel, a position that brought him into contact with many of the workers in the plant, who came quickly to respect him for his speaking ability and his militancy. He developed a reputation not just as a good speaker, but as a man who stood behind what he said. This earned him election to such key posts as business agent and president of the IUAW. Equally important to the union was Carl Nilson, who had dropped out of the University of Minnesota and tried a variety of odd jobs before catching on in 1935 with the new state Workers Education Bureau and taking an assignment in Austin. By October 1935, he was not only teaching classes on labor history and public speaking, but he was editing the IUAW's new weekly newspaper, *The Unionist*, a two-page mimeographed sheer that was distributed free to every home in Austin.[17]

Voorhees, Nilson, and the hog-kill gang were open about their interests in Trotskyism and their relationship to the Minneapolis Teamsters activists. They worked well with Ellis. They also joined in a "socialist club" with other IUAW activists, including Svend Godfredson. He combined his Danish parents' freethinking traditions with the populism of farmers of northeastern Montana, where they had homesteaded, and the Wobbly beliefs of itinerant farmhands he had met as a child. By the mid-1920s, Godfredson had abandoned formal education at a Lutheran college and moved to Chicago, where he joined the Socialist Party and participated in the unemployed movement. In July 1933, at the urging of his two brothers who were working at Hormel, he moved to Austin and got a job in the dry-sausage department, just as the IUAW was beginning to take shape. He quickly became a shop-floor leader and was soon elected to the executive board. In 1937, he succeeded Carl Nilson as editor of *The Unionist*, and he eventually became editor of *The Packinghouse Worker*, the national publication of the United Packinghouse Workers of America.[18]

In addition to Ellis, the Trotskyists, and the Socialists, there was also a group of Communists in the IUAW. Their base was in the beef kill. This department had only opened in 1931, and most of its workers were new to Austin. Among these "boomer" butchers were experienced labor militants, some of whom, like Eddie Folan and Matt Kovacic, had joined the Communist Party at some point in the 1920s. Folan had worked with Ellis in Omaha and Sioux City and had been blacklisted after leading the 1921 strike there. In the late 1920s, he had come to South St. Paul, where he met Kovacic, a Croatian immigrant who had arrived after World War I. Kovacic had brought a rich political heritage with him as the godson of Stjepan Radic, the charismatic leader of the radical peasant movement in Yugoslavia. Folan and Kovacic worked effectively with the other radicals in the IUAW well into 1936, not only holding union offices but also participating in organizing ventures into other communities.[19]

The Hormel work force was the IUAW's base, and the activists knew the importance of a strong shop-floor presence. "You worked with people who have never belonged to a union, who have never spoken back to a foreman," recalled one shop leader. The shop floor itself, he argued, held the key to dispelling the atmosphere of fear and in demonstrating the power of collective action. The IUAW relied on direct action, from the negotiation of contracts to the resolution of grievances. One veteran explained that a department would stop work whenever an issue arose and that Ellis and other union officers would support them until it was resolved. "They'd get the grievance settled right on the job." Ellis himself told an interviewer: "Most of our strikes were sitdown, sitdown right on the job and not do a damn bit of work until we got it settled."[20]

From this solid shop-floor base, the union fanned out into the wider community, into other communities, and into other activities, such as labor politics. In Austin, the IUAW included "units" of truckers, barbers and beauticians, construction tradesmen and laborers, WPA laborers, bartenders and waitresses, garage mechanics and service station attendants, retail clerks, and municipal employees. Outside Austin, the IUAW organized in more than a dozen communities. Though a stable local union was not always the result, these experiences led to labor victories in these communities for years to come.[21]

The IUAW achieved its fullest elaboration in Austin, where the potential of its model was most realized. There, they unionized every bar, restaurant, hotel, barber shop, beauty parlor, retail business, and department store. *The Unionist* was delivered free on Friday mornings to every household. Many rank-and-filers attended Carl Nilson's Workers Education classes, lectures by out-of-town visitors, participated in rallies, demonstrations, and weekly mass meetings, borrowed books from the union's library, and took part in the union's drama troupe and drum and bugle corps or attended their performances. Friday night dances brought union families together and raised money for the "relief fund," which served as an alternative to the company-dominated Community Chest. The IUAW also sponsored candidates for local elective office (both within and independently of the formal Farmer-Labor Party apparatus) and was influential within the regional Farmer-Labor Association. In 1935, the IUAW funded a mass circulation newspaper, *The Austin Ameri-*

can, hiring Walter Liggett as editor, to provide an alternative to the conservative, pro-business newspapers that dominated local discourse. The IUAW model rested on a willingness to engage consciously in class conflict, informed in part by the political ideologies that had influenced its leading activists, but it was, above all, an expression of a social movement culture. One activist explained in a 1937 editorial in *The Unionist*:

> Austin's unionization is not a shallow thing, but a master organization that penetrates far into the lives of the workers that live in Austin. . . . It is not merely a matter of wages and more money to spend. Within this program of unionization lies the basis of things that are far reaching and more important. With unionization comes a new freedom—a freedom of the individual —that will grow in importance as the organizational experience grows older. A new freedom of thought, of action and knowledge . . . .[22]

The day-to-day culture and the political climate within the IUAW promoted the free expression of ideas. Trotskyists, Socialists, and Communists put their ideas forward. In both public speeches and columns in *The Unionist*, Frank Ellis presented a Wobbly-flavored syndicalism. In the shop, all of the radicals supported plantwide seniority, 100 percent union membership, a work schedule/pay system that became known as a "guaranteed annual wage," and equal pay for equal work for women. They supported the same candidates for public office (either formally endorsed by the FLP or running simply as a "labor" candidate) and participated in efforts to spread militant unionism throughout the upper midwest. Though they disagreed about some of the issues of national and international policy, from the New Deal to the civil war in Spain, they evinced mutual respect and cooperation until late in 1936.[23]

In the fall of 1936, this movement began to come apart at the seams, as conflict grew between the AFL and the CIO. National leaders of the AFL and the CIO increased their pressure on affiliated unions as they turned their guns on each other, competing for membership and economic power. They promoted internal hierarchy and centralized authority, even to the degree of discouraging solidarity with labor organizations tied to the competing federation. In some places, leaders created paper "unions" and signed agreements with employers in order to raid the membership of their labor competitors. Both organizations undercut horizontally structured bodies, from central labor bodies and union councils to unusual formations like the IUAW.[24]

At the same time, sectarian conflicts exploded within and among the left-wing organizations in the labor movement. The temporary alliance between the Socialist Party and the Trotskyists broke down, with the latter group establishing the Socialist Workers Party. Communist Party activists increased their influence within the Farmer-Labor Party, from the newspaper *The Minnesota Leader* to the allocation of patronage positions within the state highway department. They also emerged in prominent roles within such new CIO unions at the Timberworkers and Steelworkers and within the Minnesota Industrial Union Council. These new powers alarmed other leftists, who found themselves being shut out of various undertakings and especially the circles of power within the FLP after Olson's death.[25]

Ironically, within the IUAW, both the Communists and the Trotskyists urged affiliation with outside national labor federations, even if it meant the dissolution of the IUAW itself. They were further supported by a "straight trade union" faction within the organization, which felt that wage increases at Hormel depended on the emergence of a nationwide packinghouse workers union able to raise wages at major companies like Armour and Swift. Some key union leaders, including Frank Ellis and Svend Godfredson, opposed affiliation altogether or sought to moderate its structural consequences, and they had some success in the union's internal discussions. But a series of events swept the union's membership towards a fateful decision that would permanently alter the labor movement and weaken militant pressures within the FLP.

In the early spring of 1937, a series of sit-down strikes broke out in Albert Lea, a community twenty miles west of Austin and the site of the second best organized IUAW local. Every night for three weeks, the IUAW Drum and Bugle Corps paraded the streets of Albert Lea, marching from one occupied workplace to another, serenading the sitdowners and bringing them food. Finally, the Albert Lea Chamber of Commerce put into action a plan to break the strikes. They gained an injunction from a friendly judge, recruited 150 special deputies and placed them under the control of Sheriff Helmer Myre, and propped up a back-to-work movement led by a citywide company union, the Albert Lea Employees Labor Association, which even published a daily antistrike news bulletin. The businessmen manipulated the internal tensions within the labor movement by turning to the state AFL for a charter for their company union and by featuring red-baiting "revelations" in their news bulletin.[26]

When the sit-downers left their posts and rallied outdoors on the morning of April 2, Sheriff Myre and his deputies attacked, not only dispersing the pickets with rubber hoses and tear gas but also laying siege to the IUAW headquarters. The union offices were completely destroyed. Sixty-two men were arrested. When word reached the Hormel plant in Austin, 400 men put aside their tools and streamed into Albert Lea. There, they surrounded the jail and demanded the men inside be freed. When the Albert Lea police car pulled up, the crowd "seized it, battered it into shambles, set fire to it, and tossed it into the lake." Farmer-Labor Governor Elmer Benson, on the scene to try to mediate a settlement, walked trough the crowd to the door of the jail, where he demanded the keys. He then freed all the prisoners. The crowd carried them away on their shoulders and then disarmed the deputies, forcing them to deposit their badges and weapons and then run a gauntlet of angry union members.[27]

The strikers soon lost in negotiations not only what they had won in the streets but their very organization itself. The course of events reflected the consequences of the loss of popular control over the Farmer-Labor Party. The night that the IUAW had ruled the streets, Benson sprung his proposal on the union leaders and the Chamber of Commerce. The union was to call off the strikes and return to work. The employers were to recognize the IUAW and bargain with them, on the condition that the IUAW's units affiliate with national unions within 60 days. Although this condition was put forward by the employers, Benson was encouraged to promote it by his advisors, several of whom were close to the Communist Party and eager to build the CIO, which is where they figured the major pieces of the IUAW would end up. With Ellis behind bars hundreds of miles away (and the Communist Party undermining efforts to get him out) and the Communists, Trotskyists and straight trade unionists in favor of affiliation, the IUAW leadership accepted Benson's terms.[28]

By the midsummer of 1937, the IUAW was melting away. City by city, individual units voted to affiliate with national unions or national organizing committees: the United Auto Workers, the Packinghouse Workers Organizing Committee, the Steelworkers Organizing Committee. Some connected with the AFL-affiliated Teamsters. Austin's "uptown workers"—largely women retail clerks, waitresses, hotel maids, beauticians—bounced from the IUAW to the Teamsters to District 50 of the United Mine Workers to the Gas, Coke and Chemical Workers to the Oil, Chemical and Atomic Workers, losing members each step of the way. Some units never found a home with a national union and faded away altogether.[29]

Efforts to maintain the horizontal solidarity of the IUAW were no match for the forces pulling it apart. In late 1937, Svend Godfredson's attempt to build an "Austin Central Labor Assembly" was undermined by the centrifugal tendencies of communities that feared Austin wanted to dominate them, on the one hand, and by the sectarian hostilities between the Communists and the Trotskyists on the other. A year later, an effort to link all packinghouse workers in the region in an autonomous organization was scuttled by the CIO itself and its Communist-affiliated regional director.[30]

The IUAW was a unique organization and its story was equally unique. But its experience of being built by radicals who had worked in the industry itself and initially cooperated with each other and promoted solidarity, only to be weakened by internal conflicts in the late 1930s, conflicts that left the labor movement with little independent strength to exert within the wider political process, was all too typical of the Minnesota labor movement. In Minneapolis, Communists in influential positions in various unions withheld support from the Trotskyist leadership of Teamsters Local 574 when their backs were against the wall in a struggle with the national Teamsters' leadership. In a few short years, the labor bureaucracy managed to undermine a militant union that the employers themselves had been unable to tame. Similar echoes are heard from northern Minnesota. Radicals played the central role in the organization of steelworkers and timberworkers, through their encouragement of direct action on the job and the construction of a movement culture with music, poetry, and drama in the small, formerly company-dominated towns of the Iron Range and the north woods. But, as Tom O'Connell demonstrates in his recent study, conflict between the AFL and the CIO and between the Minneapolis-based Trotskyists and the northern-based Communists engulfed the labor movement in "jurisdictional disputes, court suits, public name-calling, and physical confrontations."[31]

These developments damaged both the internal dynamics and the expansion of the labor movement and soured its political expression. The Farmer-Labor Party faded fast. In 1938, Elmer Benson received but 387,000 votes, almost 300,000 less than his tally two years earlier. He was swept out of the governor's office by Harold Stassen, and, with one exception, every FLP candidate for state and federal office was defeated. Voter analysis showed that the farm vote had stayed strongly Farmer-Labor, but the urban labor vote had either abandoned Benson or stayed home altogether. Six years later, the party's corpse was merged with the Democrats under the direction of Hubert Humphrey and his allies.[32]

The Minnesota Farmer-Labor Party died long before 1944. It lost its role as an independent political voice for the labor movement by 1936, due to dynamics internal to the party and internal to the labor movement. These dynamics splintered activists from each other, left the party's central structures in the hands of interest groups, and disempowered and alienated rank-and-file workers. A historic opportunity was lost.

NOTES

1. On third party and independent labor politics in the 1930s, see David Milton, *The Politics of U.S. Labor: From the Great Depression to the New Deal* (New York: Monthly Review Press, 1982); Hugh Lovin, "The Persistence of Third Party Dreams in the American Labor Movement, 1930–1938," *Mid-America* 58 (October 1976). For case studies of local parties, see Eric Davin, "The Very Last Hurrah? The Defeat of the Labor Party Idea, 1934–1936," and John Borsos, "'We Make You This Appeal in the Name of Every Union Man and Woman in Barberton': Solidarity Unionism in Barberton, Ohio, 1933–1941," both in Staughton Lynd, ed. *"We Are All Leaders": The Alternative Unionism of the Early 1930s* (Urbana: University of Illinois Press, 1996). On the Minnesota experience, see David Montgomery, "The Farmer-Labor Party," in Paul Buhle and Alan Dawley, eds., *Working for Democracy* (Urbana: University of Illinois Press, 1985); James Youngdale, *Populism: A Psycho-Historical Perspective* (New York: Kennikat, 1975); Millard Gieske, *Minnesota Farmer-Laborism: The Third Party Alternative* (Minneapolis: University of Minnesota Press, 1979); Richard Vallely, *Radicalism in the States: The Minnesota Farmer-Labor Party and the American Political Economy* (Chicago: University of Chicago Press, 1989).

2. John E. Haynes, *Dubious Alliance: The Making of Minnesota's DFL Party* (Minneapolis: University of Minnesota Press, 1984); Arthur Naftalin,

"A History of the Farmer-Labor Party of Minnesota," Ph.D. diss., University of Minnesota, 1948; George Tselos, "The Minneapolis Labor Movement in the 1930s," Ph.D. diss., University of Minnesota, 1970; Ivan Hinderaker, "Harold Stassen and Developments in the Republican Party in Minnesota, 1937–1947," Ph.D. diss., University of Minnesota, 1949.

3. This essay is drawn from my ongoing research on the IUAW. Part of this work has appeared as "Organizing 'Wall-to-Wall': The Independent Union of All Workers, 1933–1937," in Lynd, *We Are All Leaders." Another version of this essay appears under the same title in Shelton Stromquist and Marvin Bergman, eds., *Unionizing the Jungles: Labor and Community in the Twentieth Century Meatpacking Industry* (Iowa City: University of Iowa Press, 1997). For alternative analyses of the FLP's decline, see David Brody, "On the Failure of U.S. Radical Politics: A Farmer-Labor Analysis," *Industrial Relations* 22 (Spring 1983), 141–61, and "The Course of American Politics," in *In Labor's Cause* (New York: Oxford University Press, 1993); also, Vallely, *Radicalism in the States*. For a wide-ranging discussion of the limitations of labor activism in the 1930s, see Staughton Lynd's "Introduction" to *"We Are All Leaders"* and the symposium on the book in *Labor History* 38 (Spring–Summer, 1997), 165–201.

4. Gieske, *Minnesota Farmer-Laborism*, 138–53; Sister Mary Rene Lorentz, "Henrik Shipstead: Minnesota Independent, 1923–1946," Ph.D. diss., Catholic University of America, 1963; George H. Mayer, *The Political Career of Floyd B. Olson* (Minneapolis: University of Minnesota Press, 1951); James M. Shields, *Mr. Progressive: A Biography of Elmer Austin Benson* (Minneapolis: T.S. Denison, 1971); Steven J. Keillor, *Hjalmar Peterson of Minnesota: The Politics of Provincial Independence* (St. Paul: Minnesota Historical Society Press, 1987).

5. Mayer, *Floyd B. Olson*; Russell Fridley, "Introduction" to the 1987 reprint of Mayer's biography by the Minnesota Historical Society Press; John S. McGrath and James J. Delmont, *Floyd Bjornsterne Olson: Minnesota's Greatest Liberal Governor* (St. Paul: McGrather, 1937).

6. Floyd B. Olson, "My Political Creed," *Common Sense* (April 1935); Olson, "Why a New National Party?", *Common Sense* (January 1936); Mayer, *Floyd B. Olson*, 171ff.; Gieske, *Minnesota Farmer-Laborism*, 187–89; Haynes, *Dubious Alliance*, 9–11. See also Henry G. Teigan Papers, Floyd B. Olson Papers, Vincent Day Papers, William Mahoney Papers, Farmer Labor Association Papers, all housed at the Minnesota Historical Society, St. Paul, Minn.

7. Mayer, *Floyd B. Olson*, 14–46.

8. Mayer, *Floyd B. Olson*, 95–213; Vallely, *Radicalism in the States*, 57–66; William Millikan, "Financing the War on Labor: The Citizens Al-

liance of Minneapolis and Northwest Bancorporation," unpublished paper in author's possession (Minnesota Historical Society Press will soon publish a book by Millikan on the long history of the Citizens Alliance); Walter Bearce, "A Party Without a Program," *The New International* (March 1939), 74–78. Ward, infamous for his organized crime connections, was CEO of Brown and Bigelow, a major nonunion printing concern. Lilly was president of First National Bank of St. Paul and sat on the boards of many local corporations.

9. Walter W. Liggett, *Floyd B. Olson: Radical or Racketeer?* (Rochester: Mid-West America, 1935).

10. Liggett, *Radical or Racketeer?*, no pagination.

11. I am indebted to Marda Woodbury, Walter Liggett's daughter, for her assistance in piecing together the story of his murder and some sense of the political forces that may have lay behind it. She has completed a massive book manuscript, *Stopping the Presses: The Murder of Walter W. Liggett*, to be published by the University of Minnesota Press.

12. Haynes, *Dubious Alliance*, 71–88; Vallely, *Radicalism in the States*, 135–41; Mayer, *Floyd B. Olson*, 289–301.

13. On the conflict between the AFL and the CIO, see Irving Bernstein, *Turbulent Years: A History of the American Worker, 1933–1941* (Boston: Houghton-Mifflin, 1971), 352–431; Walter Galenson, *The CIO Challenge to the AFL* (Cambridge, Mass.: Harvard University Press, 1960). On the conflict between the Communists and the Trotskyists, see Irving Howe and Lewis Coser, *The American Communist Party: A Critical History* (New York: Random House, 1962); Harvey Levenstein, *Communism, Anticommunism and the CIO* (Westport, Conn.: Greenwood, 1981).

14. On national patterns, see Alice and Staughton Lynd, eds., *Rank and File* (Boston: Beacon Press, 1973); Wyndham Mortimer, *Organize! My Life as a Union Man* (Boston: Beacon Press, 1971); Len DeCaux, *Labor Radical* (Boston: Beacon Press, 1970); Sidney Lens, *The Labor Wars* (New York: Doubleday, 1973); Edward Levinson, *Labor on the March* (New York: University Books, 1956); Benjamin Stolberg, *The Story of the CIO* (New York: Viking, 1938). On Minnesota, see Peter Rachleff, "Turning Points in the Labor Movement: Three Key Conflicts," in Cliff Clark, ed., *Minnesota in a Century of Change* (St. Paul: Minnesota Historical Society Press, 1989); Farrell Dobbs, *Teamster Rebellion* (New York: Monad Press, 1972); Tselos, "The Minneapolis Labor Movement in the 1930s"; Charles R. Walker, *American City: A Rank-and-File History* (New York: Farrar and Rhinehart, 1937). On the IUAW, see Irene Clepper, "Minnesota's Definition of the Sitdown Strike," Ph.D. diss., University of Minnesota, 1979; Peter Rachleff, "The Role of Radicals in the Independent Union of All Workers,

1933–1937," unpublished paper, presented at the "Perspectives on Labor History: The Wisconsin School and Beyond" conference, Madison, Wisconsin, March 1990; Roger Horowitz and Rick Halpern, "The Austin Orbit," unpublished paper presented at the Missouri Valley History Conference, Omaha, Nebraska, March 1986; Larry Engelman, "We Were the Poor People: The Hormel Strike of 1933," *Labor History* 15 (Fall 1972), 483–510.

15. Frank Ellis oral history interview, Minnesota Historical Society. *Who's Who in Minnesota* (Minneapolis: Minnesota Education Association, 1941), 245; Svend Godfredson, Ralph Helstein, and John Winkels oral history interviews, United Packinghouse Workers of America Oral History Project (UPWAOHP), State Historical Society of Wisconsin; Harry DeBoer and Frank Schultz oral history interviews, Minnesota Historical Society.

16. Frank Schultz, "History of Our Union," *The Unionist*, May–June 1949; Austin *Herald*, October 16, 1936; Svend Godfredson oral interview; Jake Cooper oral history interview, Minnesota Historical Society.

17. Marian Nilson to Peter Rachleff, February 4 and March 9, 1989; Albert Lea *Evening Tribune*, July 29, 1936; Svend Godfredson oral interview; Matt Kovacic oral history interviews with Peter Rachleff, 1985–1989; *Who's Who In Minnesota* (Minneapolis: Minnesota Education Association, 1941), 246.

18. Svend Godfredson and John Winkels oral interviews; Marie Casey and Casper Winkels oral history interviews, UPWAOHP.

19. Irene Clepper, "Minnesota's Definition of a Sitdown Strike," 12–25, 43, 60; Schultz, "History of Our Union," *The Unionist*, May–June 1949; Matt Kovacic oral interviews; Peter Rachleff, "The Croatian Fraternal Union, Radicalism, and the American Labor Movement," in Matjaz Klemencic, ed., *Ethnic Fraternalism in Immigrant Countries* (Maribor, Slovenia: University of Maribor Pedagoska Fakulteta, 1996).

20. Svend Godfredson, John Winkels, Frank Schultz, and Frank Ellis oral interviews; Fred Blum, *Towards a Democratic Work Process* (New York: Harper, 1953); Frank Ellis, "Bits of Labor History," *The Unionist*, January 22, 1960.

21. *Freeborn Patriot* (Albert Lea), May 27, 1938. Shelton Stromquist conveys the continuing impact of the IUAW in Iowa in *Solidarity and Survival: An Oral History of Iowa Labor in the Twentieth Century* (Iowa City: University of Iowa Press, 1993), especially "Rebuilding the House of Labor in the 1930s," 79–122.

22. For a fuller discussion of the IUAW, see Rachleff, "Organizing Wall-to-Wall: The Independent Union of All Workers, 1933–1937," in Lynd, ed., *"We Are All Leaders."* Editorial quote from *The Unionist* July 10, 1937.

23. Sidney Wilson oral history interview, Iowa State Historical Society; Harry Buxton to *Austin American*, February 1, 1935; Ellis in *Austin American*, March 1, 1935.

24. Robert H. Zieger, *The CIO, 1935–1955* (Chapel Hill: University of North Carolina Press, 1995), 90–110. For interesting discussions of the role played by the evolving national system of labor relations, see William Forbath, *Law and the Shaping of the American Labor Movement* (Cambridge, Mass.: Harvard University Press, 1991) and Christopher Tomlins, *The State and the Unions: Labor Relations, Law, and the Organized Labor Movement in America* (Cambridge: Cambridge University Press, 1986). For particular examples of this AFL/CIO conflict, see Staughton Lynd, "Introduction" to *"We Are All Leaders"*, and John Borsos, "We Make You This Appeal in the Name of Every Union Man and Woman in Barberton," in the same collection.

25. William Z. Foster, *From Bryan to Stalin* (New York: International Publishers, 1937); James P. Cannon, *The History of American Trotskyism* (New York: Pioneer Publishers, 1944); Milton Cantor, *The Divided Left: American Radicalism, 1900–1975* (New York: Hill and Wang, 1978); Bert Cochran, *Labor and Communism: The Conflict that Shaped American Unions* (Princeton: Princeton University Press, 1977); Art Preis, *Labor's Giant Step: Twenty Years of the CIO* (New York; Pathfinder, 1972); Stephen Meyer, *"Stalin over Wisconsin": The Making and Unmaking of Militant Unionism* (New Brunswick: Rutgers University Press, 1992); Fraser Ottanelli, *The Communist Party of the United States: From the Depression to World War II* (New Brunswick: Rutgers University Press, 1991); John Haynes, *Dubious Alliance*, 16–28.

26. Albert Lea Employees Labor Association, *Labor News*, March–April 1937; IUAW (Albert Lea) *Strike News*, March–April 1937; Albert Lea *Evening Tribune*, March 19–April 2, 1937.

27. Roger Ostby, *Will Minnesota Submit to a Rule by Force and Violence?* (Albert Lea: Ostby, 1939); Albert Lea *Evening Tribune*, April 3, 1937.

28. Ostby, *Will Minnesota Submit to a Rule by Force and Violence?*; Albert Lea *Evening Tribune*, April 3, 1937.

29. *The Unionist*, August 2, 1937; Svend Godfredson interview; Rachleff, "Organizing 'Wall-to-Wall': The Independent Union of All Workers, 1933–1937."

30. "I'm Labor" series, Austin *Herald*, September 1937; Godfredson interview; Carl Nilson, ed., *The Class Struggle* 1 (September 15, 1937); John Winkels to *The Unionist*, September 3 and 10, 1937.

31. Tom O'Connell, "A House Divided: The Rise of the CIO and the Decline of the Farmer-Labor Party," unpublished paper in author's possession.

32. James Shields, *Mr. Progressive*, 217–18; John Haynes, *Dubious Alliance*, 107–124.

Bruce Nelson

5

Autoworkers, Electoral Politics, and the Convergence of Class and Race

Detroit, 1937–1945

In an address to the leadership of the Committee for Industrial Organization (CIO) in October 1937, the organization's director, John Brophy, declared that "in the brief space of its existence, the CIO . . . has brought to American political life the voice of the great mass of American workers—a voice for the first time organized and forceful." Although Brophy was clearly engaging in a bit of organizational self-promotion, his assessment was partly—though only partly—correct. In 1936, organized labor, and the CIO in particular, had played a major role in helping to mobilize the forces that led to President Franklin Roosevelt's smashing and unprecedented electoral victory over Alf Landon, and a political realignment that had been brewing for years was decisively consolidated. The working class emerged as the core constituency of the new majority, or New Deal, coalition. Brophy, his boss John L. Lewis, and other top leaders of the CIO believed that of necessity labor was in politics to stay, and that the municipal elections of 1937 in industrial cities such as Aliquippa, Clairton, Duquesne, and Homestead in western Pennsylvania, Akron and Canton in Ohio, and, above all, Detroit in Michigan would demonstrate the next stage of the CIO's forward march. When Patrick O'Brien, the CIO's mayoral candidate in Detroit, called upon labor to "seize the reins of government in every large city in America," the lines of battle became as sharply drawn in the political arena as they were in the economic.[1]

Brophy was correct to suggest that the working-class vote had become a major factor in American politics. But the force that most compellingly pulled workers into the electoral arena as a bloc was not Lewis and the CIO but Franklin Roosevelt. At the local and state levels, moreover, electoral politics sometimes accentuated the heterogeneity of American workers, the unevenness of their consciousness, and the ferocity of their institutional rivalries. In the political arena, even more than the economic, the emergence of a class-conscious labor movement not only tested the notion of a unified working class but threatened to isolate blue-collar voters from potential—and necessary—allies in the middle class.[2]

In the city of Detroit the United Automobile Workers (UAW) spearheaded the formation of a Labor Slate candidacy for the office of mayor and five seats on the nine-member Common Council in the November 1937 municipal election. The union claimed hundreds of thousands of supporters in the Motor City. Joel Seidman of the League for Industrial Democracy asserted that autoworkers and their families constituted a majority of the city's voters, and he implied that, even without the support of the more conservative American Federation of Labor (AFL), the UAW could win the election and thereby take another decisive step forward in labor's political awakening. Eli Oliver, of Labor's Non-Partisan League, was far less cautious. "Detroit, not Washington, is the capital of the United States today," he declared. "Once more the workers of Detroit are going to show the way!"[3]

But the surge of energy that had broken the open shop and built dynamic unions at General Motors and Chrysler did not translate as readily into political power. In spite of a respectable showing in the October 5 primary, none of the Labor Slate candidates was elected to office, and the UAW's choice for mayor lost to a conservative candidate by more than 100,000 votes. The *New York Times* characterized the outcome as "a crushing defeat to political unionism."[4]

The Labor Slate and its aftermath illuminate both the scope and energy of working-class insurgency and the fragility of the foundations of progressive reform. The New Deal, the CIO, the radio, the motion picture, and the emerging consumer culture all pulled industrial workers toward a "culture of unity," but there were powerful countervailing forces as well. Ethnic communities often remained inwardly-focused and, sometimes, ambivalent about the secular, rationalist underpinnings of New Deal reform. "Old" immigrants, especially the Germans and the Irish, lamented the assertiveness of

their "new" immigrant counterparts. Southern whites moving north-
ward discovered the magnetic attractions and the ominous realities
of urban, industrial society. Most ominously, from their standpoint,
African Americans were beginning to push more insistently at the
boundaries of segregation and to demand a greater share of society's
resources for themselves. The Labor Slate sought to shape these diverse and often divergent elements into a unified electoral bloc, with
results that were disappointing on election day but which held out
hope that the next round would usher in the unity that had proven
so elusive in 1937. Instead, future elections redrew the internal fault
lines of the working class in ways that the architects of the Labor
Slate could not have imagined. Race, which had been a troubling but
relatively minor factor in the 1937 election, became a major catalyst
during and after World War II. The growing African-American presence in the Motor City propelled many white workers into a political alliance with conservative Republicans and segregationist
Democrats, and Detroit became a local portent of the impending nationwide collapse of the New Deal coalition.[5]

In the wake of the UAW's historic victory over General Motors in
February 1937, Detroit emerged as the sit-down capital of the nation. Autoworkers and many others, including cigar makers, retail
clerks, hotel bellhops, and restaurant waiters and waitresses, "sat
down" in the workplace, while the *Detroit Labor News*, organ of the
local federation of labor, exhorted them to strike "while the iron is
hot, never resting, never stopping. . . . Strike on!"[6]

These festive upheavals sometimes led to sharp and bloody confrontations with the forces of law and order and served to strengthen
workers' class awareness and sense of self-reliant power. Nowhere
was this more evident that in the massive demonstration by workers
and their supporters in Cadillac Square on March 23. It came at the
crest of the wave of sit-downs and in important respects became a
declaration of labor's determination to mobilize its independent
power not only in the factories and the streets but in the political
arena as well. In the wake of what many characterized as "police ter-
ror" against Polish-American women strikers in a cigar factory, and
with Chrysler sit-downers facing a similar threat, masses of workers—the *Detroit Labor News* claimed 150,000—converged on the
square in an unprecedented demonstration of solidarity. There they
listened to Leo Kryczki, a CIO representative and Socialist Party

(SP) leader, tell them to "organize politically into a labor party" and place Detroit and Wayne County Federation of Labor President Frank Martel "in the City Hall." In a similar reference to the forthcoming Detroit municipal elections, UAW President Homer Martin shouted, "Get every worker enlisted . . . and see that every worker not only works right and strikes right, but that he also votes right in this next election." The entire meeting, said the *Labor News*, was "a portent of a new day for the workingman. . . . Labor had made its Declaration of Independence."[7]

These were strong words. They implied that the Detroit and Wayne County Federation of Labor (DFL) was prepared to unite with the UAW to wage a battle for control of Detroit's municipal government, in spite of the fact that at the national level the GM strike had contributed to the further deterioration of relations between the AFL and the CIO. The AFL had openly denounced, and had sought to undermine, the UAW's leadership of the strike. In return, Homer Martin had characterized AFL President William Green as "the modern Judas Iscariot of the labor movement."[8]

As the war of words between national AFL and CIO spokesmen escalated in the spring of 1937, the UAW and the local federation of labor nonetheless appeared to be moving toward the formation of a unified slate that would seek a full complement of nine seats on the Detroit Common Council. The UAW began by nominating Walter Reuther and Richard Frankensteen as council candidates, while the DFL proposed its own president, Frank Martel, and Ed Thal, the president of the powerful Building Trades Council. A snag developed over the endorsement of Robert Ewald, the president of the AFL Bricklayers' Union and a council incumbent whom the UAW regarded as hostile to the new unionism. But in spite of this obstacle, Martel expressed confidence that "it would be possible for us to get together." As late as mid-July, speakers from both sides at a joint mass meeting pleaded for unity "so that the Labor ticket will be victorious at the polls this fall."[9]

But events at the local and national levels intervened to drive a wedge between the Auto Workers and the Detroit and Wayne County Federation of Labor. In the wake of the intoxicating victories at GM and U. S. Steel, there was a strong impulse in the CIO not just to "organize the unorganized" but to sweep aside the "reactionary" AFL and build the CIO as a new and hegemonic labor federation in its place. On the west coast, the newspaper of the maritime unions now characterized the AFL as a "dead corpse" and equated it with "reaction, fascism, and barbarism." In Erie, Pennsylvania, a CIO regional director declared that "*All* working people in the nation must be organized and enrolled under the banner of the C. I. O." Even in Detroit, at a time when the UAW was still seeking programmatic unity with the local AFL, the *United Automobile Worker* proclaimed, "Federation Doomed While CIO Advances."[10]

More and more, the tendency to challenge AFL jurisdiction occurred not only in places like the auto industry, where the federation's claim was pathetically weak, but in industries where the AFL had functioned with varying degrees of effectiveness over long periods of time. In Flint, for example, in the spring of 1937, UAW Local 156 became a kind of One Big Union that organized workers from many different industries into its ranks. At first, the local's organizers tried to limit their outreach to workers with some relationship to the auto industry. However, once this expansion began, it was difficult to set boundaries. By mid-June, construction workers at Fisher Body, truck drivers who delivered coal to the auto plants, clerks at the city's biggest grocery chains, dry cleaners and laundry workers, waiters and waitresses, postal telegraph messengers, and local utility company workers all had received strike support from the UAW in Flint. In fact, almost all of these workers were actually enrolled in Local 156. The crescendo of this whirlwind organizing campaign came on June 9, when UAW members at the Consumers Power Company shut down all the generators in the Saginaw Valley, forcing massive layoffs and leaving hundreds of thousands of people without electricity.[11]

The Auto Workers' organizing campaign in Flint must have aroused fears that the Detroit area AFL would be engulfed by its aggressive, and seemingly insatiable, rival, especially when UAW Local 155, an amalgamated union of tool and die makers on the Motor City's east side, was engaging in a similar—although smaller—effort that was causing "jurisdictional chaos." When the CIO chartered a bakery workers' local despite the fact that various AFL craft unions had long claimed—and exercised—jurisdiction in this industry, the specter of dual unionism threatened to scuttle the joint labor slate. On July 21, at a meeting of the Detroit and Wayne County Federation of Labor, the delegates decided that "all action heretofore taken [should] be set aside" and stated that further cooperation with the CIO was unlikely unless jurisdictional disputes were settled to the satisfaction of the AFL unions involved.[12]

Later, when the federation had endorsed its own slate of candidates, Ed Thal of the Building Trades Council charged that if Patrick O'Brien were elected mayor, "the city government would be used as a weapon against the AFL Craft Unions here." Thal had good reason to fear that in conjunction with CIO organizing efforts in the construction industry, a mayor who owed his election to the CIO would pose a serious threat to the AFL's dominant position in the building trades. But, as Martel reminded his membership, the issue was not craft versus industrial unionism. "We are proud of our part in industrial unionism," he said, "but when it goes out of its way to raid and deliberately wreck established and functioning Trade Unions we must fight it." He listed a host of occupations in Detroit— including bakers, milk drivers, transit workers, the building trades, barbers, retail clerks, cigar makers, and government employees— where the CIO had encroached on AFL jurisdiction.[13]

The defeat of the AFL-supported mayoralty candidate in the October primary paved the way for a contest between Patrick O'Brien of the Labor Slate and City Clerk Richard W. Reading, a wealthy and "rigid" conservative whom the DFL had been attacking as a former employer of scab labor who was "trying to climb into the Mayor's Chair at the expense of Organized Labor." Once again the Auto Workers sought to reach an accommodation with the local labor federation, and again they failed. This time the principal factor was clearly external. In mid-October, Martel attended the AFL's annual convention in Denver and, when he returned, informed his delegates that loyalty to the parent body required them to swallow hard and support Reading. When a delegate objected, "This is too much. How could [Reading] have been our enemy three weeks ago and our friend today?" Martel responded, "This is not a contest between Reading and O'Brien. There are other elements in it, it goes deeper than that[.] I have just come from the national convention of the American Federation of Labor where the executive council of that Federation has set down principles to guide us in our political course." Martel was referring to the AFL's declaration of war on the CIO and its allies, its pledge of "renewed determination to support its friends and defeat those in public office who would . . . in any way favor, encourage or support the CIO." The leadership of the local federation now reminded its members that Reading held an honorable withdrawal card from Martel's local of the International Typographical Union and assured them that as mayor he would be both "fair" and "friendly" to the AFL.[14]

It is tempting to identify the AFL-CIO split in Detroit as one between two dramatically different kinds of unionism, drawing upon sharply divergent constituencies. Mike Davis, for example, has argued that "the [AFL's] *ancien regime* ultimately drew its solidity from the relative conservatism of its predominantly skilled, native-Protestant, and 'old immigrant' membership"; while Steve Fraser has identified a similar "anthropological fault line [that] not only divided the CIO from the AFL but ran straight through the CIO itself." However, at this particular moment, the reality of the Motor City's labor politics was not reducible to a neat anthropological fault line. The Detroit and Wayne County Federation of Labor was bitterly at odds with Father Charles Coughlin, the patron saint of many of the German- and Irish-American workers who constituted a major part of the AFL's social base. Francis Xavier Martel, himself a Catholic, referred to Coughlin as the "Raving, Ranting, Radio Racketeer of Royal Oak" who "stands convicted as the enemy of the trade union movement of America." Meanwhile, the UAW's Richard Frankensteen, a "Coughlinite" by reputation who had once characterized the famed "Radio Priest" as a person who "has done more toward educating the working class than any other living man," became a major spokesman for the undeniably left-wing Labor Slate, which Coughlin attacked publicly as the creature of "the red leaders, acting behind the scenes of the UAW."[15]

In the heyday of Detroit's working-class insurgency, the local labor federation had applauded the spirit of "rebellion" exemplified by the Cadillac Square rally, had explicitly defended the sit-downers against a host of critics that included national AFL spokesmen, and had welcomed the prospect of a "New Era of Government" in the Motor City. The retreat from this position reflected not mainly the power of an ideological and political pull to the right at the AFL's grass roots but, rather, the determination of the national AFL leadership to defend its turf against the CIO at all costs, and the apprehension in Detroit that the UAW's meteoric growth and apparently unlimited ambition would reduce a seasoned trade-union politician like Martel to a minor player and might actually render the venerable local federation extinct.[16]

With the breakdown of relations between the AFL and CIO, the Auto Workers were left with the task of developing their own program, putting forward their own candidates, and presenting both as the embodiment of an authentic and broadly based Labor Slate. The main responsibility for implementing this agenda fell to the Detroit District Council of the UAW and its Political Action Committee, headed by Alan Strachan, a Scotsman and member of the Socialist Party who became campaign director. Without actively participating in the process, the UAW inherited Judge Patrick Henry O'Brien as its mayoral candidate. O'Brien was the son of an Upper Peninsula copper miner. He had a strongly pro-labor reputation, on the bench and within the Democratic Party, and had served as Michigan's attorney general in 1933–34. But after the conclusion of the campaign Strachan could still say, "Why he was chosen and who chose him is still a mystery." Although characterizing O'Brien as "one of the finest liberals it has ever been my pleasure to meet," Strachan expressed the belief that the elderly judge "lacked the color and glamour to inspire the auto workers to really get behind him."[17]

The Common Council candidates on the Labor Slate included four local union presidents and labor lawyer Maurice Sugar. Sugar was closely identified with the Communist Party. But in part because he had already campaigned for public office on several occasions with the support of the left, the AFL, and the black community, he was the most popular of the Labor Slate's council candidates. Governor (and former Motor City mayor) Frank Murphy, who tried to avoid taking a position on the Detroit election with the argument that it was nonpartisan and a "local matter," indirectly endorsed Sugar and Richard Frankensteen, both of whom had deep and longstanding ties to the city of Detroit and political followings that went beyond their relationship to the UAW.[18]

In addition to Frankensteen, president of Dodge Local 3 and a vice president of the international union, the other UAW Labor Slate candidates were Tracy Doll, Walter Reuther, and R. J. Thomas. Doll was president of the Hudson local and a member of the international executive board. Reuther, president of the huge west side Local 174, was also a member of the UAW executive board. Thomas was president of the Chrysler local and a vice president of the international union. The *Detroit Free Press* referred to the Labor Slate council candidates as "The Five Conspirators" and characterized Reuther in particular as "one of the extreme left wing political radicals and as such one of the chief advocates of the sit-down strikes."[19]

Programmatically, the Labor Slate presented an ambitious reform agenda that, on the one hand, reflected the immediate realities of the labor wars in Detroit and, on the other, pushed at the outer limits of the New Deal. O'Brien promised that one of his first acts as mayor would be to get rid of police commissioner Heinrich "Heinie" Pickert, whom the *New Republic* described as a man of "Nazi sympathies and storm-trooper methods," and he offered assurances that Pickert's successor would "guard the people against the thugs and vigilantes of the economic royalists." The Labor Slate candidates pledged to provide full protection of First-Amendment freedoms for all Detroiters and to safeguard the right of workers—including public employees—to organize, strike, picket, and bargain collectively. For the unemployed, they favored "adequate relief for every person who is unable to find work."

In areas such as health, housing, and utilities, the Labor Slate showed a strong commitment to greater government regulation and a dramatic expansion of the public sector. Its program called for the public ownership and operation of the utilities supplying gas and electricity to the city; for the regulation of milk prices and the development of a city-owned milk distributing plant; for the establishment of a city-owned radio station to guarantee full freedom of speech; and, in response to Detroit's urgent housing crisis, for the city to buy land at reasonable prices in order to build low-cost public housing with the help of federal loans and grants. Ben Fischer, state secretary of the Michigan Socialist Party, declared that by adding a section on the ultimate aims of the SP, the Labor Slate agenda "could have been adopted as a Socialist program."[20]

But this otherwise bold agenda was remarkably cautious, and sometimes notably silent, on issues of race. Labor Slate candidates did appeal to the black vote by attempting to link their opponents with the Ku Klux Klan, which had been a powerhouse in Detroit in the 1920s. But they offered no programmatic challenge to racial discrimination in employment and housing. Their caution no doubt reflected the volatile racial dynamic in the Motor City, the auto industry and—above all—the UAW itself. Many African-American workers kept their distance from the fledgling union, waiting to see if it would live up to its stated commitment to racial equality. Many white workers had no intention of giving up their racial privileges in the shop. A few strikes actually triggered racial violence: in the course of the Dodge Main sit-down, for instance, white strikers assaulted black workers who tried to enter the plant to pick up their paychecks. And in the aftermath of the strike wave, many white workers demanded union contracts that in effect codified workplace segregation. In such circumstances, the

Labor Slate was perhaps bound to exercise care when tiptoeing through the minefield of race relations.[21]

Among the Labor Slate candidates, Maurice Sugar was basically a Communist without a party membership card, and Walter Reuther was a member of the Socialist Party who called upon the workers to develop "a permanent Labor Party in city, state, and nation." Even candidates who had no association with the left were clearly moving leftward and, in the process, pushing at the boundaries of the New Deal. Patrick O'Brien had become an ardent New Dealer who saw the Roosevelt reform program in dynamic terms, as a stepping stone toward a dramatically altered social and economic order. He told the delegates to the UAW's 1937 convention that "the New Deal is not a final thing. The New Deal does not constitute a plan for a new social system. The New Deal, rather, is an inspiration, . . . a feeling of hospitality for every suggestion, for every proposal, for every program that will improve the lot of the masses of our country." In 1938, he would tell a group of workers in Toledo that their task was to "go forward with the New Deal, expand it and amplify it to the extent of a complete and thoroughgoing reorganization of society." "Individual ownership and initiative are a thing of the past," he said. "New theories of group ownership and social activity are developing out of the debris of the capitalist system."[22]

Although he was the son of "staunch" Republican parents, the "opportunistic" Richard Frankensteen was also a New Dealer who was in the process of coming to terms with the political ferment generated by Roosevelt's charisma and the insurgent unionism of the CIO. A Detroit native, he had won all-state honors in football and served as president of his graduating class at Central High School. After attending night classes at the University of Detroit Law School for two years, he had enrolled at the University of Dayton, where he played tackle on the football team, wrote and acted in musical dramas, and earned a plaque as "the best all around man at the college." He had planned to teach school after graduation, but the depression caught up with him. He thereupon went to work at Dodge Main, where his father was a foreman. According to his friend and fellow worker John Zaremba, Frankensteen was a "good orator" and natural leader who was "appreciated as a man by everyone" in the shop. Clearly, his academic training served him well, because as an employee representative on the plant's works council "he won his point every time" in verbal confrontations with management. However, he

soon grew disgusted with company unionism and played a prominent role in forming the independent Automotive Industrial Workers
Association (AIWA). As he told the *Detroit News*, "There are lots of
lawyers and lots of school teachers, but there is a need for leaders
among the laboring men. I feel I should do all I can."[23]

Apparently fearful that the AFL and other established unions
were "infested with racketeers," Frankensteen and his fellow activists called upon Dodge workers to "join up with a clean cut crowd
of American Workmen whose ideals and principles you will be proud
of." However, their concern with autonomy and independence did not
prevent them from seeking the assistance of one prominent ally, Father Charles Coughlin. They met regularly at his home on Friday
nights and invited him to speak at their public rallies. At one such
gathering, Coughlin encouraged the assembled workers to "organize
and help yourselves," but called for an alliance (actually, a "marriage") between "industry [and] its true wife—labor" against "fi-
nance." Partly because of the Coughlin connection, experienced
unionists tended to dismiss the AIWA as "a sincere, company minded
outfit that is utterly lacking in union knowledge and background."
But the organization continued to expand, and Frankensteen defended its patron as "a man who we feel has done more toward educating the working class than any other living man." Indeed, the
AIWA's first yearbook was dedicated to "our advisor and supporter
Father Charles E. Coughlin, the friend and educator of the masses."[24]

On Labor Day weekend 1935, Frankensteen spoke before a large
gathering of AIWA members and supporters in Belle Isle Park. With
Coughlin in attendance, he delivered a nativist diatribe in which he
blamed the employers for "arbitrarily sen[ding] to Southern Europe
for illiterate, ignorant peasants to replace the good old Puritan
stock." He charged that immigrants had imported communism to
the United States and that their struggles "brought on a flow of
strikes[,] of sabotage[,] and of murders." He warned the auto manufacturers that "if experience should be the best teacher, then you will
recognize the right . . . of your employees to organize and you will
deal with them as the honest men and gentlemen they are and not
create a new class of Communists." "The automobile worker," he concluded, "is not communistic."[25]

In a radio address a year later, Frankensteen offered an even more
sweeping indictment of the foreign-born, characterizing "immigrants
from Europe and Coolies from the Far East" as "scabs." Since a very

significant proportion of the work force at Dodge Main and other Chrysler plants in the Detroit area was made up of new immigrant workers and their children, one can only wonder what they must have thought of this new "leader among the laboring men." If they were slower than native stock and old immigrant workers to respond to the appeal of the AIWA, Frankensteen's blatant nativism may have been a part of the reason. To be sure, the AIWA succeeded— partly through Coughlin's influence—in winning the allegiance of a significant number of conservative Catholic workers (some of them no doubt Polish-American) who believed that "what Father Coughlin said was infallible." Dodge Main and Local 3 would continue to be re- garded as strongholds of "Coughlinite" sentiment long after the AIWA's merger with the UAW in the summer of 1936.[26]

But the tide was turning, and Frankensteen was shrewd enough to go with the flow. In the wake of Roosevelt's unprecedented tri- umph, the election of New Dealer Frank Murphy as governor of Michigan, and the dramatic sit-down strike at Dodge Main in March and April of 1937, the ranks of Dodge Local 3 not only expanded dra- matically but a more militant style of unionism began to take hold. In comparison to the Irish immigrant and Irish Republican Army veteran Pat Quinn, and to the Communist strike leader A. J. Walden, both of whom challenged him unsuccessfully for the presi- dency of Local 3, Frankensteen remained a moderate. And at the in- ternational union level, he initially aligned himself with the more conservative of the two major caucuses. But in public at least, he abandoned his nativism and anticommunism. Indeed, his political evolution during this period would seem to stand historian Peter Friedlander's provocative hypothesis on its head. Friedlander has argued that the shop-floor militants and left-wing cadre who made up a significant proportion of the early UAW leadership were forced to become more accomodationist over time as the union expanded and brought into its ranks hundreds of thousands of European im- migrant and southern-born white workers whose world view was es- sentially conservative. Frankensteen's trajectory seems to have been just the opposite. When the AIWA merged with the UAW and work- ers poured into the CIO auto union in the spring and summer of 1937, he moved to the left, not the right. During the Labor Slate campaign, his speeches reflected the class polarization that had en- gulfed Detroit. The campaign, he said, pitted "genuine workers" and "hard working men" against "the pirate crew of Cadillac Square," whom he defined as "agents of great financial, industrial and commercial outfits, with headquarters in Detroit, Chicago and New York." In response to the constant red-baiting of the Labor Slate, he declared in a radio address that "if standing for a better and richer life for the common man makes me a radical then I submit to the title." In fact, he said in another address, "it seems to me that to be called a radical is to be complimented."[27]

Opponents of the Labor Slate were only too happy to emphasize—and exaggerate—its radicalism and to repeat ad nauseam O'Brien's statement about labor seizing "the reins of government in Detroit and in every other large city in America." Defenders of the status quo called upon the citizenry to protect their nonpartisan system of government and to safeguard their "individual liberty" against the threat of "a minority group representing the radical wing of the CIO." The *Detroit News* warned that "the CIO program calls for the election of a CIO mayor and a CIO-dominated Council; the appointment of a CIO police commissioner and corporation counsel and of CIO men to the scores of other City posts which the Charter empowers the mayor to fill." Mayoral candidate Reading chimed in with the observation that the Labor Slate platform "sounds like the voice of Red Russian revolution speaking"; and Frank Martel added the AFL's imprimatur to red-baiting by wisecracking that UAW President Martin was trying to get rid of the Communists in his union by placing them on the city council.[28]

Stung by the barbs of their critics, and placed on the defensive by charges that the Labor Slate was tantamount to a "labor dictatorship," the UAW campaign strategists chose to highlight the themes and rhetoric that had worked so well for Franklin Roosevelt in 1936, when he carried Detroit by more than 200,000 votes. They declared that their intent was to "Bring the New Deal to Detroit" and portrayed their opponents as "Reactionary Hooverist Republicans" and "millionaire carpetbaggers." In short, they tried to appropriate the language of "the people" versus "the economic royalists" in the class-tinged way that Roosevelt had, but with only limited success, in part because they really had created a *labor* slate, forged in the heat of sharp class conflict, rooted in the left wing of the diverse Roosevelt coalition, and including in its ranks men and women whose politics were considerably more radical than the New Deal's.[29]

Their opponents' ominous warnings succeeded as well as they did because Detroit, like many sections of industrial America, had undergone a major upheaval in 1937. As picket lines and sit-downs spread from the auto plants to downtown stores, restaurants, and hotels, they had an increasingly direct and disquieting effect on the lives of tens of thousands of middle-class Detroiters. Spokesmen for the middle classes sometimes found whimsy and humor in all the turbulence. An editorial in the *Flint Weekly Review* joked that "an old-timer in Michigan is a man who can remember when workmen came down to work in the morning and punched the time clock instead of the boss." But far more common were the increasingly strident calls for the protection of private property and the restoration of public order.[30]

In 1937, then, the development of a class-conscious workers' movement proved to be a two-edged sword. It won unprecedented victories over some of the world's largest industrial corporations. It enrolled millions of workers in the new—and the old—unions. But when sit-downers barricaded themselves in downtown stores, when insurgent unionists turned out the lights on half a million customers, when labor's political spokesmen called upon the CIO to seize the reins of government in every large city in the nation, an escalating wave of reaction set in. In Washington, Harry Hopkins, Roosevelt's most trusted adviser, passed along the warning that the campaign to unionize the mass-production industries was creating "a complicated situation" that was "full of all kinds of dynamite, political as well as social." The president got the message and decided it was time to stand above the fray, to declare—in the wake of the bloody confrontation at Little Steel—"a plague on both your houses."[31]

Alan Strachan saw the same dynamic at work in Detroit. "Nobody . . . could deny that the campaign wound up with a labor versus capital complexion," he said. "The vicious attacks by the newspapers had their effect on the middle class, particularly the small business man, who was led to believe that industry would move out of the city and taxes would increase. . . . [The campaign staff's] efforts [to offset the propaganda] were hardly enough to sway a group of people who were obsessed with the fear of anarchy." Socialist Party leader Ben Fischer agreed and stated even more bluntly, "The middle class went overwhelmingly to the reactionaries."[32]

The UAW had failed to achieve unity with the AFL forces in Detroit, and its leaders gradually recognized that the reality of class conflict combined with a steady drumbeat of hostile press propaganda was frightening much of the middle class into the camp of reaction. Nevertheless, Labor Slate campaign strategists calculated that by aggressively mobilizing the UAW membership, their candidates, or at least some of them, could win anyway. Initial estimates were that the auto union had 200,000 members in Detroit, with 100,000 potential members yet to be enrolled. Later, the leaders of the campaign refined their statistics and stated that the UAW had only 125,000 members in the Motor City. But—taking the adult family members of auto unionists into account—they expressed confidence that this would mean "300,000 certain votes" for the Labor Slate.[33]

The result of the October 5 primary did not justify this inflated optimism. But still the outlook remained hopeful. O'Brien finished second behind Reading, and far ahead of the AFL-supported candidate, John Smith, who, as a former mayor and current president of the Common Council, had been a formidable opponent. Out of sixty-six candidates for the council, all five of the Labor Slate's nominees finished in the top eighteen, thereby securing a place on the November ballot. Sugar and Frankensteen finished in the top nine (seventh and ninth, respectively), and even the Labor Slate's opponents conceded that both were likely to win council seats in November. Certainly, the CIO remained optimistic. Eli Oliver of Labor's Non-Partisan League declared, "What has been done in Detroit indicates what can be done in every industrial city in the country." He warned, however, that in order to succeed, "we must build a political machine that can deliver the goods."[34]

Building a machine that could deliver the goods would have been a formidable enough task for the UAW under the best of circumstances. But in the summer and fall of 1937 the circumstances—while exhilarating—hardly favored the commitment of the union's human and financial resources to the development of a parallel political infrastructure. In the wake of the GM strike, the UAW had rapidly evolved into one of the largest labor organizations in the nation. By August 1937 the union had 256 locals, 400 collective bargaining agreements, and 220,000 dues-paying members. (It claimed as many as 375,000.) The union was still trying to develop a leadership cadre to keep up with its breathtaking growth and to maintain some control of its membership whose combative spirit had already become legendary. General Motors President William Knudsen complained that the UAW's "inability to control its members" had caused more than 150 sit-down strikes in the four months following the conclusion of the GM strike.[35]

The continuing wave of unsanctioned strikes also provoked controversy within the UAW and the CIO. Meeting with a group of GM tool and die makers who were threatening a sit-down the next day, CIO official Adolph Germer warned them that "every CIO representative is looked upon as a walking strike, and . . . this epidemic is going to make it difficult to organize other industries." Tracy Doll, the president of the Hudson local and one of the five Labor Slate council candidates, recalled that in the aftermath of the initial Detroit sit-downs and the victories they brought, "My time was filled completely with attempting to keep the plants running. The people were so exuberant over [the] freedom . . . they envisioned from the yoke of the boss . . . that in many instances they even took the boss and threw him right out of the plant, which created a sort of anarchy." More tersely, Richard Frankensteen told the press, "Our men have been in a fighting mood . . . and it is sometimes difficult to stop them."[36]

UAW spokesmen charged that production was being disrupted mainly because "foremen and superintendents have deliberately and openly invited wildcat strikes on the part of the men, as part of the GM campaign to discredit the UAW and the CIO." Whatever the cause of the shop-floor turbulence, it affected the union's capacity to mobilize on behalf of the Labor Slate. Strachan readily acknowledged that the sharp and continuing conflict with management at the point of production meant that many of the most active unionists "were engaged in ironing out tense and complicated situations in their respective plants and considered the political campaign of secondary importance."[37]

The UAW's ability to mobilize its membership for political action was also severely hampered by the factional warfare that was endemic to the union's internal life. It reached a crescendo—and resulted in a wave of negative publicity—on the eve of the Detroit primary election. One highly partisan observer calculated that the actions of Homer Martin, in particular, cost the Labor Slate 20,000 votes. Although this charge is unverifiable, and almost certainly incorrect, Strachan concluded in retrospect that "no campaign should ever be run with a schism as wide as the one that existed in the International."[38]

Only two months after the conclusion of the GM strike, Adolph Germer had informed John L. Lewis that the UAW leadership was mired in a bitter factional conflict. Victor Reuther spoke of "open warfare" within the Flint UAW and declared, "It appears to me that it has at last come to a show down and we have nothing else to do but go to Detroit and fight it out." The main protagonists in this "show down" were President Homer Martin on one side and a shifting coalition of Communists, Socialists, and nonpolitical trade union militants on the other. Martin was a former Baptist minister whose speeches continued to bear the mark of pulpit oratory and middle-American values in their simplest form. In a typical homily, Martin told a meeting of shop stewards in Saginaw, "We're working to build a labor movement in this country that stands for truth and righteousness, that stands for courage and honesty, and all this will come about because our hands will be clean and our hands must be clean. With our hands clean and our thoughts pure we'll make America over to where it will be much more human." To the chagrin of his opponents, who believed he was as "inept and wishy washy . . . as a 'drunken butterfly,'" Martin remained popular with the UAW membership, especially with the large number of transplanted white southerners who were concentrated in Flint, Pontiac, Lansing, and in some of the auto plants in Detroit. His supporters, ranging from conservatives to self-proclaimed Bolsheviks, came together in the Progressive Caucus, with Martin and Richard Frankensteen serving as principal spokesmen.[39]

Leaders of the anti-Martin, or Unity, Caucus included Vice President Wyndham Mortimer, a Communist; Socialist Walter Reuther; and Vice President Ed Hall, who had no affiliation with a political party of the left. Although it was—and has remained—convenient to blame UAW factionalism on the Communists, Joe Brown, an astute and exceptionally well informed observer of auto unionism, declared, "It is not the Communists that are the cause of dissension in the UAW. It is none other than Homer Martin who is the cause of it all." A large part of Martin's animus toward the members of the Unity Caucus seems to have been based upon his fear that they were a threat to his position in the union. During the GM strike, some of them had played a far more important role than he, and the day-to-day direction of the strike in Flint had been in the hands of Mortimer protege Bob Travis and Walter Reuther's brother, Roy. Although Martin claimed at times that he knew "the profit system is doomed" and that he was as "red" as any of his intraunion opponents, he accused them of engaging in a sinister conspiracy to destroy the UAW by creating "confusion" and caus[ing] trouble." He professed to believe that the conflict was between "the International Union itself" and "some outside political group with a different policy." Meanwhile, he became increasingly dependent upon one such group, the Communist Party Opposition (CPO), led by Jay Lovestone, a former general secretary of the Communist Party who had been expelled in 1929 for the sin of "American exceptionalism." "I suggested to Homer that he rid himself of all the 'Stones,' Weinstone [head of the Communist Party in Michigan] and Lovestone alike," Germer reported to Lewis. But Martin insisted that the Lovestoneites were "willing to go along with him in good faith."[40]

At the UAW's annual convention in Milwaukee, CIO representatives went to great lengths to get the two warring factions to declare a truce. In formal terms, they succeeded. But soon after the truce agreement—in fact, within two weeks of the October 5 primary election in Detroit—Martin launched a campaign to deliver a knockout blow to his UAW opponents. In a week's time he removed seventeen members from UAW staff positions, allegedly as an economy move, and replaced them with his own supporters, many of whom were Lovestoneites who had no prior relationship to the struggles in the locals to which they were assigned. Some of these locals had been engaged in protracted guerilla warfare with management, and many of the organizers Martin removed from office had succeeded in building strong ties with the local union membership. At the GM Ternstedt plant in Detroit, for example, the local bargaining committee charged that at a perilous moment, when management was speeding up production, cutting wages, and discriminating against active unionists, "President Martin dismissed our organizer, Brother Stanley No[w]ak." Nowak, an experienced and dedicated left-winger and member of the Unity Caucus, had become something of a legend in the Detroit area UAW, in part because of his high visibility as general organizer among Polish-speaking autoworkers, but even more so because he had broken his leg is a famous altercation with "hired thugs" during a cigar industry sit-down strike in February 1937. After Martin removed Nowak from his position, the Ternstedt bargaining committee declared: "Brother Stanley No[w]ak organized Ternstedt practically single-handed. He broke his leg helping workers win a strike. For many months afterwards he worked on crutches organizing Ternstedt. When he came to this plant there were only a dozen workers in it belonging to the union. Now there are 10,000."[41]

The names of those removed from office by Martin read like an honor roll of the union's middle-level leadership during the organizing strikes of 1937. One of the victims, Victor Reuther, was the brother of Labor Slate council candidate and Unity Caucus spokesman Walter Reuther. Not surprisingly, the purge of Victor was widely interpreted as an attack on Walter. And Martin struck on other fronts as well. He and his supporters were determined to make the UAW a "responsible union," which meant not only defeating the Progressive Caucus's factional enemies but containing rank-and-file insurgency and exercising greater control of the entire union structure from the top. On September 29, Unity Caucus leader Wyndham Mortimer reported to John Brophy that the executive board had just "passed some very reactionary decisions on local unions, such as prohibiting them from printing their own local union newspapers, preventing the tool and die makers from having separate meetings to discuss problems of their trade, and other rulings of a similar nature. In fact they spent most of the time deciding what the locals were not allowed to do, instead of encouraging them to enlarge their activities." Although holding no brief for the Communist Mortimer, Joe Brown agreed that "Martin and the CPO crowd had the locals muzzled."[42]

On September 30, only five days before the Detroit primary, the UAW's internal warfare reached a comic-opera climax when, after picketing the Eddystone Hotel where Martin was closeted and waiting most of the day for a conference with him, a protest delegation led by Timken-Detroit Axle plant bargaining chairman Daniel Gallagher went to the UAW president's hotel room, with the media in tow, and knocked loudly on the door. Martin emerged and, according to the *Detroit Free Press*, "shoved the business end of a revolver against Gallagher's chest," and with "a cigaret[te] drooping from the corner of his mouth . . . warned hoarsely, 'I mean business.'" "Our people," said a member of the delegation, "were speechless at this welcome by our president" (although Gallagher did manage to say, "This is a hell of a way to treat a union man.") The press had great fun with the story, at the UAW's expense of course. Martin added to the hysterics by first justifying his brandishing of the revolver with the statement that "I thought they were coming to get me," and then, when the press discovered that he had no permit to carry such a weapon, declaring, "I never had a gun, I've never had a gun, and there was no gun in the room." Before Martin left town on a hastily arranged trip to New York, he denounced the union members who had come to his door as "thugs and gangsters" who were acting on behalf of enemies of the union. Mortimer told Brophy, "Some of our boys are still hopeful that we will come through the primaries alright, but if we do it will be in spite of [Martin] and not because of him."[43]

It is reasonable to surmise that UAW activists in Detroit who were outraged by their president's actions would have been less than enthusiastic about campaigning—or even voting for—a close Martin ally like Richard Frankensteen, who charged that at best the Eddystone Hotel protesters were "innocent dupes." But Martin had his defenders as well. In Detroit, there were numerous autoworkers who were uneasy—even angry—about the disruption and material cost of sit-down strikes. To them Martin's call for responsible unionism and his efforts to impose tighter control over local unions must have sounded like a necessary step toward the restoration of industrial peace and more regular employment. They no doubt shared his indignation at the Eddystone Hotel incident, the union members who precipitated it, and the press's treatment of it.[44]

Although Strachan recognized that factionalism was a "delicate subject," he was compelled to acknowledge its impact on the Labor Slate campaign. "The first task of the Political Action Committee," he said, "was to convince both groups to vote for the whole slate and not just for the people they liked." But it does not appear that the autoworkers cast their votes along factional lines. In the primary, for example, the top vote-getter among the four UAW candidates was Richard Frankensteen, while R. J. Thomas, his ally in the Progressive Caucus, finished last, with nearly 29,000 fewer votes. It would seem, rather, that the main effect of factionalism was on the campaign's internal cohesion and on the morale of autoworkers, only about 39 percent of whom voted in the primary (compared to a citywide average of 54 percent).[45]

In addition to the unionists who identified with one of the two major caucuses, there were many UAW members in Detroit who remained uninterested in electoral politics or who shared much of the popular animus toward left-wing ideology and a politics based upon explicit class appeals. The Motor City was famous as a magnet for young men from the rural midwest and Appalachia who flocked to Detroit in search of employment when the auto plants were hiring and drifted away when they were laid off. Detroit, said Raymond Daniell, "is not only a city of youth; it is a city of transient youth."

Beyond transiency, however, these restless migrants often brought with them a conservative ideology rooted in fundamental Protestantism and the extreme individualism of the rural petty proprietor. To many of these migrants racism, nativism, and anticommunism were second nature. They provided the social soil in which groups like the Ku Klux Klan and the Black Legion flourished. Some of them had been attracted to Father Coughlin's Catholic variant of populism—especially its resentment of the "money changers" and its fervent anticommunism—and to the nativist strains evident in independent auto unions such as Frankensteen's Automotive Industrial Workers'Association.[46]

Would these workers even vote? And if so, would they cast ballots for Labor Slate candidates such as Maurice Sugar, a Jewish attorney who was closely identified with the Communist Party, and Walter Reuther, an outspoken Socialist who had worked in an automobile plant in the Soviet Union? In fact, would they be inclined to vote for anyone on a slate whose members were under constant public attack as instruments of subversion and dictatorship? Joel Seidman may have stated the issue too melodramatically, but he recognized that the campaign propaganda about 300,000 sure autoworker votes for the Labor Slate was blatantly misleading. As he put it, "Most of the thousands of automobile unionists who are providing the mass base of [the Labor Slate] had never been in any labor organization until a few months ago. . . . Many of them followed the Coughlin banners but a short time ago. Raw and untrained, they may be marshaled into a genuine workers' political movement or swept off their feet by some silver-tongued demagogue."[47]

The city's African-American community—about 9 percent of Detroit's population in 1937—posed a different set of problems for the Labor Slate. Excluded from most jobs, even in the lower reaches of the auto industry, locked into a narrow strip of ghetto near downtown, subject to white violence on the streets and in the factories, black Detroiters had every reason to be skeptical about an all-white insurgent movement claiming to speak for the "common man." To overcome African-American doubts, the Labor Slate would have had to promise a substantive attack on segregation. To do that, however, would have run the risk of losing white working-class votes.[48]

November 2 saw the largest electoral turnout in Detroit's history, as more than two-thirds of the city's 625,000 registrants voted. The Labor Slate endured what its adherents characterized as a near miss but most others chose to call a humiliating defeat. Patrick O'Brien received 154,000 votes for mayor, a greater total than any previous candidate except Frank Murphy. But Richard Reading received almost 107,000 votes more than O'Brien (62.9 percent to O'Brien's 37.1 percent). Even more painful was the defeat of all the Common Council candidates. After their primary showing, Sugar and Frankensteen had been given an excellent chance of winning seats in November; they were, according to the *New York Times*, "sure winners." But Sugar finished tenth, with 145,342 votes, almost 14,000 behind the successful ninth-place candidate. Frankensteen finished eleventh, with 141,414 votes. Doll (128,979), Reuther (126,323), and Thomas (126,126) followed, in thirteen, fourteenth, and fifteenth places, suggesting that the Labor Slate's supporters very clearly voted as a bloc.[49]

Martin explained the outcome by saying that the UAW had 175,000 members in the city, and that about 35,000 of them were "not politically minded and did not vote." His statement implies that the Labor Slate bloc was composed almost entirely of UAW members and excluded their wives (or husbands) and other family members, other CIO unionists, and members of AFL unions in the city. At the very least, the outcome must be analyzed in broader terms that take account of ethnicity, gender, and race. It would appear that a much higher percentage of autoworkers voted in the November election than in the primary, although in general working-class participation was considerably lower than in WASP middle-income districts (where the turnout was sometimes as high as 89 percent). By far the greatest vote for the Labor Slate occurred in Polish neighborhoods. O'Brien carried only four of the city's twenty-two wards. Three of them were overwhelmingly Polish in character, and the fourth, Hungarian. In the Polish wards his margin of victory was three to one and the council candidates finished one-two-three-four-five. The Polish community was mainly working class in character, and although historically it was also family centered, inward looking, and devoutly Catholic, the combined force of the depression, the New Deal, and the insurgent unionism of the CIO had stimulated a period of intense political ferment in Detroit's "Poletown" and in Hamtramck, an overwhelmingly Polish municipality surrounded by the Motor City. The electoral success of left-wingers like Stanley Nowak (who a year later would win a seat in the state senate) and Mary Zuk suggests that a class- and ethnic-based Popular Front mentality was taking root among many Polish-Americans. Therefore it is hardly surprising that, along with other new immigrant groups, they would provide the Labor Slate with its most solid support.[50]

Apparently skilled workers, especially the members of tool and die locals 155 and 157, who were disproportionately old immigrant in character and whose leadership was mainly left-wing, were strongly committed to the Labor Slate. The same would appear to be true of the more heterogeneous membership of the amalgamated West Side Local 174, where the internal mobilization on behalf of the campaign was especially impressive and the membership allegedly "idolize[d]" their president, Walter Reuther. The local's newspaper, the *West Side Conveyor*, claimed that "in number of election workers, in amount of money raised, in energy and talent of its committees, in enthusiasm and cooperation of its membership, West Side led the parade."[51]

Reading did especially well among Detroit's large number of white native-born Protestants. It is reasonable to assume that the unskilled and semi-skilled autoworkers from this group, most notably the southern migrants among them, were far from unanimous in their support of the UAW's candidates. Statistical evidence also suggests that women voted disproportionately for Reading. Outside of tightly knit ethnic communities it may be that in many instances the wives of autoworkers shared the general fear that a Labor Slate victory would mean more strikes and unemployment and voted accordingly.[52]

Reading won the black vote by an overwhelming margin, even though the Labor Slate candidates made a vigorous attempt to tie him to the Ku Klux Klan. In spite of the UAW's strong effort to appeal to black voters, only Sugar, who had a long history of providing legal service to the black community, did well in African-American precincts. The UAW's effort in the black community was seriously undermined when one of its local unions held a dance in a segregated hotel and refused to fight for the right of its black members to attend the function. Black newspapers reported the incident with banner headlines that read, "Jim Crowism in the UAW," and hopes of building upon a stronger than expected showing in the primary evaporated.[53]

Ford workers presented the UAW with a special challenge. The union had failed to penetrate Ford, where the firm's aging patriarch ran a semi-feudal, quasi-fascist regime, with the help of the notorious Ford Service Department. Although the UAW publicly scoffed at the claim of one of Ford's "independent" unions to represent more than 20,000 of the 80,000 workers at the giant River Rouge complex, it is likely that significant numbers of Ford workers were either intimidated into inaction or were actively opposed to the UAW and CIO. In October 1937 there were 9,825 black workers at the River Rouge complex, where they made up nearly 12 percent of the labor force and remained "remarkably loyal" to the company. Even after the UAW's successful strike for union recognition in 1941 22,322 River Rouge workers voted against affiliation with the UAW. Wyndham Mortimer was certainly correct in stating that "the Ford problem is THE problem facing us now and for some time to come," and Ford's ability to stave off the UAW and reinforce his authoritarian regime must have affected the participation of autoworkers in the municipal election.[54]

Was the outcome a crushing defeat for political unionism, and for the UAW and the CIO in particular? Does it suggest the impossibility of independent labor politics in the 1930s? From the vantage point of the union's inflated claims for its candidates and the CIO's expectation that Detroit would represent a decisive step toward labor control of the politics of major industrial cities, it is clear that the UAW suffered a significant setback. But given the AFL's defection; the fear, verging on hysteria, among much of the middle class; the factional divisions in the UAW; the refusal of President Roosevelt, Governor Murphy, and much of the local Democratic Party to endorse the Labor Slate; and the fact that the Labor Slate program and some of its candidates were considerably to the left of the New Deal, Alan Strachan was correct to emphasize that the Labor Slate succeeded in marshaling "150,000 votes that all the propaganda and vilification of the reactionaries [could] not shake."[55]

From the standpoint of November 1937, the Labor Slate campaign appeared to have provided a solid foundation for future efforts in the realm of independent labor politics. Strachan made the vitally important point that "the basis for organization has been laid"; and the *West Side Conveyor* declared that "the bosses and bankers . . . [a]re already worrying about the next election." But a far more basic issue—the survival of the union—soon cast "the next election" onto the far horizon. By December 1937, Detroit was again devastated by an economic downturn. In spite of its less ominous name, the "Roosevelt recession" wreaked havoc on automobile production and employment. December saw the sharpest monthly drop in car sales in GM history. And by the end of January 1938, the UAW was estimating that of 517,000 production workers in the auto industry, 320,000 were jobless and 196,000 were on short time. It would have been difficult enough to maintain internal cohesion—and any bargaining power—under these circumstances, but the union was weakened even further by the intensification of its factional wars. According to Irving Bernstein, "For all practical purposes the international union had ceased to function" by June 1938. It would recover in 1939, after a painful schism in which Martin flew the coop with a relative handful of followers. But then World War II intervened to create a new set of problems and responsibilities, one of which was the demand that the union pull together with the rest of the nation in a great campaign to defeat the fascist menace abroad. In such circumstances, independent politics that emphasized the division of society into hostile class forces was very much out of favor.[56]

If the pursuit of independent labor politics was jeopardized by these developments, the issue of race cut even deeper and exposed the extreme fragility of the New Deal coalition. During the war, the pace of black migration to the Motor City accelerated. While Detroit's white population declined by 2 percent between 1940 and 1944, its black population increased by 41.5 percent. By the end of the war there were more that 210,000 African Americans in a city of 1.8 million. They crowded into dilapidated ghettoes, jostled with whites on buses and street corners and in public parks, and found both unprecedented opportunity and rampant discrimination in the labor market. Black advancement organizations grew as rapidly as the city's African-American population, and Detroit's NAACP chapter, which increased its membership from 2,860 to 20,500 between 1938 and 1944, became the largest in the nation.[57]

White reactions to the enhanced black presence ranged from acceptance to apprehension to outright hysteria. Black workers' attempts to move from casual labor and service employment to semi-skilled factory work sometimes precipitated "hate" strikes, including one that involved 90 percent of the 25,000 workers at a Packard assembly plant. When African Americans sought decent housing beyond the confines of the ghetto, they encountered even sterner resistance. The opening of the Sojourner Truth Homes to black occupancy in April 1942 was, of necessity, accompanied by a massive show of force: 1,600 troops with fixed bayonets and 1,400 city and state police officers. "Detroit is dynamite," *Life* magazine declared, and the entire city seemed to "blow up" in June 1943, when a race riot left thirty-four people dead (twenty-five of the victims were black) and caused some two million dollars in property damage.[58]

In negotiating its way through the home front's racial mine fields, the UAW leadership temporized and retreated at times but on the whole demonstrated far more resolve than the leaders of most predominantly white organizations. The union engineered the discharge of hate strikers, supported civil rights initiatives in the community, and forged a close and enduring alliance with the NAACP. "It was in the UAW," said historians August Meier and Elliot Rudwick, "that the black community found its warmest and most dependable ally."[59]

Inevitably, the union again turned to the electoral arena, where "crime" and "housing"—code words for the politics of race—had superseded the issue of "labor dictatorship." In 1945, UAW Vice President Richard Frankensteen ran for mayor of Detroit against the incumbent Edward Jeffries. Once a liberal ally of labor, Jeffries had shifted dramatically to the right during World War II. He consolidated his position by defending the racial "common sense" of his white constituents and red-baiting anyone who challenged his policies. During the 1945 mayoral campaign, he warned that Frankensteen was a "red" who would aid and abet "racial invasions" of white neighborhoods. Trade union membership had grown dramatically during the war. The CIO claimed 350,000 members in the Motor City; the AFL, another 100,000. Thus, on paper at least, labor should have been in an even stronger position to "seize the reins of government" than it had been in 1937. But once again the house of labor was divided. The AFL endorsed Jeffries; and within the UAW bitter infighting between "left-wing" and "right-wing" factions kept the leadership in turmoil. (This time Frankensteen was associated with the union's left wing and Reuther with the right wing.) The most important divide, however, came within labor's rank and file, and the principal fault line was racial. Ninety percent of the black community's votes went to Frankensteen. But many white workers cast their ballots for the incumbent mayor, in spite of almost universal dissatisfaction with his record. In the poorest "native white" neighborhoods, Jeffries captured 55 percent of the vote (compared to 82 percent among middle-class "native whites"). In the city's Polish neighborhoods, Frankensteen won 61 percent of the vote, but this represented a significant erosion of Polish-American support in the eight years since 1937. "Mayor Jeffries is Against Mixed Housing," his campaign posters proclaimed, and for many Detroiters that was enough to turn the tide in his favor. He won the election by more than 57,000 votes.[60]

Nineteen thirty-seven had offered a moment of disappointment mixed with hope. Nineteen forty-five revealed that the quest for independent labor politics remained as precarious as ever, despite (to some degree, because of) the extraordinary growth of the trade union movement. But 1945 also foreshadowed the breakup of the New Deal coalition. For many white workers, their very sense of themselves as "working people" remained racialized; indeed, it became more so as African Americans demanded access to the jobs, schools, neighborhoods, and public space that whites claimed as their own. In that sense of white entitlement, and victimization, the seeds of a major political realignment were germinating.[61]

 NOTES

1. "Address of John Brophy on Progress of Organizing Drives," Atlantic City, N.J., October 13, 1937, box 4, Briggs Local 212 Collection, Archives of Labor and Urban Affairs, Walter P. Reuther Library, Wayne State University, Detroit, Mich. [hereafter ALUA/WSU]; O'Brien quoted in *Newsweek*, October 18, 1937, 12.

2. For a summary of these developments, see Richard J. Oestreicher, "Urban Working-Class Political Behavior and Theories of Mass Electoral Politics, 1870–1940," *Journal of American History* 74 (March 1988), 1257–86. A good introduction to the vast literature on the formation of the Roosevelt coalition and the emergence of the Democrats as the majority party is Kristi Andersen, *The Creation of a Democratic Majority, 1928–1936* (Chicago: University of Chicago Press, 1979). On the 1936 election, see James McGregor Burns, *Roosevelt: The Lion and the Fox, 1882–1940* (New York: Harcourt, Brace & World, 1956), 276–88; William E. Leuchtenburg, *Franklin D. Roosevelt and the New Deal, 1932–1940* (New York: Harper & Row, 1963), 183–96; Robert McElvaine, *The Great Depression: America, 1929–1941* (New York: Times Books, 1984), 275–82. On 1940, an even more important election than 1936 in solidifying the

working-class vote as the critical component of the Roosevelt coalition, see Irving Bernstein, "John L. Lewis and the Voting Behavior of the CIO," *Public Opinion Quarterly* 5 (June 1941), 233–49; Samuel Lubell's, "Post Mortem: Who Elected Roosevelt?" *Saturday Evening Post*, January 25, 1941, 9–11, 91–94, 96; Richard Jensen, "The Cities Reelect Roosevelt: Ethnicity, Religion, and Class in 1940," *Ethnicity* 8 (June 1981), 189–95; Bruce Nelson, "'A Class Across the Face of American Politics'? Workers, Organized Labor, and the Presidential Election of 1940" (paper presented at the Organization of Historians Annual Meeting, St. Louis, April 1989). On municipal politics, an outstanding case study is Daniel Nelson, "The CIO at Bay: Labor Militancy and Politics in Akron, 1936–1938," *Journal of American History* 71 (December 1984), 565–86. See also Karen L. Steed, "Unionization and the Turn to Politics: Aliquippa and the Jones and Laughlin Steel Works, 1937–1941" (seminar paper, University of Pittsburgh, 1982).

3. Joel Seidman, "Detroit's Labor Slate," *Nation*, September 11, 1937, 261; *United Automobile Worker*, September 25, 1937, 4.

4. F. Raymond Daniell, "Detroit—Our Laboratory of Social Change," *New York Times Magazine*, November 14, 1937, 5.

5. Lizabeth Cohen offers an eloquent and innovative articulation of the "culture of unity" perspective in *Making a New Deal: Industrial Workers in Chicago, 1919–1939* (New York: Cambridge University Press, 1990). In sharp contrast to Cohen, Peter Friedlander, Steve Fraser, and Nelson Lichtenstein emphasize the continuing balkanization of the industrial working class and the unevenness of working-class consciousness in the 1930s. See Friedlander, *The Emergence of a UAW Local, 1936–1939: A Study in Class and Culture* (Pittsburgh: University of Pittsburgh Press, 1975); Fraser, "The 'Labor Question,'" in Fraser and Gary Gerstle, eds., *The Rise and Fall of the New Deal Order, 1930–1980* (Princeton, N.J.: Princeton University Press, 1989), 55–84; Fraser, *Labor Will Rule: Sidney Hillman and the Rise of American Labor* (New York: Free Press, 1991); Lichtenstein, *The Most Dangerous Man in Detroit: Walter Reuther and the Fate of American Labor* (New York: Basic Books, 1995). On the emergence of race as a pivotal issue, see Alan Clive, *State of War: Michigan in World War II* (Ann Arbor: University of Michigan Press, 1979), 130–69; Dominic J. Capeci, Jr., *Race Relations in Wartime Detroit: The Sojourner Truth Housing Controversy of 1942* (Philadelphia: Temple University Press, 1984); and, above all, Thomas J. Sugrue, "Crabgrass-Roots Politics: Race, Rights, and the Reaction Against Liberalism in the Urban North, 1940–1964," *Journal of American History* 82 (September 1995), 551–78, and Thomas J. Sugrue, *The Origins of the Urban Crisis: Race and Inequality in Postwar Detroit* (Princeton, N.J.: Princeton University Press, 1996).

6. *Detroit Labor News*, quoted in Carlos A. Schwantes, " 'We've Got 'em on the Run, Brothers': The 1937 Non-Automotive Strikes in Detroit," *Michigan History* 56 (Fall 1972), 183.

7. Christopher J. Johnson, *Maurice Sugar: Law, Labor, and the Left in Detroit, 1912–1950* (Detroit: Wayne State University Press, 1987), 214–15; *Detroit News*, March 24, 1937, 4; *Detroit Labor News*, March 26, 1937, 1, 7, 12; "Mr. Homer Martin's Speech in Cadillac Square, March 23, 1937," box 11, Henry Kraus Collection, ALUA/WSU.

8. Sidney Fine, *Sit-Down: The General Motors Strike of 1936–1937* (Ann Arbor: University of Michigan Press, 1971), 183–85, 289–90, 330.

9. Michael Craine, "Labor in the 1937 Detroit Municipal Election" (seminar paper, University of Michigan, Ann Arbor, 1971), 16–17; Alan Strachan, "A History of the Work of the Political Action Committee in the Detroit Municipal Elections, 1937," 1–2, box 11, Maurice Sugar Collection, ALUA/WSU.

10. *Voice of the Federation* (newspaper of the Maritime Federation of the Pacific Coast) quoted in Bruce Nelson, *Workers on the Waterfront: Seamen, Longshoremen, and Unionism in the 1930s* (Urbana: University of Illinois Press, 1988), 232; Ralph W. Tillotson, "To the Marchers on Labor Day, 1937," *The CIO Files of John L. Lewis*; *United Automobile Worker*, September 18, 1937, 5.

11. The Consumer Power workers' bold maneuver won them union recognition but also provoked the intervention of Michigan governor Frank Murphy, the UAW's Homer Martin, and CIO Director John Brophy, which put an end to this moment of militant insurgency in Flint. Ronald Edsforth, *Class Conflict and Cultural Consensus: The Making of a Mass Consumer Society in Flint, Michigan* (New Brunswick, N.J.: Rutgers University Press, 1987), 181–82.

12. Steve Babson, "Pointing the Way: Skilled Workers and Anglo-Gaelic Immigrants in the Rise of the UAW," Ph.D. diss., Wayne State University, 1989, 455–56; Craine, "Labor in the 1937 Municipal Election," 18; "Minutes of the Detroit and Wayne County Federation of Labor," July 21, 1937, box 10, series I, Metro Detroit AFL-CIO Collection, ALUA/WSU.

13. *Detroit Labor News*, October 22, 1937, 1. Thal's statement reflects the AFL's recognition of the new realities in the realm of collective bargaining. For many years the AFL's stance had been to ask the government to refrain from interfering in the relationship between labor and capital. But as state intervention in the economy grew apace, the government's attitude toward questions of jurisdiction and organization became critical. As early as 1931, Frank Murphy, who was then mayor of Detroit, had cooperated with

the AFL's successful efforts to organize public employees, and the local federation had been happy to give Murphy "no small part of the credit." Philip Taft, "Labor's Changing Political Line," *Journal of Political Economy* 45 (December, 1937), 634–50. The best study of the AFL's, and the CIO's, changing attitude toward the role of government in labor-management relations is Christopher L. Tomlins, *The State and the Unions: Labor Relations, Law, and the Labor Movement in America, 1880–1960* (New York: Cambridge University Press, 1985).

14. Sidney Fine, *Frank Murphy: The New Deal Years* (Chicago: University of Chicago Press, 1979), 472; *Detroit Labor News*, September 24, 1937, 1, October 22, 1937, 1; Strachan, "A History of the Work of the Political Action Committee," 3; *United Automobile Worker*, October 23, 1937, 1.

15. Mike Davis, *Prisoners of the American Dream: Politics and Economy in the History of the U.S. Working Class* (London: Verso, 1986), 71; Fraser, "The 'Labor Question,'" 72; Frank X. Martel to Robert Kendall, April 2, 1934, box 3, series I, Metro Detroit AFL-CIO Collection; *Report of Proceedings of the Fifty-fourth Annual Convention of the American Federation of Labor*, San Francisco, October 1–12, 1934, 372; Richard Frankensteen, address to "Friends of the Automo[tive] Industrial Workers Association," August 31, 1935, box 1, Richard Frankensteen Collection, ALUA/WSU; Craine, "Labor in the 1937 Detroit Municipal Election," 37.

16. *Detroit Labor News*, March 26, 1937, 1; Davis, *Prisoners of the American Dream*, 69–70. Homer Martin publicly credited Martel with having "fought in the American Federation of Labor the first real battles for industrial unionism for the automobile workers of America." *United Automobile Worker*, September 11, 1937, 3.

17. "Vote Labor: Labor Ticket Enters Field," n.d., box 2, Frankensteen Collection; International Union, United Automobile Workers of America [hereafter UAW], *Proceedings of the Second Annual Convention*, Milwaukee, August 23–29, 1937, 57–59; Strachan, "A History of the Work of the Political Action Committee," 13–14.

18. Johnson, *Maurice Sugar*, 152–76, 187–90; Fine, *Frank Murphy: The New Deal Years*, 482.

19. "Vote Labor: Labor Ticket Enters Field"; *Detroit Free Press*, October 29, 1937, clipping in box 7, Frankensteen Collection.

20. "O'Brien Greases Skids for Dictator Pickert," *Vote Labor*, September 20, 1937, 1; oversize folder–1, Kraus Collection; Frank Winn, "Labor Slate in Detroit," *New Republic*, November 3, 1937, 364; "Vote Labor: Our Candidates, Our Platform," folder 17, box 11, Maurice Sugar Collection, and other campaign materials in the same folder; Ben Fischer, "The Lessons of Detroit's Labor Campaign," *Socialist Review* 6 (January–February 1938), 15.

21. Steve Babson, *Working Detroit: The Making of a Union Town* (New York: Adama Books, 1984), 44–45; August Meier and Elliot Rudwick, *Black Detroit and the Rise of the UAW* (New York: Oxford University Press, 1979), 34–38; Kevin Boyle, " 'There Are No Union Sorrows That the Union Can't Heal': The Struggle for Racial Equality in the United Automobile Workers, 1940–1960," *Labor History* 36 (Winter 1995), 8–9.

22. Johnson, *Maurice Sugar*, especially 99; Walter P. Reuther, "Detroit Can Be Workers' City," *Socialist Call* (Special Detroit Campaign Edition), October 2, 1937, 3, oversize folder–1, Kraus Collection; International Union, UAW, *Proceedings of the Second Annual Convention*, 58; Patrick H. O'Brien, "Labor in Politics" (Toledo, Ohio, March 26, 1938), box 13, Kraus Collection.

23. "Dick Frankensteen Goes After Henry Ford," *St. Louis Post-Dispatch*, July 18, 1937, clipping in box 7, Frankensteen Collection; "Vote Labor: Labor Ticket Enters Field"; Oral History of John Zaremba, 8–9, ALUA/WSU; *Detroit News*, undated clipping in box 7, Frankensteen Collection. For portrayals of Frankensteen as a consummate opportunist, see Joe Brown to Edward Wieck, box 10, Edward A. Wieck Collection, ALUA/WSU; Irving Bernstein, *Turbulent Years: A History of the American Worker, 1933–1941* (Boston: Houghton Mifflin, 1970), 557.

24. Oral History of John A. Zaremba, 12, 14; leaflet addressed to "Automotive Industrial Workers Association Members," n.d., box 16, Kraus Collection; Steve Jefferys, *Management and Managed: Fifty Years of Crisis at Chrysler* (Cambridge: Cambridge University Press, 1986), 55–67; Steve Jefferys, " 'Matters of Mutual Interest': The Unionization Process at Dodge Main, 1933–1939," in Nelson Lichtenstein and Stephen Meyer, eds., *On the Line: Essays in the History of Auto Work* (Urbana: University of Illinois Press, 1989), 109–10; *Detroit Free Press*, July 1, 1935, clipping in box 7, Frankensteen Collection; Benjamin Linsky to Edward Wieck, September 25, 1935, box 10, Weick Collection; Frankensteen address to "Friends of the Automo[tive] Industrial Workers Association," August 31, 1935; *First Year Book and History of the A.I.W.A.* (Detroit: n.p., n.d.), box 1, Frankensteen Collection. It is important to remember that Coughlin remained enormously popular in 1935. No less a person than Frank Murphy, soon to be governor of Michigan, characterized himself as a "close friend and admirer" of the Radio Priest, while Homer Martin, the Baptist preacher in search of a larger (union) congregation, wrote to Coughlin in 1935, "I listen at every opportunity to your broadcasts and have done so since you started." Martin Halpern, *UAW Politics in the Cold War Era* (Albany: State University of New York Press, 1988), 18–19, 275–76, 278.

25. Frankensteen address to "Friends of the Automo[tive] Industrial Workers Association," August 31, 1935.

26. Richard Frankensteen, "Radio Broadcast," July 17, 1936, box 6, Kraus Collection; Oral History of John A. Zaremba, 15–16; Jefferys, " 'Mat-

ters of Mutual Interest,'" 115–16. In his address to the South Bend convention of the United Auto Workers in April 1936, before the AIWA merged with the UAW, Frankensteen continued to defend the AIWA's relationship to Coughlin, saying that "we make no apologies for having him speak to us as a guest speaker—that person has done a great service." International Union, UAW, *Proceedings of the Second Convention*, South Bend, Indiana, April 27–May 2, 1936, 141.

27. Jefferys, *Management and Managed*, 71–80; Friedlander, *The Emergence of a UAW Local*, 111–31, especially 127; "Radio Talk of Richard T. Frankensteen," October 28, 1937, box 4, Frankensteen Collection; Richard Frankensteen, "Labor Slate Broadcast," October 30, 1937, ibid.; Richard Frankensteen, "Who Is the Big Bad Wolf?" (radio address), October 31, 1937, ibid.; Richard Frankensteen, "Radio Address," n.d., ibid.

28. *Detroit Free Press*, October 29, 1937, clipping in box 7, Frankensteen Collection; *Detroit News*, October 3, 1937, 1; Craine, "Labor in the 1937 Municipal Election," 30,44.

29. *Civic Searchlight*, October 1937, box 2, Frankensteen Collection; "Bring the New Deal to Detroit," n.d., box 11, Sugar Collection; *West Side Conveyor*, October 19, 1937, 2.

30. Schwantes, " 'We've Got 'em on the Run, Brothers' "; *Flint Weekly Review*, August 20, 1937, 2, oversize folder–1, Kraus Collection.

31. Harry Hopkins to [Franklin Roosevelt], July 2, 1937, with enclosure (Pierce Williams to Harry Hopkins, July 1, 1937), box 11, Official File 407B, Franklin D. Roosevelt Papers, Franklin D. Roosevelt Library, Hyde Park, N.Y.; Melvyn Dubofsky and Warren Van Tine, *John L. Lewis: A Biography* (New York: Quadrangle/New York Times Book Co., 1977), 314.

32. Strachan, "A History of the Work of the Political Action Committee," 15; Fischer, "The Lessons of Detroit's Labor Campaign," 17.

33. Seidman, "Detroit's Labor Slate," 261; Strachan, "A History of the Work of the Political Action Committee," 7; *New York Times*, November 1, 1937, 10.

34. *Detroit News*, October 6, 1937, clipping in box 7, Frankensteen Collection; *Detroit News*, October 16, 1937, 1–2.

35. Bernstein, *Turbulent Years*, 554; *Detroit News*, June 20, 1937, clipping in box 7, Frankensteen Collection.

36. Germer to Lewis, April 14, 1937; Oral History of Mr. Tracy Doll, 27, ALUA/WSU; *Detroit News*, October 14, 1937, clipping in box 7, Frankensteen Collection.

37. Ternstedt Bargaining Committee, West Side Local 174, UAW, "In Reply to President Martin," n.d., box 12, Kraus Collection; Strachan, "A History of the Work of the Political Action Committee," 17.

38. Robert Cantwell, "Communists and the CIO," *New Republic*, February 23, 1938, 65; Strachan, "A History of the Work of the Political Action Committee," 18. While lamenting the impact of factionalism on the campaign, Strachan credited Martin with using the financial resources of the international union to aid the entire Labor Slate at critical moments, and in public at least, Martin vigorously supported the entire slate. He characterized Maurice Sugar, an ally of his factional opponents, as "in every sense of the word one of us," and he emphasized that "it is of utmost importance that every UAW member in Detroit vote for each candidate on the ticket." Strachan, "A History of the Work of the Political Action Committee," 6; Homer Martin, "To All Locals in Detroit Affiliated with the United Automobile Workers of America," September 9, 1937, box 39, Briggs Local 212 Collection.

39. Germer to Lewis, April 14, 1937; Victor Reuther to Ed Hall, April 5, 1937, unnumbered box on Small Collections M–R, Victor Reuther Collection, ALUA/WSU; Bernstein, *Turbulent Years*, 508–9; Fine, *Sit Down*, 78; "Mr. Martin's Speech to Shop Stewards," Saginaw, Mich., July 1, 1937, box 3, Homer Martin Collection, ALUA/WSU; Joe Brown to Edward Wieck, January 24, [1938], box 10, Wieck Collection; Johnson, *Maurice Sugar*, 222, 226–30; Friedlander, *The Emergence of a UAW Local*, 127–31; Edsforth, *Class Conflict and Cultural Consensus*, 178–79, 184–85.

40. Joe Brown to Edward Wieck, February 5, 1938, box 10, Wieck Collection; Bernstein, *Turbulent Years*, 555; Carl Haessler, "Martin's Gunplay Brings UAW Strife into Spotlight" (Federated Press release), October 1, 1937, box 12, Kraus Collection; "Mr. Martin's Speech to Shop Stewards," July 1, 1937; Germer to Lewis, April 14, 1937.

41. Bernstein, *Turbulent Years*, 560–61; "Martin Shifts Flint Leader [Robert Travis]," *Detroit News*, September 25, 1937, clipping in box 7, Frankensteen Collection; Ternstedt Bargaining Committee, "In Reply to President Martin." Nowak broke his leg after jumping out of a second-story window when goons attacked him and Hamtramck councilwoman Mary Zuk during a meeting of sit-down strikers. "This incident became an instant legend," said Christopher Johnson in 1987, "and to this day more people remember Nowak's leap than any other event in his illustrious career." Johnson, *Maurice Sugar*, 210.

42. Fischer, "The Lessons of Detroit's Labor Campaign," 16; Wyndham Mortimer to John Brophy, September 29, 1937, box 12, Kraus Collection; Joe Brown to Edward Wieck, September 10, 1939, Wieck Collection.

43. *Detroit News*, October 1, 1937, 1; *Detroit Free Press*, October 1 and October 2, 1937, and *Detroit News*, October 2, 1937, clippings in box 7, Frankensteen Collection; Ternstedt Bargaining Committee, "In Reply to President Martin"; Wyndham Mortimer to John Brophy, October 2, 1937, Kraus Collection.

44. *Detroit Free Press*, October 1, 1937, clipping in box 7, Frankensteen Collection; Homer Martin to "All Local Unions, and All Organizers and Representatives," October 8, 1937, box 12, Kraus Collection.

45. Strachan, "A History of the Work of the Political Action Committee," 17–18; *Detroit News*, October 6, 1937, clipping in box 7, Frankensteen Collection; Fischer, "The Lessons of Detroit's Labor Campaign," 16.

46. Daniell, "Detroit—Our Laboratory of Social Change," 5, 18; Johnson, *Maurice Sugar*, 161, 181–86; Friedlander, *The Emergence of a UAW Local*, 127–28; Louis Adamic, *My America, 1928–1938* (New York: Harper & Brothers, 1938), 363–66; Jefferys, "Matters of Mutual Interest," 109–10.

47. Seidman, "Detroit's Labor Slate," 262.

48. Richard W. Thomas, *Life for Us Is What We Make It: Building Black Community in Detroit, 1915–1945* (Bloomington: Indiana University Press, 1992), chapter two; Babson, *Working Detroit*, 44–45; Sugrue, *The Origins of the Urban Crisis*, 23–24.

49. *New York Times*, November 1, 1937, 10, November 4, 1937, 16; [Alan Strachan], "Analysis of Vote—November 2, 1937 Elections—City of Detroit," box 12, Kraus Collection; Donald S. Hecock and Harry A. Trevelyan, *Detroit Voters and Recent Elections* (Detroit: Bureau of Governmental Research, 1938), 36.

50. *New York Times*, November 4, 1937, 16; Craine, "Labor in the 1937 Detroit Municipal Election," 47–50; Johnson, *Maurice Sugar*, 207–10. Tenerowicz, a physician and the son of a Pennsylvania coal miner, was elected mayor of Hamtramck, and then to the U.S. House of Representatives from a district that included Hamtramck and parts of Detroit. Zuk, a former autoworker at Dodge Main, was elected to the Hamtramck city council on a "progressive slate" in 1936. See Rudolph G. Tenerowicz to Richard Frankensteen, March 12, 1936, box 1, Frankensteen Collection; Rudolph G. Tenerowicz to John A. Zaremba, box 5, John A. Zaremba Collection, ALUA/WSU; Friedlander, *The Emergence of a UAW Local*, 14.

51. Babson, "Pointing the Way," especially chapter 6; Joe Brown to Edward Wieck, April 10, 1938, box 10, Wieck Collection; *West Side Conveyor*, November 9, 1937, 1.

52. Craine, "Labor in the Detroit Municipal Election of 1937," 47–50; Hecock and Trevelyan, *Detroit Voters and Recent Elections*, 13.

53. Hecock and Trevelyan, *Detroit Voters and Recent Elections*, 46; Strachan, "A History of the Work of the Political Action Committee," 9, 18.

54. *Detroit News*, October 2, 1937, clipping in box 7, Frankensteen Collection; August Meier and Elliott Rudwick, *Black Detroit and the Rise of the UAW* (New York: Oxford University Press, 1979), 6; Nelson Lichtenstein, "Life at the Rouge: A Cycle of Workers' Control," in Charles Stephenson and Robert Asher, eds., *Life and Labor: Dimensions of American Working-Class History* (Albany: State University of New York Press, 1986), 241; Bernstein, *Turbulent Years*, 746; Wyndham Mortimer to John L. Lewis, October 22, 1937, box 12, Kraus Collection. Nelson Lichtenstein points out that the Labor Slate "won no wards" on Detroit's west side, "where Ford's sway was most pronounced." Lichtenstein, *The Most Dangerous Man in Detroit*, 91.

55. [Strachan], "Analysis of Vote," 2.

56. Strachan, "A History of the Political Action Committee," 11; Alan Strachan (Committee for the Formation of Detroit Labor's Non-Partisan League) to "Dear Sir and Brother," November 8, 1937, box 4, Briggs Local 212 Collection; *West Side Conveyor*, November 9, 1937, 1; Bernstein, *Turbulent Years*, 562, 565; Nelson Lichtenstein, *Labor's War at Home: The CIO in World War II* (New York: Cambridge University Press, 1982).

57. Clive, *State of War*, 130–69; Gloster B. Current, "The Detroit Elections: Problem of Reconversion," *Crisis* 52 (November 1945), 321; Carl O. Smith and Stephen B. Sarashohn, "Hate Propaganda in Detroit," *Public Opinion Quarterly* 10 (Spring 1946), 25; Robert Korstad and Nelson Lichtenstein, "Opportunities Found and Lost: Labor, Radicals, and the Early Civil Rights Movement," *Journal of American History* 75 (December 1988), 797–98.

58. Clive, *State of War*, 141–50; Capeci, *Race Relations in Wartime Detroit*, 135–36.

59. Meier and Rudwick, *Black Detroit and the Rise of the UAW*, 206.

60. Henry Lee Moon, "Danger in Detroit," *Crisis* 53 (January 1946), 12–13, 28–29; B. J. Widick, *Detroit: City of Race and Class Violence* (Chicago: Quadrangle Books, 1972), 153–54; Robert Conot, *American Odyssey* (1974; reprt., Detroit: Wayne State University Press, 1986), 393–94; Clive, *State of War*, 168; Sugrue, "Crabgrass-Roots Politics," 569–70; Sugrue, *Origins of the Urban Crisis*, 80; Smith and Sarasohn, "Hate Propaganda in Detroit," 47–50.

61. David Halle, *America's Working Man: Work, Home, and Politics among Blue-Collar Property Owners* (Chicago: University of Chicago Press, 1984); Kenneth Durr, "'You Make Your Own Heaven': White Working-Class Citizenship in Baltimore, 1946–1964" (paper delivered at the Organization of American Historians Annual Meeting, San Francisco, Apr. 19, 1997); Kevin Boyle, "The Kiss: Racial and Gender Conflict in a 1950s Automobile Factory," *Journal of American History* 84 (September 1997), 496–523. A major book on race and political realignment is Thomas Byrne Edsall with Mary D. Edsall, *Chain Reaction: The Impact of Race, Rights, and Taxes on American Politics* (New York: Norton, 1990). It should be read, however, in conjunction with studies that trace the breakup of the New Deal coalition to events that occurred well before the 1960s. See, especially, Sugrue, "Crabgrass-Roots Politics," and Arnold Hirsch, "Massive Resistance in the Urban North: Trumbull Park, Chicago, 1953–1966," *Journal of American History* 82 (September 1995), 522–50.

Part Two

The Labor-Liberal
Alliance at Work

Stephen Amberg

———————— 6 ————————

The CIO Political Strategy in Historical Perspective

Creating a High-Road Economy in the Postwar Era

The widespread invocation of globalization, whether in praise or curse, has framed the public debate about the relationship of markets and politics. The global broadening of market competition allegedly compels workers, unions, firms, and governments to adjust in some particular way. Americans have been expected to accept wage compression with workers in the developing world, to cut protective work rules, and to endure higher rates of unemployment, union decline, and social service cutbacks. If the market rules, political action to halt the slide of labor standards is impossible.

But for much of the previous fifty years in the United States, an alternative conception of political economy challenged this market orthodoxy. According to this alternative view, unionization and rising social standards fostered the market economy's success. Still today, after the rate of unionization has collapsed to its lowest level since the advent of the New Deal, many Americans are searching for ways in which unionism can contribute to a new prosperity. Union supporters have observed that labor movements in some other democratic capitalist countries are surviving comparatively well during market restructuring and therefore have proposed industrial relations reforms modeled on foreign experiences. They most often compare the U.S. system with that of Germany.[1] Thus, the Clinton administration's Commission on the Future of Worker-Management

Relations recommended legal and institutional changes to establish a semblance of the German works council, through which workers participate in decisions affecting work methods, technology, plant layout, work assignments among plants, plant closings, and benefit policies.[2]

But it is misleading to advocate changes in the institutions of U.S. labor regulation in the hope that they will lead to a stronger labor movement. Industrial relations institutions are part of a broader package of national political institutions and ideological commitments. In Germany, the works council law was legislated by conservative political leaders who hoped to forestall even greater labor influence over industry. Even so, the unions were able to turn the law to their benefit.[3] In the United States, in contrast, virtually no employers supported the Worker-Management Commission's proposals. Nor is there a political party championing the advance of workers' power as there had been in postwar Germany.[4] In the United States today, unions are willing (as always) to deal but are having trouble finding bargaining partners. Consequently, they must either make concessions of their contractual rights or become economic spoilers. To understand how this situation came to pass, it is necessary to see how the labor movement shaped and was shaped by American politics.[5]

This chapter argues that the union strategies of job control and Democratic partisanship were constituted during the long crises of the Great Depression, World War II, and the cold war. This is not an exceptional argument.[6] But unlike other scholars, I contend that organized labor adopted these characteristics not merely as strategies but as identities. They did so because of specific political circumstances. These identities then became established in two key arrangements: the institutions of pluralist industrial relations and the labor-Democratic Party alliance. Now that pluralist industrial relations and Democratic politics have been substantially undermined, workers' identities are increasingly freed from the institutions that previously shaped them even as union organizations remain intertwined with those institutions.

This chapter resurrects the strategic politics of the Congress of Industrial Organizations (CIO) leadership to help explain why the American labor movement became one of the weakest in the industrialized world at the end of the twentieth century. I am far from suggesting that the CIO's strategy is solely responsible for labor's perilous state; on the contrary, the strategy that I outline below was highly successful for a long time, and the problems besetting the labor movement have been significantly directed from forces outside of the trade unions. But I do insist that technological change, trade competition, or recent partisan electoral losses are properly understood as important parts of the context for strategic action rather than uncaused causes. Strategic action presupposes some settlement of questions of what workers' interests are. This in turn has much to do with perceptions of the proper place of workers in the polity and economy and the role of unions in it.[7] Periodically—in the 1930s and 1940s or the present day—the political economy is transformed and the identities and interests of workers, unionists, employers, government officials, and others are transformed with it. Economic change itself is constructed through a political process in which economic agents interpret and define their work according to their ideas about the economy, society, and the state. Economic change, that is, should be understood as a series of political struggles over the legitimate nature of social order. The settlement of those struggles establishes institutional frameworks of industrial governance that shape basic political and economic practices, particularly the boundaries of authority in the workplace and the contours of electoral coalitions.[8] The modern American labor movement was shaped through the transformations of identity and interest associated with the Great Depression and the cold war. Unlike the German labor movement, organized labor in the United States after the 1930s came to focus on job control and a particular style of partisanship. In particular, American unions became administrator/advocates for workers' citizenship rights at work and partisan allies of the Democratic Party and its agenda of reformist Americanism. But these established interests were theoretically only one of the possibilities for the constitution of the union movement. This chapter focuses on the ideological and strategic choices of postwar unionism because it is precisely those choices—job control and Democratic partisanship—that are so much challenged by the current transformations of the political economy.

The first part of the chapter outlines the institutional patterns of industrial order that were established after World War II and remained stable until the 1970s. As I show in the chapter's second part, the industrial order did not reflect the unilateral preferences of organized labor. Instead, adverse political conditions and electoral rules pushed union leaders to rethink the labor movement's strategic direction between the 1930s and the late 1940s. Third, I discuss subsequent developments of this strategy and the responses of the labor-Democratic alliance partners to the onset of the current structural crisis. Finally, I identify the twin industrial and political dilemmas that face American unionists in the current period.

Industrial Relations and Electoral Politics

The term, "industrial order," refers to the manifold relations between industry and society that determine the ways in which labor and capital are combined.[9] A prominent feature of industrial order that is highlighted by current industrial restructuring is the degree and scope of worker participation. There is widespread appreciation for (if not action to achieve) the productivity gains that can come from greater involvement by lower-level employees in managing their work.[10] Worker participation can alter the competitive quality of labor. Workers are more productive because they are more flexible in responding to changing market conditions and are more satisfied with their jobs. But current debates also reveal how industrial organization is linked to social and political institutions that establish the terms of employment, decision-making authority and income. For worker participation to succeed, there must be appropriate coordination with these broader institutions.

The American political economy coordinated worker participation in the postwar era through collective bargaining between national industrial unions and individual, integrated manufacturing corporations.[11] Union contracts detailed wage and work rules for all of the plants of each company, although local supplementary agreements on working conditions were made as well. Union representatives acted as advocates for workers in disputes over work rules. When negotiations failed, unions and employers often resorted to strikes and lockouts to resolve their differences. The system established workers' economic security through three interrelated rules: seniority, job classifications, and wage rules. Seniority in specified job categories determined one's rights in layoffs, recalls, and promotions; these categories or classifications were pathways that linked types of jobs together and placed other types off-limits. Pay also was tied to specific job categories; in some core industries like automobiles, moreover, wage rules included price-indexing and productivity gain-sharing. Job classifications described exactly what was required by workers in specific jobs and thereby established a defense against supervisory discipline. But workers and unions were not involved in designing jobs, ordering the flow of work through the plant, planning the introduction of new technologies, or other work organization issues.

The pattern of industrial relations was highly segmented by industry and geography.[12] Although many of the large, integrated firms accommodated union demands that personnel policy be placed on a contractual basis, most employers never conceded workers' rights to collective bargaining. Private sector unionization peaked at about 35 percent in the postwar era. A vast nonunion segment of the economy persisted in peripheral manufacturing, in services, even in some core firms and generally across the southern states. Industrial relationships in these areas were only loosely regulated by the government, and worker participation was sharply circumscribed. Some twenty states restricted union efforts to organize employees, effectively placing whole regions off-limits to unions, while the same states also sustained only the most minimal standards for unemployment compensation and other income supplements.

National industry and macroeconomic policies supported the core firms. The United States maintained a historical antitrust, procompetition policy that could be used to regulate the large firms. But because the federal government's implementation of this policy was based on assuring consumers reasonable prices, the state supported the large firms' "Fordist" strategies of standardizing products and driving-down unit costs of production. As long as its products delivered value for price, a large firm like General Motors could extend its market share virtually with impunity. Macroeconomic policy similarly supported the core industrial relationships. The national government's Keynesian policy to achieve a "high" level of employment largely ignored the structures of the economy in favor of broad fiscal and monetary steering of aggregate consumer demand.[13] Extending the consumer market reinforced and rewarded "Fordist" strategies and the unions' wage standardization bargaining programs. From 1948 to 1973, the national economy grew at a robust annual rate, average annual unemployment hovered at 4.5 percent, and real average family income doubled.

As Richard Oestreicher notes in this volume, workers' participation in the polity was also structured by the form of government in the United States: highly active semi-independent national institutions, such as the Federal Reserve, operating in a decentralized federal system. The two-party electoral system, driven by plurality election rules and personal voter registration requirements, influenced worker participation as well. Although labor leaders did not accept that these features of the political system necessarily limited their influence, the institutional organization of the state did establish high hurdles for any group trying to gain control of national policy making. An inability to secure such control could preclude corporatist arrangements that would divide administrative office between capital and labor. The political system reinforced the dispositions of economic blocs to engage in interest group pressure tactics.[14] Organized labor's diffuse structure and internal divisions reinforced these tendencies.[15] At various times throughout the postwar era, some of the largest and most active unions were either not part of the AFL-CIO or carried on independent legislative operations.

The AFL-CIO centered its political activity in two departments. The Legislative Department handled the federation's lobbying of Congress and worked to coordinate the legislative work of the various unions.[16] The Committee on Political Education (COPE), successor to the CIO's Political Action Committee and the AFL's Labor's League for Political Education, assumed responsibility for mobilizing union members in elections. In the decentralized labor federation, COPE was organizationally dependent on the leaders of affiliated and local unions to carry out its various programs of money raising, voter registration, education, and outreach to minorities.[17] Each state and local central labor committee was responsible for encouraging local union participation in COPE activity, organizing rank and file involvement in campaigns, endorsing candidates and collecting voluntary campaign contributions. Because of its dependency, COPE had to accommodate local leaders' primary focus on bilateral collective bargaining with employers. Many local unions never affiliated with central city and state labor councils. Nonetheless, organized labor devoted enough resources to political action from the late 1940s to the 1970s so that COPE became a formidable participant in politics in key areas of the country. While voter participation by the general public was modest—in part as a result of registration restrictions—union members and their families voted in a more consistently partisan way (pro–Democratic Party) and at higher rates than nonunion household workers.[18]

The two-party electoral system contributed to these patterns. Plurality electoral rules and historical patterns of party identification allowed the two major parties, the Democratic and Republican Parties, to dominate public life. The parties normally operated as "constituent" multiclass organizations, collecting votes from almost whoever they could get them, then turning them into recognition and support.[19] The parties did not compete to mobilize all voters. The two parties had somewhat different mass support profiles throughout the postwar era, the Democrats drawing more low-income voters and the Republicans doing better among upper-income voters. But partisan identities were not strictly class based. Businesses, for instance, invested in both parties: corporations contributed more to the Democratic Party than did the AFL-CIO.[20] And though members of organized labor sat on the Democratic National Committee and some labor leaders were very close to leading politicians, only in 1982 did the party give the AFL-CIO seats on its executive committee. National leaders of both parties agreed on government policies that favored business expansion, contained Soviet Communism, made mild progress on social issues and civil rights, and maintained federal support for collective bargaining. Through most of the era, the Democratic Party consistently prevailed in elections and dominated national government institutions. The Democrats lost control of Congress for only four years from 1932 to 1980; they held the presidency for thirty-two years during the same forty-eight-year period; and they dominated Supreme Court appointments. The Democrats used their power to expand the working classes' opportunities for social mobility by distributing the gains from economic growth. One of the favorite conundrums of postwar political science was to explain the statistical observation of class-skewed voting and the comparative dearth of class rhetoric and identity.

Crisis and Commitment

What really matters is what the union movement made of its circumstances and opportunities during the long crises of the 1930s and 1940s, when its modern identity was formed, and again during the contemporary crisis. As I have suggested, the key question is not how union leaders optimized their interests but rather what union leaders and members thought about their situation. How did they perceive the world and their place in it? Labor leaders developed their strategic commitment to job control collective bargaining institutions and Democratic Party partisanship based on their assessments of the political and economic contexts in which unions could make progress. Labor leaders wanted a lot more authority over the labor process initially. In the end, they did not get all they wanted. But the gains they won in the postwar era were very valuable for the leaders, union organizations, and workers. These gains sustained a more specific labor identity that was closely bound to the institutionalized expression of the leaders' strategic interests.[21]

What were the conditions for progress as labor leaders understood them in the postwar decades? First consider what the CIO's leadership echelon wanted to accomplish. In the 1930s and 1940s they repeatedly stated their desire for a form of economic democracy that they called "industry councils."[22] There were diverse sources for this goal—syndicalism, Catholic labor teaching, varieties of socialism, craft unionism, and industrial unionism—which it is not important to weigh here. CIO leaders believed that the worker's role was as a producer in a democratic polity, the full development of which had been blocked by the power of employers to set the terms of work unilaterally. A new form of industrial relations had to be created to secure just working conditions and assure workers honorable labor citizenship in the broader democratic society. To accomplish these goals, it was critical that organized labor "take its rightful place," as John L. Lewis said,[23] at all levels of economic decision making. The CIO formally advanced a scheme to achieve that goal in 1940 to the National Defense Advisory Commission, casting the proposal as the CIO's plan for the governance of industry for the duration. The CIO received a stinging rebuff from the war planners, a rebuff repeated for many years after the war. Top union leaders nevertheless repeatedly affirmed that labor's role should be properly established in industry councils and a national planning board.

The council plan envisioned a structure of industrial governance based on union representation through plant-level councils, company councils, industry councils, and a national planning board. It was a far-reaching program for union co-management of industry, not unlike the contemporaneous German labor movement's demand for co-determination. But unlike Germany, where political leaders across the ideological spectrum debated how to structure labor's role in governing industry, virtually no American politicians and policy makers expressed sympathy with the CIO's industry council plan. On the contrary, those experts and intellectuals who reviewed it in the late 1940s were scornful or dismissive.[24] The CIO leaders learned very quickly just how limited a role the unions were to be accorded in American society.

As their plan died a quiet death in the immediate postwar years, CIO leaders faced two contrary conceptions of industrial relations offered by employers. Many employers sought to adjust the legal framework created by the Wagner Act, so as to regulate much more fully the rights and obligations of workers and unions. At the same time, employers sought to use social science research into group dynamics to regain employees' loyalties to the corporation. Labor leaders, reassessing their situation in light of these employer offensives, soon turned to other tactics. They consolidated and extended the unions' collective bargaining position through direct action, and they sought an electoral alliance with the Democratic Party.

The regulatory approach, pushed by "realistic" members of the National Association of Manufacturers (NAM), proved most immediately successful.[25] Union membership had grown enormously during World War II, but the restructuring and layoffs that accompanied postwar reconversion challenged the unions' newly won gains. The revival of the corporations' symbolic capital during the war mobilization added to the labor movement's weakness. Bruce Catton derided them as the "warlords of Washington," but corporate leaders' new authority in Washington enabled them to stymie the federal government's postwar planning.[26] The labor movement's internal divisions hampered the CIO's ability to counter the corporate resurgence. When the CIO proposed a national wage agreement to President Truman's Labor-Management Conference in September 1945, the AFL and independent Mineworkers' president John L. Lewis joined with employer representatives in rejecting the idea. The unions' subsequent massive strikes incurred the wrath of leaders in both major political parties. The Truman administration intervened in several strikes during the winter and spring of 1945 and 1946, badly compromising the unions' positions.[27] The Democratic-controlled Congress overwhelmingly passed antilabor legislation, the Case bill, in 1946, although Truman vetoed the measure. Then the Republican Party rousted the voting public to bring in a solid GOP victory in the fall congressional elections. The Republican-controlled Congress proceeded to pass the NAM-drafted Taft-Hartley Act in 1947.

Among the many provisions that debilitated union representation, the Taft-Hartley Act virtually banned industrywide bargaining, sympathy strikes, and secondary boycotts; it redefined industrial union bargaining units; and it allowed states to pass laws more restrictive of unions than the federal statute.[28] Taft-Hartley also banned union participation in elections, although this was quickly overturned in federal court. Significantly, the Act did not override the Wagner Act. Rather, Taft-Hartley conceded that workers and managers had conflicting interests. It simply sought to limit a union's ability to represent the workers' interests. This concession was a compromise position within the NAM; whereas some NAM members accepted unionization, many others completely opposed collective bargaining. Take the automobile industry as an example. Executives at Studebaker encouraged their employees to join the UAW, General Motors executives tolerated the union, and Chrysler officials offered brass-hat opposition to the UAW. One key provision of the act reflected the die-hard opponents' views: the requirement that new union representation elections be held to determine if workers wanted to throw off union leadership. The National Labor Relations Board stopped enforcing the provision after unions won these representation elections by overwhelming margins. It seemed clear that workers, too, believed they had interests that conflicted with management.

Unions faced another tactic by employers, both unionized and nonunion alike, in the immediate postwar era. Across industrial America, employers implemented "human relations" programs to resolve conflicts by changing workers' attitudes about their jobs, fairness, and workplace relations. Social science studies had shown that workplaces were composed of small, informal work groups defined by norms of effort and intragroup loyalty. This group solidarity could powerfully affect individual behavior and, when harnessed, could strengthen either unions or corporations. Prominent academic allies of unions who were proponents of industrial relations pluralism fiercely combated human relations-style labor relations. They vigorously argued that conflicts of interest were not rooted in social-psychological dynamics but were structured by modern industrialism. The organized and regulated expression of these conflicts actually contributed to political freedom and economic growth.[29] Almost all union leaders responded in similar fashion, rejecting the human relations analysis of industrial conflict, particularly its premise that the employee properly was part of a management team responsible for achieving company goals. Instead, union officials insisted that distinctive worker and union interests in the workplace required contractual protection.

In this sense, some manufacturing employers and union leaders agreed on the need to bureaucratize labor relations. This was far different from the kind of accommodation claimed later by the industrial pluralists themselves and by some New Left critics of industrial pluralism, who saw a smooth maturation of industrial relations institutions, tempered by wartime experiences and sealed by the pragmatic collaboration of union leaders in industry management. Nor was the labor-management accommodation the fruition of a natural rank-and-file preference for legalistic approaches to labor relations.[30] Instead, the political situation of the immediate postwar years made it virtually impossible for the CIO leaders to attain the broader role for labor they had wanted. Most union leaders came to agree with their pluralist intellectual allies on the need to emphasize the procedural and economistic (wages and benefits) dimensions of labor relations. There is no doubt that the identity of workers was shaped by these conditions-in-the-making. But the bureaucratic representation of workers' interests clearly captured only part—the politically feasible part—of workers' practical experiences.

The dominant "right-wing" leaders of the CIO sought to consolidate their unions' positions in industry. In a series of contracts signed in 1946, 1947, 1948, and 1950, the United Automobile Workers (UAW) won a number of contractual guarantees from employers: formal committeeman organization in the shops, maintenance of union membership, specified work rules and job descriptions, grievance procedures. And they won major economic concessions, most notably wage rules that protected employees from inflation, allowances that shared productivity gains, and private welfare plans that supplemented social security. The United Steelworkers, the Electrical Workers and other unions followed suit with similarly detailed agreements.[31] These contracts helped resolve many conflicts that arose as a result of the routine conflicts of industrial labor and the large unions' social diversity. More fundamentally, they ensured the unions' continued place at work.

But there was another side to the CIO leaders' response to postwar political conditions. The "right-wing" leaders developed an electoral strategy based on realigning constituency groups among the

Republican and Democratic Parties to make the latter a truly progressive political party. This was a risky effort, as it required disciplining wayward congressmen without making the government even more hostile to unions in the short run. The CIO could have attempted to discipline Democratic House members by running candidates against them. The CIO candidate did not necessarily have to defeat the Democrat: labor leaders could hope that simply running an independent candidate would force a half-hearted Democratic candidate to move to the union position to win back labor votes. Or the CIO could seek to replace wayward Democrats with a labor party candidate. But because of the shape of electoral institutions, either strategy was fraught with difficulties. If the CIO ran a "labor" candidate simply to sensitize a Democratic congressman to labor's perspective, the "labor vote" would be split between the Democratic candidate and the union-backed candidate. That would all but ensure the victory of the Republican candidate, who was more likely to be an anti-labor legislator. With plurality election rules, it is winner-take-all: the losers—although possibly a majority of the voters split between two candidates—get nothing. If the CIO sought an outright victory for a labor party candidate, they knew they would have to overcome the rank-and-file's overwhelming identification with the Democratic Party. Even if some labor candidates could be elected, the locality-based congressional elections would under-count labor votes nationwide and the House would be overwhelmingly nonlabor. Electoral rules thus all but prevented labor leaders from running independent candidates as a means of disciplining government officials. That left the CIO with two other options. They could attempt to change the electoral institutions themselves or they could accept the institutional arrangements and find a partner among one of the two existing party organizations so as to influence representatives elected across the country, even in those districts where union organization was weak. The latter is just what the CIO (and later the AFL) did.

In particular, the "right-wing" CIO leaders allied with liberal Democratic politicians, such as Hubert Humphrey, and with the organizations those liberals had constructed, such as Americans for Democratic Action (ADA). The alliance sought to protect the labor rights won in the New Deal, which they considered critical to maintaining economic balance, and to force the partisan realignment of the Democratic and Republican Parties. "Liberal" forces, they believed, should shift to the Democrats while the "reactionaries" would align with the Republicans.[32] The new labor-liberal alliance focused its strategy, logically enough, on presidential politics, reasoning that the White House controls nominations to the NLRB and other regulatory agencies and to the federal courts. The presidency thus was the key to influencing the political framework that determined the industrial order.

The terms of labor-Democratic Party alliance made all the difference. Top CIO leaders did not accept the Democratic Party status quo (which was complex, in any case). Even the "right-wing" leaders could be scathingly critical of Truman and the Democratic Party. The "right-wing" CIO leaders wanted an alliance with liberal Democrats so as to transform the party into a programmatic reformist party that would promote a full-employment welfare state program.[33] For example, a more programmatic Democratic Party, led by a sympathetic president, could take a party-line vote to overturn the Taft-Hartley Act. In fact, union leaders thought this would be accomplished in 1949 after the Democrats won the 1948 congressional and presidential elections. When this failed to occur, the "right-wing" leaders were very bitter toward the "leftists" who they accused of splitting the pro-labor vote.[34] Although they were wrong—the continuing opposition to unions by (mostly) southern Democrats accounted for the failure to repeal Taft-Hartley—the events of 1949 made it clear that the realignment strategy required a long-run engagement with party leaders to create a solid pro-union bloc. Over the next decade, this urge for broad unity led the CIO to merge with the AFL in 1955 and to take the lead in the new labor federation's Committee on Political Education. It also led labor social democrats to join with liberal Democrats in their commitment to civil rights and to anti-Communist patriotism. These were at one and the same time tactical and principled.

A crucial piece of the realignment strategy was to break the grip of white supremacists on the southern wing of the Democratic Party by pushing the party to commit itself to equal rights for African-Americans. This was difficult because the Democratic Party was not programmatic but more of a "constituency" party that sought to integrate powerful groups based on locale and industry into the national political process. To influence local southern party politics, unionists provided votes for liberal initiatives inside the party that would confront conservatives with the options of surrendering to liberals or quitting the party. An early spectacular example was gaining the endorsement by the Democratic national convention in 1948 for a platform plank supporting civil rights. This caused many southern delegates to bolt and form the States' Rights Party.[35] However, pushing out the conservatives became a drawn-out process of escalating the pressure because southerners in their local districts could ignore national party rhetoric with impunity. This is the truth of later assertions by union spokesmen and by critics like Herbert Hill of the NAACP: some of organized labor should be credited with being there at the beginning of the modern civil rights movement, but they were there for strategic reasons. It is also true that progress in civil rights law was very cautious, but claims that the cautiousness is rooted in the defeat of the "left-wing" unionists have not been well substantiated.[36] This interpretation slights the partisan context. Even the liberal Democratic presidential candidate Adlai Stevenson backpedalled on race when he needed southern campaign support in 1952 and 1956.[37] The CIO's partisan strategy involved it in similar intraparty compromises. Not until the late 1950s and early 1960s did federal intervention in local race relations begin to change political alignments. Another, more aggressive side of the CIO strategy was to initiate a massive unionization drive in the south, but after bitter struggles and expensive litigation spawned by the Taft-Hartley Act, the drive was largely abandoned. The drive's defeat then reinforced the electoral elements of the strategy.[38] In sum, in the postwar era the CIO and the new AFL-CIO helped to create a web of institutional arrangements and a labor identity that was economistic, contractualist, patriotic, and strategically racially egalitarian. Labor's identity was progressive in the strict sense that labor leaders believed that unions had an achievable mission to improve conditions for the working classes. At the same time, the boundaries of the worker's role at work and in the broader society were powerfully influenced by the institutions to which the labor movement was committed. In the manufacturing heartland of the country, unionized workers' relations to management came to be defined by extensive contracts. Outside of work, they became the centerpiece of the affluent society, buying houses, cars, and appliances and sending their children to college. Outside of the industrial core was the periphery, which lacked union representation and enforceable workplace rights, a gap overlaid with cultural messages rooted in the history of race, ethnicity, and gender.[39] The salience of core-periphery boundaries increased with the shift of industry to the south and with the mobilization of the civil rights and women's movements. Labor leaders' strategic action to represent the selected interests of organized workers also helped to shape the ways workers related to one another, to their employer, and to politics as well as how they understood their own position. In short, the representation of workers—interests and image—by leaders contributed to the workers' practical apprehension of the social world.[40]

Labor in American Politics

During the 1950s and into the 1960s, the political order became routinized. The interests of organized groups were firmly established, and there was little movement in one direction or another. The connection between workers' role at work and the well-being of the broader society slipped below public consciousness. This occurred for several reasons. National economic performance began to achieve unprecedented levels of mass affluence, which strengthened workers' consumerism at the same time that it reinforced policy makers' belief that their technical skills had enabled them to master the economy. Unions had dug in their positions in the postwar years to protect themselves from resurgent managerial authority; most union officials devoted most of their attention to administering contracts offering steady improvements in pay and benefits. Regulators and judges administered labor law so as to emphasize stable labor-management relations, forestalling the overt politicization of industrial relations by insisting on arbitration.[41] The ideological consensus on anti-communism and democratic capitalism, moreover, created the impression that Americans had made disagreements over political fundamentals a thing of the past, something the nation had thankfully outgrown by the mature achievement of modernity. In the 1960 presidential race, for instance, it was hard to perceive the policy differences between Richard Nixon and John Kennedy; the election result was a virtual tie.

Union leaders in this era of philosophical complacency focused on strategy and tactics for moving the Democrats, and through them the American polity, toward support for labor's policy proposals. It was not to be. The Democratic Party won large majorities in several congressional elections in the 1960s and 1970s, but these new partisan majorities did not prove to be pro-labor majorities. There were significant breakthroughs for civil rights, but political support for unions peaked and then declined. As the pace of economic growth quickened and then as foreign competition impinged on the United States, policy makers did indeed begin strategizing about how to re-structure industry and politics. But they focussed their attention on welfare services and affirmative action for minorities and women. And when industrial relations appeared as a critical matter for gov-ernment policy, unions were told to limit their collective-bargaining demands, and Congress turned a deaf ear to the unions. Finally, the realignment of electoral forces, heavily stimulated by race issues, fa-vored the Republicans, not the Democrats.

As already noted, the AFL-CIO political effort was conducted by its Legislative Department and COPE. We should not identify labor politics exclusively with these efforts because top labor leaders also were members of Americans for Democratic Action, the Conference on Economic Progress, the National Planning Association, the Ur-ban League, and a host of other liberal Democratic groups that sought to shape the party's agenda. But the CIO's major hope for progress lay in pressure politics. The AFL-CIO did not gain or seek formal representation in Democratic Party councils. Instead, it fo-cused on electioneering and lobbying. During the height of liberal Democratic dominance of national politics in the mid-1960s, labor's lobbying effort was competitive with other groups' lobbying.[42] The AFL-CIO was able to influence the Congress and executive branch on a wide range of issues of interest not only to union members but to the broader working class. Moreover, the prominent attention given by American presidents to AFL-CIO president George Meany and to Walter Reuther, the president of the largest member union and of the AFL-CIO Industrial Union Department, reinforced the perception that the union movement was at the center of national politics. The Democratic Party continually burnished its New Deal image as the party of the people. In the 1970s and 1980s, the AFL-CIO increased its investments in congressional leaders, through both lobbying and campaign contributions.

For their part, workers continued to believe that the Democrats were the party of the people.[43] Working-class Americans overwhelm-ingly identified themselves as Democrats and voted accordingly. See Table 6.1.

Analysts of voting in America repeatedly noted that partisan identities were the most reliable predictors of how a person would

Table 6.1
Share of the Vote by Union Households, 1948–96

Year	Presidential Vote	Congressional Vote
1948	80%	—
1950	—	—
1952	56	61%
1954	—	65
1956	53	62
1958	—	78
1960	64	69
1962	—	—
1964	83	80
1966	—	68
1968	56	58
1970	—	63
1972	43	62
1974	—	71
1976	64	72
1978	—	70
1980	55	65
1982	—	70
1984	57	62
1986	—	64
1988	59	60
1990	—	63
1992	55	66
1994	—	61
1996	59	63

Notes: Sources are Everett Carll Ladd, ed., *America at the Polls 1994* (Storrs, Conn.: The Roper Center at the University of Connecticut, 1995); John Thomas Delaney and Marick Masters, "Unions and Political Action," *The State of the Unions*, ed. George Strauss, Daniel G. Gallagher and Jack Fiorito (Madison, Wisc.: Industrial Relations Research Association, 1991) and the *New York Times*. Voters who lived in households with at least one union member were asked how they voted. The question is framed this way because political scientists who study voting use a social-psychology model similar to that used by human relations specialists. Union members were even more pro-Democratic.

vote. Surveys of working-class voters in the 1950s and later further noted that voters based their decisions in elections almost solely on the partisan affiliation of the candidates. Blue-collar voters knew little about the specifics of government policy and the operations of government institutions. They tended to work from general images of the parties: Democrats were New Dealers and Republicans were the party of the Great Depression. Needless to say, Democratic Party leaders encouraged such images. The low level of political cognition was worrisome for those committed to a republican ideal of citizenship. But from another, less-demanding perspective, observers argued that voters had had substantial experience with the two major parties and only needed to confirm their past decisions about which of the two was most likely to act in their interests.[44] In this view, voter support for the Democrats was firm but conditional on performance.[45]

COPE's task was to mobilize union members to vote and to support the candidates that COPE had determined were friends of the union movement. Again, COPE had to operate through the independent member unions of the federation and the state and local labor councils. In fact, participation in COPE activities by member labor organizations was neither extensive nor deep. Although some unions were enthusiastic supporters of COPE initiatives, in general the operation was orchestrated from Washington. The highly charged political activity of organized labor in Michigan was exceptional.[46] Social scientists differ about the extent of union influence on electoral behavior and election outcomes.[47] But whatever labor's real impact on elections, COPE's reputation for influencing campaigns, registering voters, and getting voters to the polls on election day made a strong impression on politicians. The evidence is clear that compared to nonunion workers, unionized workers voted more Democratic and as a group voted at higher rates.

COPE's standards for evaluating candidates depended largely on an index of "pro-labor" votes in Congress. The usefulness of the results depends on what factors went into the index. Pro-labor votes meant votes supportive of the strategy of partisan realignment; that is, the COPE index comprised votes that helped unions specifically plus those votes that furthered the interests of groups with which organized labor wanted to be allied, such as the elderly and racial minorities.[48] Alan Draper argues that this broader and vaguer agenda alienated union members in the 1960s and he claims that a more focused "social democratic" message would have been more effective.[49] In the 1970s, 1980s, and 1990s, pro-labor votes also could mean votes against anti-labor bills in Congress. COPE could almost always find a candidate who should be supported over another candidate who was even more hostile to labor but that was not the same as saying that the favored candidate was pro-union.[50]

Impressive Democratic majorities in Congress did not necessarily translate into pro-union majorities. There were only three periods during the New Deal era when liberal Democrats held a majority of the seats in the House of Representatives: the middle of the Great Depression (1932–1936), the middle of the era of postwar growth (1960, 1964–66), and the post-Watergate years (1974–78). Each time, the liberal bloc was largely composed of northern Democrats. During all other years, a coalition of conservative Democrats and Republicans dominated key labor and social policy votes. See Figure 6.1.[51]

It seemed that only a northern liberal majority could pass clearly pro-union legislation without debilitating compromises to southerners and Republicans. Yet much depended on what the Democratic Party's priorities were, and in the course of the period they changed. In 1965, after the Democratic landslide of the previous year, Lyndon Johnson and the Democratic Congressional leadership prevailed on the AFL-CIO to shelve its insistence on repealing Taft-Hartley's restrictions on union organizing. The Congress then passed other widely popular laws, such as Medicare and Medicaid, which were strongly supported by organized labor. In 1975–78, when northern Democrats regained their majority in the wake of the Watergate affair, they were not the pro-labor group they once had been. The number of House members with very high COPE scores dramatically declined in 1976. See Figure 6.2.[52]

As labor's advocates declined, labor's opponents increased their power and cohesion.[53] Democrats lost control of the White House for 20 of 24 years from 1968 to 1992. White voters in the old Confederate states began to shift their allegiance to the Republican Party in presidential elections and increasingly in congressional elections as well.[54]

Labor Beyond Liberal Keynesianism

The top leadership of the AFL-CIO believed that collective bargaining as practiced in the United States could not resolve all of the

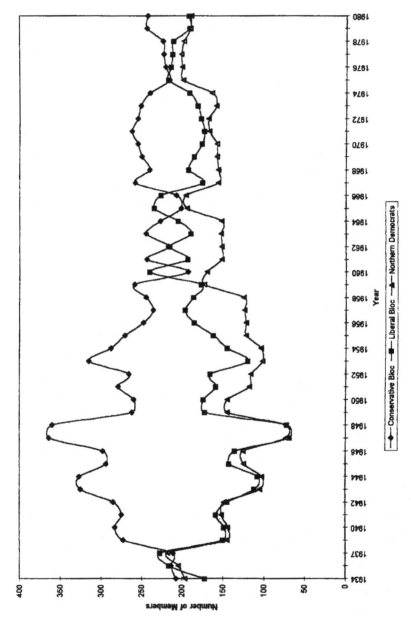

Figure 6.1   Conservative Power in the U.S. House of Representatives, 1934–1980

problems facing American workers, such as dislocation because of technological change and job losses from trade competition. Beginning with the 1955 merger of the AFL and CIO, the unified labor movement persistently urged the federal government to adopt Keynesian policies to increase economic growth and facilitate job creation. And while the AFL-CIO stressed the importance of collective bargaining by individual unions to distribute aggregate economic growth, it also sought "Keynes-plus" labor market policies to deal with the obsolescence of skills, trade adjustment, and underemployment. Once the Democratic Party regained control of the presidency in 1960, labor-liberal Democrats planned to more closely coordinate labor strategy and party-government policy.[55] However, the task of coordination between a decentralized labor movement and a decentralized party proved complex. There were two ambitious attempts in the 1960s to explicitly broker broad intergroup agreements for a more just form of economic development. One was the Kennedy-Johnson wage-price policy and the other was a set of tripartite arrangements to racially integrate the skilled trades. Such semicorporatist initiatives are difficult to sustain in virtually any democratic capitalist environment, but in the American context it was particularly difficult to gain compliance from a broad enough range of interests and, ultimately, to justify the purposes of corporatist policy making.

The Kennedy administration worried that robust economic growth would ignite inflation and hurt the American balance of payments. To ensure noninflationary growth, the Democratic administration tried to head off workers' demands for large pay increases by enlisting the voluntary cooperation of labor and corporate leaders to moderate wages and prices. Some union leaders, such as the UAW's Walter Reuther, were eager to make a deal that would establish a broader incomes' policy which would include profits, dividends, and other capital income. He pressed this position with the Johnson administration, but he found no takers in the White House or in the business community. At the same time, Reuther came under increasing criticism for playing partisan politics from business unionists and rank-and-file militants.[56] Throughout the 1960s the leaders of cooperating unions were squeezed between members' wage demands, which were expressed directly up the line to local and national union officials, and employers' mounting concern about inflation. The Kennedy and Johnson administrations repeatedly intervened in collective bargaining negotiations, mostly behind the scenes, but by 1966 the Democrats' wage-price policy was in collapse. When the Republicans regained control of the presidency in 1968, the Nixon administration engineered a recession and then imposed a wage freeze in 1971. The unions successfully fought the freeze in court, but in the process presented themselves to the public as a special interest group.[57] Even when they lost their grip on the presidency in the late 1960s, the Democrats maintained control of the Congress. But as Gary Fink's essay in this volume demonstrates, the Democratic Congress was often unwilling to support trade unionism. In 1974, for example, the Democratic Congress passed a bill to reform collective bargaining in the construction industry in a corporatistic direction to control inflation, but the Republican president, Gerald Ford, vetoed it. Later, when Democrat Jimmy Carter was in the White House, the Democratic Congress refused to pass the bill again. The Carter administration's wage-price policy, moreover, was a dismal failure. By the late 1970s, it is clear, labor-liberal industrial leadership was exhausted.

The other example of labor-liberal Democrats' attempts to extend the scope of reform was in the critical area of equal employment opportunity for blacks (and later also for women and Hispanic-Americans). As we have seen, the progressive union leadership considered progress on civil rights to be critical to their entire realignment strategy. The CIO made its merger with the AFL in 1955 conditional on member unions ending their racial discriminatory practices. At the 1961 convention of the combined labor federation, the AFL-CIO went on record for equality among the races. But despite the rhetoric, discrimination persisted within the AFL-CIO. A few unions maintained racial discrimination clauses in their charters until 1964; many more unions practiced discrimination in particular cases, especially but not exclusively in the apprenticeable skilled trades. Thus, progressive union leaders faced a double task: unions had to clean their own houses as they pushed the country at large to end white supremacy.

With the strong backing of organizations of black trade unionists such as the Trade Union Leadership Council and of industrial unions like the UAW, the civil rights movement forced the issue in the legislative arena, winning the Civil Rights Act of 1964 and the Voting Rights Act of 1965. After the passage of the latter act, Reuther wrote to Willy Brandt, the Social-Democratic leader of

Berlin, predicting that "the achievement of democratic franchise and full citizenship rights by millions of southern Negroes will drastically shift the balance of political power in the thirteen southern states. . . . This will accelerate the historic process of bringing about a fundamental political realignment of forces in the United States."[58]

But the labor movement's claim to leadership of the progressive coalition had to be proved by the integration of the unions themselves. The Civil Rights Act created the Equal Employment Opportunity Commission (EEOC) to enforce labor-market equality. The EEOC involved the federal government in the details of company and union agreements. In response, union leaders accelerated their efforts to comply with the act. Plumbers' Union president Peter Schoemann argued that "the recently adopted affirmative action program of the Building and Construction Trades Department . . . is more important than COPE donations, more important than getting our people registered and out to the polls on Election Day."[59] By 1969, fifty-five communities had federally supported union outreach programs to recruit minority youth for apprenticeships in the construction industry.[60] Unions made modifications in job classifications and training qualifications to ease minority entry into unionized jobs. The absolute number of workers involved was quite small, however. In manufacturing industries like automobiles, where most members were not skilled tradesmen, union leaders already had achieved access to craft jobs for unskilled assembly line workers. Now they reached out to the community with preapprenticeship programs. Again progress was slow. The autonomy of building-trade locals, whose white members were skeptical of changes in apprentice rules and who were often racist in their outlook, undermined union leaders' efforts to implement voluntary affirmative action programs. "Tripartite" administrative arrangements, in which representatives of black workers gained an "equal" vote with local building-trades officials and employers, led local unions to join forces with employers against minorities. Black workers in many places walked out or split from their ostensible union allies.[61] By the early 1970s, federal administrators and judges began ordering unions to change apprentice programs and other parts of collective bargaining agreements to ensure that goals and timetables for minority participation would be met. This more aggressive state action alienated many white unionists. As workers resisted integration, unions lost some of their middle-class political allies.

As these examples suggest, the broader labor-Democratic alliance was breaking down throughout the late 1960s and 1970s. This was not a clean break between the partners but rather a multidimensional split within each group. When the Democratic Party began to adopt affirmative action goals for its internal party deliberations in 1972, the AFL-CIO, led by George Meany and COPE director Al Barkan, denounced the move. But eleven unions broke with the federation and allied themselves with black activists and feminists within the party to win the new rules. The Meanyites regrouped with centrist and conservative Democrats in the Coalition for a Democratic Majority, which pursued a rearguard strategy against the "New Politics" wing of the party.[62] The New Politics group was successful at first but was still unable to move the party toward a commitment to economic planning and labor law reform, two key goals of progressive unions. Both wings of the party agreed to give the AFL-CIO seats on the Democratic National Committee, now greatly expanded in size, yet both agreed to back off from basic procedural reforms as instituting an off-year issues convention. As already related, the Democratic majority in the Congress noticeably cooled to labor's agenda in the mid-1970s; moreover, it began to retreat from consumer, environmental, and occupational health and safety reforms in an effort to ease the regulatory burden on employers.

Conflicts over employment policy, racial integration, and income distribution raised a more fundamental issue: the purpose of politics. Until the 1970s, organized labor was part of a coalition which believed that justice required full employment, racial equality, income redistribution, and government regulation of corporate-dominated markets to safeguard the public interest. Then it became less clear how to achieve these goals because the background conditions for a politics of distribution changed. The performance of the economy became less certain and companies began to shift to new strategies to maintain profitability. The AFL-CIO lost its way during these years, but it was not alone. Government leaders, administrators and federal judges, professionals, businessmen, and many others began to doubt that the old pluralistic system was justifiable or practicable. When it came to the regulation of business, many powerful figures began to argue that deregulation of markets might be a pro-consumer policy. Federal courts began to doubt the legal and technocratic bases for the laws relied upon by regulatory agencies.[63]

Employers, meanwhile, rapidly mobilized to block union wage demands and to escape the union presence and government regulation. They also allied with new right-wing forces in the Republican Party to promote a new ideology which proclaimed that "markets should trump politics." That ideology rewrote the social map of relationships among groups and classes.[64] Many Democrats and liberal professionals came to accept the new view (and the campaign contributions that came with it) that corporations had to be free to adjust to "markets" and that unions no longer served the cause of progress. These groups pointed to the AFL-CIO's mounting opposition to free trade as further proof that organized labor was nothing more than a special interest group.[65]

In this new political context, under pressure from both employers and members, many union leaders sought new accommodations in their industries. In some unions, such as coal mining, steel, and trucking, the union leaders' efforts only inflamed militant insurgencies. In other industries, like automobiles, union leaders were able to keep control while seeking to develop a new relationship with employers to humanize work and increase productivity through greater worker participation. But the declining position of unions and the mounting employer disregard for its employees generally undermined even the most creative of efforts.[66] In the political sphere, unionized workers still voted Democratic, but there were fewer unionized workers. The new uncompromising ideology associated with the Reagan Republican Party quickly emerged victorious. In the 1980s, intense import competition and hostile labor-law administration combined to tempt employers to undermine unions, which confirmed militant critics' charges that cooperative labor leaders were selling out workers' interests.[67] In truth, it had become increasingly difficult to determine workers' interests. Many observers believed that union members had been pushed to the margins with other workers in a world-spanning marketplace.

Labor Politics in Retrospect and Prospect

The strategy of partisan realignment which guided the CIO leaders' involvement in politics failed. That does not mean that there will be no connection between organized labor and the Democratic Party. It does mean that the old basis for alliance has played out. A new strategy, like the old one, will be made up of perceptions of worker and union interests, perceptions that arise from a sense of group identity, itself built from union members' relation to other groups in the political economy: nonunionized workers, managers, and investors.

The CIO unions established specific job-control and collective-bargaining institutions in significant part because of the ways that the political context shaped worker identities. In the 1930s, the country was sharply divided politically and regionally, an explosive racial cleavage laying underneath. Unlike the nonpartisan postwar German labor movement, the regionally based CIO became closely allied with the northern Democratic Party in a strategy designed to nationalize the labor movement by promoting civil rights in the south. In the event, they got little from the Democrats in the area of economic participation (that is, the right to help shape economic matters), but the Democrats did support very significant procedural rights for "core" workers. Those workers used these rights to restrict management authority in collectively bargained contracts. The accompanying ideology of industrial pluralism said that workers and managers had antagonistic interests but their struggles could be channeled in ways which protected group interests and contributed to the general welfare. Moreover, labor leaders and policy makers expected that pluralistic industrial relations would spread as the economy modernized nationwide. Democratic officials protected union rights and the mini–class struggle as long as the outcomes were beneficial. But the pluralists' expected outcomes were not acceptable to southern employers, so the South was not unionized. A mobilized national employers class in the 1970s proved effective in moving Democratic Party leaders away from the unions and in focusing its attention on rebuilding the Republican Party. The South realigned, but in the wrong direction.

Beyond the partisan context, another source of job-control unionism was the corporate strategy of drawing a sharp boundary between workers and managers and carefully delineating management authority. Corporate employers conceded that workers would form unions and bargain collectively. Though Murray and Reuther broached the producers' ideology, the comparative case of Germany reveals just how much would have had to be different in the United States to transform ideology into policy. To make their producers' alternative a reality, the CIO leaders need the support of sympathetic government officials and a much more intense and widespread labor solidarity of the right kind—a solidarity not based on occupations, for example—to force capitalists to accept limits on their authority.

The fate of the CIO's producerism also highlights the labor relations system that did get established, the understandings that underpinned that system, and why changes in competitive conditions in the 1970s posed such difficult political questions for American unions. The procedural rights that unions secured were nibbled away throughout the postwar era in the sheltered realm of industrial relations. Those rights were never completely eradicated: even in 1995 the Supreme Court affirmed that employers cannot fire union organizers.[68] More fundamentally, the American political economy is now dominated by a post–New Deal understanding of industrial governance that much more narrowly defines a business' obligations to society and that undermines unions' claims to a share of business gains.[69] Americans commonly see the new ideology as a reflection of much more intense global competition, which requires limits to be placed on workers' income and job security even as it privileges investors. A logical response to this new order is to establish new standards for corporate behavior.[70] But the situation is more complicated than that. It is not so clear to managers what should be done.[71] And the suggested "new standards" also pose difficult questions for organized labor. What rights and obligations should workers and unionists have in the firm? What rights and obligations do workers have toward laborers in developing countries?[72] Since the industrial relations settlements of the postwar 1940s, American workers and unions have had carefully prescribed contractual rights and obligations linked to work and wage rules. Indeed, local unionists have used these rules as the defensive line against managerial power. But the line has been breached in a thousand places. A new offensive move toward the managerial line would be contingent on rethinking what it means to be a worker and a manager. If the labor movement conceives and organizes a new identity, a new set of interests in industrial governance would gel and a political strategy for achieving them could be developed.[73]

ACKNOWLEDGMENT

I wish to thank Rikke Smith for valuable research assistance.

NOTES

1. Katherine G. Abraham and Susan N. Houseman, *Job Security in America: Lessons from Germany* (Washington, D.C.: Brookings Institution, 1993); Lowell Turner, "Industrial Relations and the Reorganization of Work in West Germany: Lessons for the United States," Lawrence Mishel and Paula Voos, ed., *Unions and Economic Competitiveness* (Armock, N.Y.: M. E. Sharpe, 1992); John T. Addison, Kornelius Kraft, and Joachim Wagner, "German Works Councils and Firm Performance," Bruce Kaufman and Morris M. Kleiner, ed., *Employee Representation: Alternatives and Future Directions* (Madison: Industrial Relations Research Association, 1993), 305–38; Stephen Amberg, "The Contrasting Consequences of Institutions and Politics: Labor and Industrial Relations in the United States and Germany," *Political Power and Social Theory* 10 (1996), 195–227.

2. Commission on the Future of Worker-Management Relations, *Fact Finding Report* (May 1994) and *Report and Recommendations* (December 1994).

3. Andrei Markovits, *The Politics of the West German Trade Unions: Strategies of Class and Interest Representation in Growth and Crisis* (Cambridge: Cambridge University Press, 1986); Peter Swenson, "Union Politics, the Welfare State, and Intraclass Conflict in Sweden and Germany," Miriam Golden and Jonas Pontusson, ed., *Bargaining for Change: Union Politics in North America and Europe* (Ithaca: Cornell University Press 1992), 45–76; Kathleen Thelen, *Union of Parts: Labor Politics in Postwar Germany* (Ithaca: Cornell University Press, 1991).

4. David Moberg, "Management Care," *In These Times* (February 6 1995), 24–26; Moberg, "Forward Looking," *In These Times* (April 3, 1995), 4–5; *Labor Notes* (1995). Having "no takers," it should be noted, is different from criticizing the commission's proposals because they would sacrifice contractual guarantees of workers' job rights and legalize nonunion employee participation plans.

5. Steven Greenhouse, "Labor Chief Asks Business for a New Social Compact, *New York Times*, December 7, 1995, A 10.

6. Michael Goldfield, *The Decline of Organized Labor in the United States* (Chicago: University of Chicago Press, 1987).

7. Gary Herrigel, "Identity and Institutions: The Social Construction of Trade Unions in Nineteenth-Century Germany and the United States," *Studies in American Political Development* 7 (Fall 1993), 371–94; Charles F. Sabel, *Work and Politics* (New York: Cambridge University Press, 1982); Pierre Bourdieu, "Social Space and the Genesis of Classes," Pierre Bourdieu,

ed., *Language and Symbolic Power* (Cambridge, Mass.: Harvard University Press, 1991), 229–51.

8. Thanks to Gerald Berk for suggesting this formulation to me. It is not enough to note that union leaders and members have sometimes divergent interests and to argue that the key to understanding labor's perilous state is the dead hand of union bureaucracy restraining the spontaneous resistance of the rank and file to corporate power. Glenn Perusek and Kent Worcester, eds., *Trade Union Politics: American Unions and Economic Change, 1960s–1990s* (Atlantic Highlands, N.J.: Humanities Press, 1995); Mike Davis, *Prisoners of the American Dream: Politics and Economy in the History of the U.S. Working Class* (London: Verso, 1986). That claim only shifts the question to another set of actors.

9. Stephen Amberg, *The Union Inspiration in American Politics: The Autoworkers and the Making of a Liberal Industrial Order* (Philadelphia: Temple University Press, 1994).

10. Mishel and Voos, *Unions and Economic Competitiveness.*

11. Thomas Kochan, Harry Katz, and Robert McKersie, *The Transformation of American Industrial Relations* (New York: Basic Books, 1986); Katherine Van Wezel Stone, "The Postwar Paradigm in American Labor Law," *Yale Law Journal* 90 (1981), 1509–81; Sumner Slichter, James Healy, and E. Robert Livernash, *The Impact of Collective Bargaining on Management* (Washington, D.C.: Brookings Institution, 1960).

12. Goldfield, *The Decline of Organized Labor in the United States.*

13. Robert Collins, *The Business Response to Keynes* (New York: Columbia University Press, 1981); Margaret Weir, *Politics and Jobs* (Princeton: Princeton University Press, 1992).

14. Richard Oestreicher, "The Rules of the Game: Class Politics in Twentieth Century America," in Kevin Boyle, ed., *Organized Labor and American Politics, 1894–1994* (Albany: State University of New York Press, 1998); Jeremy Richardson, ed., *Pressure Groups* (New York: Oxford University Press, 1993); Robert H. Salisbury, "Why No Corporatism in America?" in *Trends Toward Corporatist Intermediation* (Beverly Hills, Calif.: Sage, 1982) 213–30; David Vogel, "Why Businessmen Distrust Their State: The Political Consciousness of American Corporate Executives," *British Journal of Political Science* 8 (1978), 45–78; Frances Fox Piven, ed., *Labor Parties in Postindustrial Societies* (New York: Oxford University Press, 1992).

15. Alan Draper, *A Rope of Sand: The AFL-CIO Committee on Political Education, 1955–67* (New York: Praeger, 1989); Perusek and Worcester, *Trade Union Politics*, 3–21.

16. Derek C. Bok and John T. Dunlop, *Labor and the American Community* (New York: Simon and Schuster, 1970); John Thomas Delaney and Marick F. Masters, "Unions and Political Action," in George Strauss, Daniel Gallagher, and Jack Fiorito, ed., *The State and the Unions* (Madison: Industrial Relations Research Association, 1991), 313–45.

17. Draper, *Rope of Sand.*

18. Harry M. Scoble, "Organized Labor in Electoral Politics: Some Questions for the Discipline," *The Western Political Quarterly* 3 (September 1963), 666–85; Delaney and Masters, "Unions and Political Action," tables 4 and 5.

19. William Nisbet Chambers and Walter Dean Burnham, eds., *The American Party System* (New York: Oxford University Press, 1975).

20. Thomas Ferguson, *Golden Rule: The Investment Theory of Party Competition and the Logic of Money-Driven Political Systems* (Chicago: University of Chicago Press, 1994); Delaney and Masters, "Unions and Political Action."

21. Debates about union voluntarism or contractualism are debates about the ontological status of workers' interests, industrial relations institutions, and governing frameworks. David Brody, "Workplace Contractualism in Comparative Perspective," in Nelson Lichtenstein and Howell John Harris, ed., *Industrial Democracy in America: Ambigious Promise* (New York: Woodrow Wilson Center Press/Oxford University Press, 1993), 176–205; Robert Zieger, *The CIO, 1935–55* (Chapel Hill: University of North Carolina Press, 1995). Thus, the question of whether American workers prefer (now and always) "contractualism" or workers' control or again whether the postwar "accords" reflected timeless voluntarism or a settlement of the conflicting (static) interests of labor and capital can be seen afresh. Workers' and unions' preferences are constituted by an interpretation of a specific political context that contributes to a strategic orientation. Rather than focus on disputes between the "left" and "right" in the CIO, we can shift attention to the conditions under which CIO leaders thought they were operating for the achievement of their goals and which led, eventually, to a new orthodoxy of unionism associated with the "right."

22. M. L. Cooke and Philip Murray, *Organized Labor and Production* (New York: Harper, 1941); Milton Derber, *The American Idea of Industrial Democracy* (Urbana, Ill.: University of Illinois Press, 1970); George G. Higgins, *Organized Labor and the Church* (New York: Paulist Press, 1993); Amberg, *The Union Inspiration in American Politics.*

23. Ruth L. Horowitz, *Political Ideologies of Organized Labor: The New Deal Era* (New Brunswick, N.J.: Transaction Books, 1978), 215.

24. Neil Chamberlain, *The Union Challenge to Management Control* (New York: Harpers, 1948); Charles Lindblom, *Unions and Capitalism* (New Haven: Yale University Press, 1949); Leon Keyserling, "Everybody's Problem: Prices, Wages, Profits," *Harper's Magazine* (March 1948).

25. Howell John Harris, *The Right to Manage* (Madison: University of Wisconsin Press, 1982), 119–35.

26. Bruce Catton, *The Warlords of Washington* (New York: Harcourt Brace and World, 1948).

27. Amberg, *The Union Inspiration in American Politics*.

28. Harry Millis and Emily Clark Brown, *From the Wagner Act to Taft Hartley* (Chicago: University of Chicago Press, 1950).

29. Bruce E. Kaufman, *The Origins and Evolution of the Field of Industrial Relations in the United States* (Ithaca: ILR Press, 1993).

30. I am not suggesting that there were no antecedants for postwar labor relations. On this point, see Steven Fraser, *Labor Will Rule* (New York: Basic Books, 1991),which is all about anticipating the industrial relations system that eventually emerged. Contrast Amberg, *The Union Inspiration in American Politics*, chapter 2.

31. Amberg, *The Union Inspiration in American Politics*.

32. Alonzo Hamby, *Beyond the New Deal: Harry S. Truman and American Liberalism* (New York: Columbia University Press, 1973).

33. Indicative of the hopes and myth making surrounding the labor leaders' goals is that they continually called the Employment Act of 1946 the Full Employment Act. The latter was the name of the original bill, but the former name became more accurate after the full-employment commitment was stripped before final passage. Labor leaders still hoped that the Democrats would become committed to full employment, and they worked to make it happen. The myth making has also slipped into the historiography of the postwar years. Melvyn Dubofsky, for example, fails to catch his use of the Full Employment phrase in his otherwise excellent book, *The State and Labor in Modern America* (Chapel Hill: University of North Carolina Press, 1994), 197. Such lapses only confuse the assessment of how the relationship between organized labor and the Democrats came to be structured and represented.

34. Gerald Pomper, "Labor and Congress: The Repeal of Taft-Hartley," *Labor History* 2 (1961), 323–43.

35. Robert Garson, *The Democratic Party and the Politics of Sectionalism, 1941–1948* (Baton Rouge: Louisiana State University Press, 1974).

36. Hugh Davis Graham, *The Civil Rights Era: Origins and Development of National Policy, 1960–1972* (New York: Oxford University Press, 1990); John Frederick Martin, *Civil Rights and the Crisis of Liberalism: The Democratic Party, 1945–1976* (Boulder, Colo.: Westview, 1976). Michael Goldfield, "Was There a Golden Age of the CIO? Race, Solidarity and Union Growth during the 1930s and 1940s," in Perusek and Worcester, ed., *Trade Union Politics*, 78–110, carefully reviews evidence for the differences between "left"-led and "right"-led unions in the southern unionizing drive, but curiously downplays left-wing temporizing with racism as a "strategic mistake" (p. 91) while labelling right-wing behavior as tacitly racist (pp. 102–03). An important example in the north, the UAW, undermines these generalizations. Oral histories of black unionists Buddy Battle and Shelton Tappes at the Archives of Labor and Urban Affairs, Wayne State University, do not support any easy contrast between "left" and "right" on racial issues.

37. Rodney Sievers, *The Last Puritan? Adlai Stevenson in American Politics* (Port Washington, N.Y.: Associated Faculty Press, 1983).

38. Amberg, *The Union Inspiration in American Politics*.

39. Samuel Lubell, *The Future of American Politics* (New York: Harper, 1952); Elaine Tyler May, "Cold War—Warm Hearth: Politics and the Family in Postwar America," in Steve Fraser and Gary Gerstle, ed., *The Rise and Fall of the New Deal Order* (Princeton: Princeton University Press, 1989), 153–81; Jonathan Rieder, "The Rise of the Silent Majority," in Fraser and Gerstle, ed., *The Rise and Fall of the New Deal Order*, 243–68.

40. This conception contrasts with that of some New Leftists, who conceived of class as a voluntaristic act. That is, workers "armed" with a marxist rhetoric would become a class-for-themselves, playing their structured role, instead of seeing the specific historical context of class formation. See, for instance, James Geschwender, *Class, Race and Worker Insurgency* (New York: Cambridge University Press, 1977).

41. Stone, "The Postwar Paradigm in American Labor Law."

42. J. David Greenstone, *Labor in American Politics* (New York: Vintage, 1969); Bok and Dunlop, *Labor and the American Community*, 411–12; Dubofsky, *The State and Labor in Modern America*, 226.

43. Lubell, *The Future of American Politics*; Arthur Kornhauser, Harold Sheppard, and Albert Mayer, *When Labor Votes* (New York: University Press, 1956); Angus Campbell, Philip Converse, Warren Miller, and Donald Stokes, *The American Voter* (New York: Wiley, 1960); Richard Trilling, *Party Image and Electoral Behavior* (New York: Wiley, 1976).

44. V. O. Key, *The Responsible Electorate: Rationality in Presidential Voting, 1936–1960* (Cambridge, Mass.: Belknap Press, 1964). Unlike Key, some scholars have argued that political leaders had substantial freedom to shape the perceptions of voters and the specific policies of government. Campbell, et al., *The American Voter*, 282–83; Ferguson, *Golden Rule*.

45. Kornhauser, et al., *When Labor Votes*; Morris Fiorina, *Retrospective Voting in American National Elections* (New Haven: Yale University Press, 1981).

46. Greenstone, *Labor in American Politics*; Draper, *Rope of Sand*.

47. E. E. Schattschneider, *The Semi-Sovereign People* (New York: Holt, Reinhart, and Winston, 1960); Scoble, "Organized Labor in Electoral Politics"; Bok and Dunlop, *Labor and the American Community*.

48. Greenstone, *Labor in American Politics*.

49. Draper, *Rope of Sand*, 99.

50. Delaney and Masters, "Unions and Political Action."

51. Blocs calculated from Mack C. Shelley, *The Permanent Majority: The Conservative Coalition in the United States Congress* (University, Ala.: University of Alabama Press, 1983).

52. *Congressional Quarterly* (various years).

53. Thomas Byrne Edsall, *The New Politics of Inequality* (New York: Norton, 1984).

54. James Sundquist, *The American Party Systems*, 2d edition (Washington, D.C.: Brookings Institution, 1982); Paul R. Abramson, John H. Aldrich, and David W. Rohde, *Change and Continuity in the 1992 Elections* (Washington, D.C.: CQ Press, 1995).

55. Amberg, *The Union Inspiration in American Politics*.

56. B. J. Widick, *Labor Today* (Boston: Houghton Mifflin, 1964).

57. Amberg, *The Union Inspiration in American Politics*.

58. Walter Reuther To Willy Brandt, June 18, 1965, Walter P. Reuther Collection, Archives of Labor and Urban Affairs, Wayne State University, Detroit, Mich.

59. Quoted in Bok and Dunlop, *Labor and the American Community*, 117.

60. Bok and Dunlop, *Labor and the American Community*, 131.

61. Amberg, *The Union Inspiration in American Politics*; William Gould, *Black Workers in White Unions* (Ithaca: Cornell University Press, 1977); Geschwender, *Class, Race and Worker Insurgency*.

62. William J. Crotty, *Political Reform and the American Experiment* (New York: Thomas Crowell, 1977).

63. Richard B. Stewart, "The Reformation of American Administrative Law," *Harvard Law Review* 88 (June 1975), 1667–1711; James B. Atleson, *Values and Assumptions in American Labor Law* (Amherst, Mass.: University of Massachusetts Press, 1983).

64. Sar Levitan and Martha Cooper, *Business Lobbies: The Public Good and the Bottom Line* (Baltimore: Johns Hopkins University Press, 1982).

65. Thomas Ferguson and Joel Rogers, *Right Turn* (New York: Hill and Wang, 1986); James B. Womack, Daniel T. Jones, and Daniel Roos, *The Machine That Changed the World* (New York: Rawson Press, 1990).

66. Kochan, Katz, and McKersie, *The Transformation of American Industrial Relations*.

67. Mike Parker and Jane Slaughter, eds., *Working Smart: A Union Guide to Participation Programs and Reengineering* (Detroit: Labor Notes, 1994).

68. Linda Greenhouse, "High Court Protects Union Organizers From Dismissals," *New York Times* (November 29, 1995), A17.

69. Margaret Blair, *Ownership and Control: Rethinking Corporate Governance for the Twenty-First Century* (Washington, D.C.: Brookings Institution, 1995).

70. Commission on the Future of Worker-Management Relations, *Report and Recommendations*; Robert Reich, "How to Avoid These Layoffs," *New York Times* (January 4, 1996), A13.

71. Bennett Harrison, *Lean and Mean: The Changing Landscape of Corporate Power in the Age of Flexibility* (New York: Basic Books, 1994).

72. Alice Amsden, "Debate With Richard Rothstein: International Labor Standards: Protectionism or Simple Decency?" *Boston Review* 20 (December 1995–January 1996), 3–11.

73. Howard Wial, "The Emerging Organizational Structure of Unionism in Low-Wage Services," *Rutgers Law Review* 45 (1993), 671–738; Charles F. Sabel, "Social Democratic Trade Unions and Politics: Can the

End of the Social Democratic Trade Unions be the Beginning of the New Kind of Social Democratic Politics," in Stephen R. Sleigh, ed., *Economic Restructuring and Emerging Patterns of Industrial Relations* (Kalamazoo: Upjohn Institute for Employment Research, 1993), 137–66; Bill R. Fletcher Jr., "Debate: Inside or Outside the Democratic Party," *Labor Research Review* 22 (1994), 87–98; Jose Padin, "Sustainable America: A Strategic Initiative for Economic Justice," *FIRR News* 1 (1995), 10–11; Dan Cantor, "New Party Time," *The Progressive* (January 1995), 26–27.

Gilbert J. Gall

----------------- 7 -----------------

Thoughts on Defeating Right-to-Work

Reflections on Two Referendum Campaigns

In November 1958 tens of thousands of black voters went to the polls in Ohio and cast their ballots against a business-sponsored right-to-work proposal. In the relatively rural counties of Franklin, Ashland, and Miami, the "overwhelming Negro vote against . . . was responsible for the narrow margin of defeat," labor's African-American political operative, Philip Weightman, reported to James L. McDevitt, the AFL-CIO's director of the Committee On Political Education (COPE). Furthermore, in various wards and precincts in the state's more highly urban regions, predominantly black districts supported the labor position on the referendum question by large percentages. In Akron, for example, five wards "with heavy Negro population" totaled 35,556 votes against versus 9,106 for, an 80-to-20 percent margin. Seven Negro precincts in Columbus voted 901 against to 97 for, a 90-to-10 percent divide. Fourteen wards in Cleveland tallied 88,422 ballots against right-to-work to 12,939 in support, an 87-to-13 percent breakdown. And finally, six predominantly black wards in Cincinnati compiled a 1,442 votes against to 95 votes for, a 94-to-6 percent split. According to Weightman's report, a "conservative estimate would place the Negro vote as 8–1 against with as high as 20–1 in some spots." As Weightman pointed out to McDevitt, the "Negro people in Ohio showed their loyalty to labor over and beyond the call of duty." Remarkably, most of these African-American voters were not union members themselves.[1]

Similarly, in the 1978 Missouri right-to-work referendum battle, organized labor mobilized pro-union voting strength in unexpected places. Essentially, labor's campaign directors aimed to cast the potential voter net beyond the union member and his or her family towards low-to-middle-income working-class people, towards small-farm ruralists, towards urban blacks, and towards politically liberal middle-class professionals. And they succeeded. Labor won particularly strong backing from African-American districts in the St. Louis and Kansas City areas, from whites in the rural regions of the state where small farms predominated, and from the broader (i.e., nonunionized) working class.[2]

The question tying both of these campaigns together is why were so many working-class voters who had only loose ties to labor unions motivated to support the union position on right-to-work referendums. This cannot be simply explained by the union variable alone. Many, if not most, of those African-American voters, for example, were not in unions and had not been union members. Indeed, more than a few of them had experienced union-related racial discrimination at some point in their working lives or knew someone in their community who had. While overt union discrimination may have been less salient in Missouri in 1978 as it pertained to African-American workers, unions in certain sectors, such as the skilled trades, still struggled against the poor public image created by past racial and gender discrimination. Equally as interesting, why were Missouri's small family farmers persuaded to vote against the anti-union security measure? Small farmers often labored under the impression that the high costs they incurred for their farm equipment, for example, resulted from the inflated wage levels of highly unionized agricultural implement companies. Why would they be persuaded to side with labor on what was, after all, an institutional issue that some likened to "special interest" legislation? What exactly was it about both the Ohio and Missouri anti-right-to-work campaigns that mobilized working-class voters—urban and rural—effectively? Why should small farmers, nonunion white working-class people and African-Americans—or any other members of a potential electoral coalition on behalf of labor—have not responded with disinterest, if not opposition, to the anti-right-to-work position?[3]

As the history of right-to-work referendum voting has shown, whenever organized labor has succeeded at the polls in defending itself against union security restrictions—as in Ohio in 1958 and Missouri in 1978—it has been able to muster broad voter support, especially within the working class. Since in most places and at most times organized labor has represented a minority of the labor force, out of necessity labor leaders had to appeal to a broader array of political forces in an effort to form an effective electoral defense of union security prerogatives. This essay will examine these two historical case studies—Ohio and Missouri—in the hope of discerning commonalities in the campaigns that led to the victories. And in so doing, it further hopes to reflect upon the general nature of effective labor politics in defense of basic trade union rights.

The 1958 Ohio Right-to-Work Campaign

The 1958 Ohio right-to-work election was part of the broadest-based electoral effort by right-to-work forces to establish the legitimacy of restricting union security either before or since that date. The modern right-to-work movement began in the early 1940s in Texas when the right-wing publisher of the *Dallas Morning News*, William Ruggles, convinced equally conservative public relations specialist Vance Muse to adopt the theme as a method of undercutting growing union economic power. Ruggles and Muse founded the Christian American Association to publicize their cause and began a propaganda campaign and literature distribution efforts in several southern states. Before long other business groups such as state affiliates of the National Association of Manufacturers (NAM), local chambers of commerce, and the agribusiness-oriented Farm Bureau Federation took up the banner, increasingly joined by pro-business legislators. At this stage in the development of the right-to-work movement, many national unionized corporations avoided publicly promoting the legislation, though as William Canak and Berkeley Miller note, their silence did not signify corporate support for the position of organized labor on the issue. In the 1950s, the movement expanded as the national offices of NAM and the U.S. Chamber of Commerce attempted to stimulate right-to-work initiatives wherever feasible, claiming concern for the individual rights of nonunion workers. There was never any doubt, though, that a coalition of business people in local and regional manufacturing, retailing, processing, and agribusiness concerns provided the main funding and consistently represented the driving energy behind the agitation up to 1958.[4]

In that year, six states—Ohio, California, Washington, Idaho, Colorado, and Kansas—held right-to-work elections. In all but Kansas, voters turned down the proposals. In 1958 the right-to-work issue was, in effect, a national issue of broad scope and public visibility. Initially, it was also an issue that was fought in what was ostensibly a conservative, anti-labor political climate. Coasting on the reelection popularity of President Eisenhower, some liberal Republicans— in the 1950s this was not the oxymoron it has since become—even believed that in 1956 they had made significant inroads into the labor vote in many areas, promising continued Republican success in the future. Furthermore, the 1957 Senate McClellan Committee hearings into labor racketeering and corruption played a large role in encouraging right-to-workers to take the ballot route in 1958. In sum, it was not a climate in which the general public viewed organized labor with much sympathy. Yet, in spite of all of this, unionists won on the right-to-work issue resoundingly and in the process helped elect many liberal Democrats. The key to that success was that labor leaders, spearheaded by the efforts of United Auto Workers (UAW) president Walter Reuther, adopted campaign themes which made it possible not only to obtain the endorsements of other political groups but also effectively enhanced the mobilization of the members of the other political groups. That development politically energized the nonunion working-class vote.

Reuther's involvement stemmed from the passage of a right-to-work bill in the Indiana legislature in 1957, an event that prodded him into action the following year. Organized labor in Indiana was both numerically strong and putatively powerful in the state legislature, even if still divided at that point into AFL and CIO camps. In 1955, the Indiana labor movement consisted of over 400,000 members: 220,000 in the CIO (in 25 internationals and 420 locals); 141,000 in the AFL (in 100 internationals and 1,000 locals); and the balance in unaffiliated unions. Together, unions had 36 percent of the work force unionized with 78 percent of their contracts containing some form of union security. More importantly to Reuther, however, Indiana had many UAW local unions. That anti-union security advocates could establish a beachhead in such an industrialized state sounded a clarion call to industrial union leaders such as Reuther, who had heretofore regarded right-to-work as a phenomena of the south or rural, nonindustrialized Plains states. Previously, the UAW chief had understood its threat to craft unions, but he thought it posed little danger to large, industrial unions with national contracts. Now that circumstance had seemed to change.[5]

In addition to presenting Walter Reuther with the specter of right-to-work encroachments into the industrial heartland, the success in Indiana sparked the interest of conservative political figures in lobbying for a *national* right-to-work law. Most visible among such advocates was Senator Barry Goldwater, Republican of Arizona, who personally undertook a campaign to convince President Eisenhower to push for such legislation in spite of the opposition of his secretary of labor, James P. Mitchell. Goldwater, whose conservative family ran an Arizona department store and fit the profile of right-to-workers socially, was also moved by ideological concerns, like many supporters. Union power had grown so much in the 1940s and 1950s that it had come to represent the driving force behind the seemingly ever-enlarging welfare state and creeping socialism and thus the destruction of American individualism and the protection esconced in the Constitution to protect that individualism. "There is one more part of the Constitution that I would like to touch on," Goldwater informed a Senate committee in a mid-1950s speech. "That is contained in the First Amendment which relates to the freedom of association." Eisenhower reacted negatively, having been attuned to the potential political ramifications by Secretary Mitchell. "God damn it, Barry, I believe as much in [the] right to work as you do," snapped the president at one point, "but I have to live with my Secretary of Labor!"[6]

Perhaps equally troubling to Reuther was the apparent increase in activity by the nascent National Right to Work Committee (NRTWC), which had been formed in 1955 but had recently expanded operations by opening new branches across the country. Here again, mostly small-to-medium-size businesses took the lead; executives from Lone Star Steel, ARMCO Steel, Thorington Construction, Timken Roller Bearing were prominent among NRTWC backers, as was conservative southern textile industrialist Roger Milliken. Later, larger corporations selectively joined in various state campaigns, GE and Boeing in Washington state, for example. The committee rounded out its membership by letterheading a number of conservative academics and clergy as well. Soon the NRTWC began founding state affiliates, as in Illinois, where Ira Latimer, a former Marxist who eventually became an anticommunist Baptist minister, ran the operation. He formed an alliance with the Illinois Conference of Small Business in Chicago and worked hard to raise the necessary funds—the lion's share from businesses—to do the or-

ganization's necessary anti-union security PR work. His appeals ev-
idenced not only hostility to union security in the workplace, but an
ideological fervor against union political power in society which, he
believed, had been the prime motive force in the expansion of the liberal welfare state. These proselytizers armed themselves rhetori-
cally for combat against union power in its many forms. "I have seen
so many so-called executives tossing an occasional creampuff from
behind the cloistered protection of the private club," wrote one fiesty
executive. Business leaders, particularly small-business leaders,
should fight union encroachments, in the manner of "high-class in-
dividualists like Herbert V. Kohler," the Wisconsin plumbing fixture
industrialist then locked in a bitter strike with the UAW. In addition, the NRTWC was always interested in visibly highlighting the
membership of any rank-and-file worker who it could attract to its
cause. These disgruntled unionists offered perfect public relations
cover for charges that the NRTWC was simply a corporate shill that
opposed unions, instead of a principled organization dedicated to
fighting compulsory union membership. "This is an organization
that bears close watching," UAW public relations director Joe Walsh
wrote local unions in 1957, "and one which could conceivably visit serious harm" on the labor movement.[7]

The combination of these factors provided more than enough
stimulus to attract Reuther's concern and prod him into action. The
UAW leader, who had an AFL-CIO power base as president of the Industrial Union Department (IUD), pressed federation president
George Meany to expand the AFL-CIO's anti-right-to-work involvement in two areas. First, Meany promised to appoint a high-level
committee to plot strategy, tactics, and campaign funding in fighting
right to work in 1958. Second, Reuther won agreement from Meany
that labor should try to get allies to set up national and state citizens
committees to help promote labor's position. At the national level,
those efforts took the form of the National Council for Industrial
Peace (NCIP), co-chaired by prominent liberals Eleanor Roosevelt
and Senator Herbert Lehman, the New York Democrat. The NCIP
would later contribute strategic political analysis, research, and
publicity in alliance with the labor movement when it was fighting a
right-to-work initiative.

Though he had won federation backing for the 1958 battles,
Reuther was wary of the level of actual resource commitment that
the AFL-CIO would make at the national level. Therefore, he used

the offices of the IUD to carry forward his vision of the proper way in which unions and their allies should respond. He enunciated his central themes in an address to the May 1958 conference of the Industrial Union Department, a meeting entirely devoted to the issue of the forthcoming right-to-work elections.

The title of the conference—"The Union Shop and the Public Welfare"—encapsulated the central message of the anti-right-to-work thrust Reuther and industrial unionists would promote over the next several months. In short, the right-to-work struggle was a struggle between the forces of progressivism and the forces of reaction; it was a broad struggle between *workers* and those *antiworker elements of the business and political community* that wanted to attack the economic gains working people had made since the New Deal and the rebirth of the labor movement.

The UAW president outlined his specific evaluation of the controversy in his keynote address. The modern right-to-work movement, he argued, owed its existence to much more than opposition to union security per se. If "you begin to look behind the scenes you will find very quickly what really motivates these people," he told his audience. In his view, the widespread agitation against union security resulted from organized labor's extensive lobbying for social-welfare legislation, a phenomenon now some two decades old. Labor's foes, he informed his union brothers and sisters, preferred "a narrow labor movement that restricts itself to narrow issues. They believe that they can manage that kind of movement." However, when "the labor movement attempts to act responsibly at the bargaining table and in the political field, out of a conviction that labor's interests are inseparably bound together with the interests of the whole community and that labor can make progress only as we facilitate progress for the whole," it was "at that point we become dangerous in the eyes of the men. That is why they would destroy us" by attacking the right of union organizations to exist. And this was dangerous to everyone who worked for a living. "[W]hen you weaken the American labor movement and its ability to conduct collective bargaining effectively, you tamper with our ability to maintain a dynamic, expanding economy," he insisted.

In Europe, Reuther pointed out, unions did not concern themselves with union security. Their social-democratic origins in the struggle to achieve political freedoms for working people had made them an "important part of the economic, social and political fabric of the nation." After those political freedoms had been won, European unions' "right to live as organizations was not under constant attack. They were not threatened constantly, as has been the American labor movement," the IUD president observed. In contrast, he noted, in "America we are being tolerated. We have not been fully accepted." Consequently, "union security took on a much more significant aspect in America."

Only by continuing to weave itself into America's political and social fabric—by in effect becoming a champion of all workers, not just those organized into unions—would organized labor be able to fight off the attacks of right-to-work advocates such as Goldwater. "It would be a tragic tactical mistake," Reuther cautioned, "to fight the 'right-to-work' conspiracy on a purely negative, defensive basis." Those who opposed the union shop, he declared, were "just as wrong when they fight aid to education, housing, social security, unemployment compensation, economic aid programs and farm legislation. These people are wrong on issue after issue," he proclaimed, "because they represent the economic and political and social forces of America who have fought every forward step we have tried to move from the dark and insecure past to a better, more secure tomorrow."

Unionists everywhere must oppose the temptation to look at the struggle as one of trade unionists, pure and simple. "The answer to the 'right to work' problem is a practical job of political education. It is a practical job of getting the American people to see the issues in their right perspective and to let them know who are the forces who are fighting for this. . . . We must make this fight on a positive basis in which we put all these issues in their proper relationship[,] one to the other[,] and then equate them with the forces pushing the 'right-to-work' laws." "Our job is basically a job of education and communication, getting people to understand that they can protect their interest as trade unionists at the bargaining table only as they act together with men and women of good will as political citizens," he closed.[8]

Clearly the campaign theme that Reuther preferred dealt with an articulation of the social and economic roles which the labor movement played in achieving a rising standard of living for everyone who worked for a living. It was, in effect, a definition that attempted to step beyond a narrow consideration of what could not or should not be legal in a labor contract and to move the debate into a new arena. It attempted to put forth a broader perspective by tying the "public welfare" in a variety of areas—aid for education, civil rights, income support, employment security, wage levels, rural prosperity—to the fortunes of the labor movement that had supported and struggled with others in partnerships trying to achieve those goals, at least since the 1940s. It placed the blame for failures in those areas on the shoulders of those conservative and business leaders who, Reuther claimed, evangelized for the right-to-work movement as well. Essentially, the UAW president's vision of the union security battle strove to make the working-class public realize that if rising water lifted all boats, unions were responsible for making sure that water was flowing in from the dam.

This was the message that the Ohio labor movement took to the people of the Buckeye state. Ohio unionists faced a right-to-work initiative inspired by some of the more conservative segments of the business community, including such prominent unionized employers as GE, Timken Roller Bearing, ARMCO Steel, and Cincinnati Milling Machine. The proposal had also received public support from the Republican governor running for reelection. Although anti-union security activists began meeting in late 1957, it was not until February 1958 that these forces congealed into the Ohioans for Right to Work (ORTW).[9]

The political directors of the newly merged Ohio AFL-CIO, however, were well aware of the actitivies of their fellow citizens. Labor representatives from the state federation and unaffiliated unions had met as early as November 1957 to discuss how to respond. This grouping later became known as the United Organized Labor Committee of Ohio (UOLO). In February 1958 the UOLO sponsored an anti-right-to-work conference to explore initial strategies and funding for the anticipated referendum vote. The UOLO then retained the services of Charles Baker and the Burr Agency, a Toledo public relations firm with ties to the UAW. Baker noted that the right-to-work slogan, by itself, blended well with the basic American value systems and that polls showed the general public supported right to work by two to one.

He believed a winning campaign program would have to get its themes out in front of the opposition. He reasoned, with Reuther, that labor should make right to work a public issue instead of a narrow labor issue. If the UOLO could round up the support of civic, fraternal, and religious organizations, it would put the opposition in the position of criticizing respected community groups. Eschewing complicated explanations, he advised the UOLO to construct a campaign of "minimal explanation and maximum punch," centering on general economic loss to the whole state if the referendum passed and the labor movement weakened.

Despite the vocal backing of Republican governor William O'Neill for the proposition, by late September 1958 the UOLO leadership began to suspect they would emerge victorious. Activism among the mid-level leadership echelon of the labor movement—perhaps stimulated as much by ear as by anything else—swelled. Late polls showed 31 percent of voters against to 29 percent in favor, with 40 percent still undecided. Baker wrote a friend that he saw a "rank-and-file response that makes me feel like I'm working the West Side of Detroit." A campaign worker wrote state federation official Elmer Cope that "from all sorts of normally inactive places . . . there are reports of zip . . . [and] activity: loud speakers, trips into cities to pick up literature . . ." and so on. "There's a *hell of a scrappy defensive action [out] there, and make no mistake about it!*" That activity brought both record voter registration numbers and money into UOLO coffers. It also forced the ORTW committee to abandon its former refined campaign themes and descend into a blatant anti-union tirade focusing on labor corruption and racketeering.[10]

Labor's campaign also drew in allied citizens groups in the liberal community and the religious community, and it pitched its arguments broadly so as to attract working-class voter support beyond the union membership connection. It is worthwhile to examine Philip Weightman's work in the African-American community in a bit more detail in order to observe how campaign themes tapped into the concerns of a crucial group of voters in labor's hoped-for electoral coalition.

Initially, black trade unionists had to overcome the doubt among some members of the Ohio State Federation of Labor's executive board that black voters' interest in opposing right to work could be aroused. Once that battle had been won, black unionists set up a program to increase registration, canvass neighborhoods, and get out the vote. Most important, however, were their efforts to persuade African-American voters of the righteousness of labor's position on the right-to-work proposal. This was not going to be easy. Anti-union security backers were quick to play the race card in their campaigns, as they believed groups suffering high unemployment would see increased job opportunities inherent in ridding the state of protective union devices like the union security clause. It was also not going to be easy because of the skeptical attitude that many in the black community had towards some unions which had historically practiced de facto racial exclusion. For example, many African-Americans in Ohio were aware of the well-publicized case of Theodore Pinkston, an African-American electrician who struggled unsuccessfully for five years to break the color line and gain admittance into the International Brotherhood of Electrical Workers (IBEW).

The anti-right-to-work campaign in the African-American community took place in beauty and barber shops, in churches and pulpits, and in the community press. Quickly, Weightman and his colleagues realized the need to tailor their message to the audience. The general campaign material, even if pitched towards broader themes, seemed not to be working and "was not making the impression we wanted. We knew that we had to have something with a special appeal to Negro voters that would dramatize just how the issue would affect him, since a good many felt that unions were of no particular benefit to them," he reported to McDevitt. The result was a brochure designed in collaboration with the National Council for Industrial Peace. Entitled "It Could Happen Here," the promotion piece featured anti-right-to work statements "from prominent national Negro leaders . . ." More particularly, the brochure "exploded the false claims being made by the RTW supporters that the bill contained little in the way of fair employment practices guarantees," the COPE operative informed his director. "The tremendous impact of this one piece of literature cannot be adequately described. . . . this was the turning point in our campaign. It generated interest where hundreds of speeches couldn't," he reported. "From that time on, 'Right-to-Work' became a burning issue in the Negro communities." Eventually Weightman's labor activists distributed nearly a million copies.[11]

The African-American press proved especially friendly to organized labor, also due to the work of the black trade unionists. They undercut the effect of a ORTW-sponsored story about how the Indiana right-to-work law had supposedly increased employment opportunities for black workers by publishing in advance a feature story in the *Cleveland Courier*, "Report from Indiana," which countered "with facts, figures, and pictures to offset their claims." Subsequently, the right-to-workers attempted to publish a four-page paper, "Freedom Voice," which tried to tap into the ill feeling still resident due to the Pinkston case, along with several other stories of union racial discrimination. "Fortunately we were able to get [pro-labor] statements from . . . Pinkston [himself] . . . about RTW . . . to counteract 'Freedom Voice' and get them published in the Negro press."

The experience was a formative one for Weightman. He quickly realized that labor's appeal had only been accepted because labor was able to make it *a broad community appeal* within the African-American community in Ohio. By effectively relating specific concerns to the broader campaign themes—that the same employer groups which were right-to-work backers had also been especially active in defeating a previous FEPC bill in the state legislature, for example—Weightman succeeded in bringing this element of the anti-right-to-work coalition into the fold. In particular, he argued to McDevitt, black trade-union activists played a crucial role, unfortunately hampered by their sometimes ambiguous leadership positions within the labor movement. Negro "representatives in the unions must have leadership [positions] because they do not have the authority or respect within the unions to otherwise move out into the community as they should. . . . As a result of this campaign Negro labor representatives have shown that the Negro vote can be rallied behind a [union] candidate or issue and that they as representatives can influence votes," he reported. Moreover, he "further suggested that they take part in church and other organizational activities so that when labor has some issue or candidate to see, it can do it in the community as part of the community and not as late comers."

In closing, he informed McDevitt, "it is impossible for labor to do the job by itself. Only with the support and enthusiasm of the community were we able to turn the tide against 'Right-To-Work'. . . . We cannot give too much praise to the courageous leadership of most of the ministers and just plain little people who went all out in the fight. . . . It would be a real pity if we were to lose the gains we so carefully made during the campaign," he pointed out, "by again becoming indifferent and isolated form the rest of the community. If labor is to remain victorious, we must hold on to these contacts and participate in every phase of community life to let the people know that we are aware of their problems and that we are concerned, and are grateful for the confidence shown."

The efforts of Weightman and others working different aspects of coalition building helped produce an impressive electoral victory for labor. By a 63-to-37 percent margin (2,001,520 against to 1,160,320 for), Ohio unionists captured 74 of the states' 88 counties in a win that stunned right-to-work advocates. In a subsequent analysis of the county-level voting patterns, political scientist John Fenton found "the existence of class division" in the voting. Working-class economic strata from all regions responded to labor's appeal—even in rural, small-farm counties and towns. These farmers "often supplemented their income" by periods of work in industrial centers, he noted, "and thus their attitudes" were "shaped as much by their labor status as by their farm residence." Moreover, "many of them saw 'right-to-work' as a rich man vs. poor man issue and voted for their economic kith and kin," he believed.[12]

The 1978 Missouri Right-to-Work Campaign

As in Ohio in 1958, during the 1978 Missouri campaign an umbrella organization, the United Labor Committee (ULC), unified the AFL-CIO and the unaffiliated United Auto Workers, United Mine Workers (UMW), and Teamsters of Missouri. In the intervening years the pro-right-to-work rhetoric had shifted in emphasis. As Paul Sultan noted in *Right-to-Work Laws: A Study in Conflict*, several traditional themes could be found in proponents' rhetorical appeals. The traditional themes argued along one or more of the following lines: union security clauses deprived individuals of their right to work for a living; that it was discriminatory; that it imposed indefensible hardships on nonmembers; that it denied them their freedom of association and political and civil liberties. Furthermore, it contributed to union monopoly, undermined union democracy, and forced member support of unions' harmful economic policies. By the late 1970s, much more attention started to be given to role that right-to-work laws played in attracting and/or keeping jobs within a given state, and what kind of jobs as well. Along with this shift away from the question of ideological/political freedom to economic impact came a much more sophisticated approach to the practical challenges of mobilizing a pro-labor, anti-right-to-work vote among the electorate. In Missouri, state union activists engaged political consultants who used polling and targeting refinements not available in 1958 to devise campaign themes that in the end proved similar to the ones used in Ohio. Using geodemographic census data cross tabulated against opinion survey results, the campaign's strategists identified a number of neighborhood areas with large amounts of "persuadable" voters: working-class urban African-Americans, small-town family farmers, and low-to-middle-income ethnic (white) urban and suburban blue-collar workers, among others. These voters, the campaign's leaders believed, would respond favorably to the kinds of "value of unions" arguments conceived by Walter Reuther in 1958. However, labor's political consultants also wanted to avoid potential countermobilization by conservative political elements in Missouri who might respond with alarm to mass-media appeals. Therefore, strategists directed their troops' efforts to repeated, targeted communication to the persuadable focus groups among the working class.[13]

Again, the campaign's effort to arouse a positive response among the state's urban African-American workers, among its family farmers, and among the members of the nonunionized working class deserves further analysis. Campaign literature focused on the broad message of how right-to-work restrictions would weaken unions *and thus harm the interests of everyone.* "Amendment 23 Doesn't Affect Me . . . Or Does It?" proclaimed one ad, showing a photo of quizzical white, working-class male apparently lost in thought. The ad noted that wages were less in right-to-work states than in non-right-to-work states. "When the wages of working people go down," it noted, "their spending power is reduced." This meant that farmers' and small-business owners' incomes declined, less money existed for education, health care, and public transportation, and the "families of wage earners . . . *both union and non-union* . . . can expect to adjust their standard of living—DOWN."[14]

Two pieces of campaign literature specifically focused on the African-American worker. " 'Black workers will be the first and most brutalized victims,' " one ad announced, quoting African-American trade union leader A. Philip Randolph, next to a photo of a likely low-income black male worker. If unions were crushed, the ad asserted, black workers would suffer more than other workers. "What it boils down to is this—do you want to live in a state where labor is strong, where you can get a good job with good pay?" it asked. Another flyer, handsomely produced, centerpieced Dr. Martin Luther King's statement against right-to-work laws. "A great man had a dream. That man is dead. Keep his dream alive, Missouri," ad copy proclaimed next to a sharply posed black-and-white photograph of King before a microphone. Using King's words, the ad warned against those right-to-work promoters who insisted that their proposal was related to civil rights in employment. It pointed out that the measure was more accurately devised to weaken unions and collective bargaining, not to ensure black workers' rights to employment free from union discrimination.[15]

Also noteworthy were the ULC ads directed at small farmers. Supported in their efforts by the liberal National Farmers Union and the American Agricultural Movement organizations, campaign strategists produced a multipage flyer called "Reality" magazine. This flyer stressed former President Harry Truman's opposition to right-to-work laws, which of course played well in rural, small-farm counties throughout the state. It included a special farm-oriented insert relating the right-to-work issue to small-farmer concerns. For example, "The Big Wheels and the Big Lie" ad noted how some consumers blamed farmers for the high price of food. Accompanied by a photo of a small farmer leaning against a not so state-of-the-art tractor, the ad argued that "[w]e in organized labor know the farmer's not at fault. Middlemen cause high food prices. The farmer and the consumer should be allies—and we've said so. Now we ask you to watch out for a Big Lie—the lie that workers and their unions are to blame for the high cost of farm machinery. *It just isn't so."* The ad noted that while farm machinery prices rose 34 percent from 1973 to 1975, only 9 percent of that increase came from union wage negotiations, which had not even been enough to keep pace with inflation during that period. The balance of the increase came from record profit taking by the farm equipment companies. The giant farm implement concerns favored a cheap food policy, strove to turn consumers against farmers, and "farmers against workers." It was a "Divide and Rule" strategy. "All of us—farmers, workers, consumers—must stick together for a better life," ad copy asserted, asking farmers not to "punish labor for a crime it didn't commit." Additional farm ads featured statements from four small farmers from various Missouri counties, either affirming the benefits of unions and higher wages or denouncing the intentions of the right-to-work proposal's business and conservative backers. The connection between farmers' income levels and the ability of other working people—particularly union members—to achieve good wage levels was a common thread through all the statements. Ermil Steiner of Amity, Missouri, concluded that "All around here you see kids leaving the farm. Most are going into industrial work. When they get there, they find out how much they need a union." Marvin Sloop of California, Missouri, remembered that before organized labor arrived on the scene, shoes only cost $2.65 a pair, "but no one bought shoes" because "they weren't paying near enough in the cities. They want to divide the farmer against the worker," he asserted. "But we're all the same. We all have to work for our living."[16]

As in Ohio, the ULC's efforts proved quite effective. Missouri labor defeated the right-to-work proposal by a 60-to-40 percent margin (944,071 against to 630,764 for). Sixty-six of Missouri's 114 counties (a 58 percent margin) voted for the labor position. Particularly strong support was generated in St. Louis and Kansas City African-American districts, in generally blue-collar working-class areas and in a number of counties that were largely rural. In the ten predominantly black wards of North St. Louis, for instance, there had been only a 50 percent turnout of nearly 64,000 voters. But of that turnout about 93 percent voted against the proposition, accounting for approximately 28 percent of the total "no" vote in the entire city of St. Louis. Black ministers, politicians, and union members had carried the pro-union message to the larger, non-unionized African-American working class. In many such wards in both urban areas, the vote was four to one against right to work.[17]

The "greatest surprise," according to the Service Employees International Union (SEIU) representative Kim Fellner, "came from out-state. On election day, 871,364 voters" outside of the largest urban areas turned down the measure by a "57 to 43 percent" division. "Even if labor had only broken even in its urban strongholds, the rural counties would have carried the day." In many of these places, the residents had children who had moved to the city and who worked in unionized shops for good wages. Thus, along with the broad working-class appeal of the campaign literature, Missouri labor was able to activate a network of personal ties to agricultural residents which reinforced the message that unions were good for all working people, even if they were not personally members.[18]

Labor in Missouri thus succeeded in building an effective electoral coalition, but, some observed, it had not been easy. One retrospective report noted that "the difficulty of doing so in this crisis proved the necessity for labor to build these coalitions, not just in an emergency, but on a continuous basis, year after year. In some cases potential allies met labor's overtures with cynicism" because of a lack of former contacts and work on issues of joint concern. If organized labor had been doing so all along, the report argued, it "would have been in a position to call for reciprocity. The performances and support of the past are better recalled than promises of future support."[19]

Thus, in reflecting on these two successful campaigns, one could form the following generalization. In order for organized labor to achieve a political victory *even* on a trade-union policy issue of special institutional interest—such as union security—it had to first use the challenge to develop a *public articulation of the labor movement's self-value to the community.* It then had to move that articulation into opinion-shaping channels (usually through organizations which are potential coalition allies), and from there, in tandem with its internal communication, it had to reach the broader working class with its campaign theme. Given unionism's current membership levels, only by reaching *that* segment of the electorate can it ever succeed politically, for it is precisely there that enough votes exist to overcome conservative opposition. A successful electoral coalition, even on labor relations issues such as right to work, then, is really a coalition of the organized segment of the working class with the unorganized segment, brought into being through the intermediary efforts of allied organizations.

Mark Erlich's detailed campaign history of the 1988 Massachusetts prevailing wage campaign, *Labor at the Ballot Box*, also supports this appraisal. This referendum victory on a basically narrow labor-relations policy issue of special concern to skilled trade unionists, he wrote, "hinged on the creation of a coalition that could transform the prevailing wage battle from a union issue into a community and class issue. . . ." Massachusetts labor leaders had "to capture the imagination of the public by asking people to identify with those who would be hurt by repeal" of the prevailing wage law. "Making that empathetic leap," Erlich argued, "required intermediaries—both individual leaders and established organizations who were prepared to say publicly that their interests and the larger public interest would not be served" by repeal. In the final pages of his detailed case study, which remarkably seems to bear out many of the generalizations gleaned from the two right-to-work referendum campaigns studied in this essay, Erlich concludes:

> Perhaps the lesson to be learned is that the labor movement will arrest its decline and reassert its potential when it once again— as it has done in its finest hours—identifies unions with the desires and aspirations of the entire working community and with the broader crusade for social and economic justice. Unions have their greatest appeal when they simultaneously serve the daily

needs of their members and incorporate a larger vision that can attract potential new members and the general working public.[20]

Perhaps the most important lesson that can be learned about labor politics from victorious right-to-work campaigns is that in order to prevail, labor leaders must continuously reexamine themselves and their activities to ensure that they and their organizations attempt to live up to their role as representatives of the aspirations of *all* workers, that they work to *communicate* their achievements in this area on a day-to-day basis, and that they do not retreat into the rampant selfishness that enraptures so much of American society, becoming only one among many self-obsessed interest groups. The "people are watching to see whether labor will take steps to more vigorously end discrimination within its ranks and thereby repay the loyalty of the Negro people," Weightman wrote to McDevitt in 1958. "Just as a personal observation it sort of brought a lump to my throat when" Theodore Pinkston—the black electrician denied IBEW membership—came to labor's rescue in the Ohio right-to-work campaign, "in spite of what happened to him" in his dispute with the craft union. He "still wistfully hopes that some day he can become a card-carrying union member," the COPE representative observed. "Unless we do show these people that we mean the right thing and that we will repay their loyalty," he warned, "the day may come when we will go to them again for support and we may not get it." Having lived through the last fifteen years of conservative political domination—including the significant inroads that movement has made into the American working class—we know how prophetic those words have become. And it is precisely for that reason that the arrival of new leadership within the national AFL-CIO, seemingly convinced of this necessity of consistently practicing this broader approach in labor politics, that union political activists may once again look with hope to the future.[21]

NOTES

1. Philip M. Weightman to James L. McDevitt, "Report on Ohio Campaign Against Right-to-Work," December 1, 1958, 110-9-1-8, Texas AFL-CIO Collection, Texas Labor Archives, University of Texas at Arlington, Arlington, Tex. (hereafter TLA).

2. See Gilbert J. Gall, "Union Security Rights at the Polls: A Call for Modeling Right-to-Work Voting," *Employee Responsibilities and Rights Journal* 9 (March 1, 1996): 41–56.

3. For a general overview of labor's political response to right-to-work legislation from the 1940s to the 1970s, see Gilbert J. Gall, *The Politics of Right to Work: The Labor Federations as Special Interests, 1943–1978* (Westport, Conn.: Greenwood Press, 1988). On right-to-work referendum voting, see Gilbert J. Gall, "Right-to-Work Referendum Voting: Observations on the Aggregate Historical Statistics," *Labor Law Journal* (December 1988): 805–12.

4. George N. Green, *The Establishment in Texas Politics, 1938–1957* (Westport, Conn.: Greenwood Press, 1979), 61–66, 104–107; Gall, *The Politics of Right to Work*, 18–19; William Canak and Berkeley Miller, "Gumbo Politics: Unions, Business and Louisiana Right-to-Work Legislation," *Industrial and Labor Relations Review* 43 (January 1990): 258–71; Elizabeth Fones-Wolf, *Selling Free Enterprise: The Business Assault on Labor and Liberalism, 1945–1960* (Urbana: Ill.: University of Illinois Press, 1994), 261–74.

5. The membership figures cited are from Fred Witney, "The Indiana Right-to-Work Law," *Industrial and Labor Relations Review* 11 (July 1958): 507, 517. Much of the summary and analysis of the 1958 right-to-work elections is drawn from my book. See Gall, *The Politics of Right to Work*, 93–128 passim. A more detailed summary of the Missouri referendum is found in Gall, "Union Security Rights at the Polls."

6. Goldwater quote from J. Weston Walch, comp., *Debate Handbook on Right-to-Work Laws* (Portland, Maine: J. Weston Walch, 1957), 94–95; Gall, *The Politics of Right to Work*, 98.

7. Gall, *The Politics of Right to Work*, 75, 101; Fones-Wolf, *Selling Free Enterprise*, 272; Memo, Joe Walsh, Assistant Director of Public Relations, UAW, to all UAW Officers, Regional Directors, and Department Heads, Re: National Right to Work Committee, September 24, 1957, Box 11, UAW Citizenship Department, Roy Reuther Files, Archives of Labor History and Urban Affairs, Walter P. Reuther Library, Wayne State University, Detroit, Mich., hereafter ALUA.

8. AFL-CIO Industrial Union Department, *Proceedings of the 2nd Annual Industrial Relations Conference: "Union Shop and the Public Welfare,"* May 17–18, 1958, 12–18, copy in Box 25, John W. Edelman Collection, ALUA. Also see the summary of remarks in Industrial Union Department, *Bulletin,* "Union Shop and [the] Public Welfare," Conference Summary, July 1958, Box 2, Charles Baker Collection, ALUA.

9. Glenn W. Miller and Stephen B. Ware, "Organized Labor in the Political Process: A Case Study of the Right-to-Work Campaign in Ohio," *Labor History* 4 (Winter 1963): 51–57; John Fenton, "The Right-to-Work Vote in Ohio," *Midwest Journal of Political Science 3* (1959): 241–53. Also see Gall, *The Politics of Right to Work,* 113–15.

10. Gall, *The Politics of Right to Work,* 115.

11. Weightman to McDevitt, "Report on Ohio Campaign Against Right-to-Work." Unless otherwise noted, all information about the coalition campaign in Ohio's black communities are taken from this memo.

12. Gall, *The Politics of Right to Work,* 119; Fenton, "The Right-to-Work Vote in Ohio," 246–47. Fenton also found that Catholics voted in large numbers across the board against the proposal, further strengthening the observation of a responsive working-class-based vote.

13. Paul Sultan, *Right-to-Work Laws: A Study in Conflict* (Los Angeles: University of California at Los Angeles, Institute of Industrial Relations, 1958), 63–74. The specific targeting system used was the CLARITAS cluster system, designed by Jonathan Robbin. See Jonathan Robbin, "Geodemographics: The New Magic," *Campaigns & Elections* (Spring 1980): 25–34, and Gall, "Union Security Rights at the Polls," 48–49. On the changing nature of the composition of business support for right-to-work laws, see Canak and Miller, "Gumbo Politics," 258–60.

14. Italics added. See Missouri Right-to-Work Campaign Documents (hereafter MRTWCD), 1978. Documents regarding the anti-right-to-work campaign by Missouri labor were provided through the courtesy of state federation of labor president Daniel "Duke" McVey.

15. MRTWCD, 1978.

16. Ibid.

17. Kim Fellner, "The Missouri Right-to-Work Campaign," n.d. [1979?]. Report to the Service Employees International Union. Copy provided through the courtesy of Walter Pearson, Research and Education Director, Bakery, Confectionery, and Tobacco Worker Unions. Copy in possession of the author. Also see MRTWCD, 1978.

18. Fellner, "The Missouri Right-to-Work Campaign."

19. MRTWCD, 1978.

20. Mark Erlich, *Labor at the Ballot Box: The Massachusetts Prevailing Wage Campaign of 1988* (Philadelphia: Temple University Press, 1990), 96, 205.

21. Weightman to McDevitt, "Report on Ohio Campaign Against Right-to-Work." See David Brody's analysis of the factors underlying the disassembly of the post–World War II liberal-labor political alliance and the marginalization of unionism, in public opinion, into a special interest lobby protecting unionized workers often as the expense of the working class, in "The Uses of Power II: Political Action," *Workers in Industrial America: Essays on the 20th Century Struggle*, 2d ed. (N.Y.: Oxford University Press, 1993, orig. ed. 1980), 215–55.

Kevin Boyle

8

Little More than Ashes

The UAW and American Reform in the 1960s

For much of his adult life, Brendan Sexton was a true believer in the labor movement's power to transform the American political economy. A committed socialist, he spent the late 1930s travelling from mill town to mill town as an organizer for the Steelworkers' Organizing Committee. He moved to the United Automobile Workers in 1941, convinced that it, more than any other union, could lay the groundwork for social democracy. As he rose in the UAW hierarchy over the next twenty years, from local union president to director of the union's substantial education department, Sexton's faith began to weaken, so much so, in fact, that in 1962 he considered leaving the UAW to become director of the more pristine, and powerless, League for Industrial Democracy.[1]

The stunning political changes of the mid-1960s—particularly Lyndon Johnson's promise of an unrelenting war on poverty—restored Sexton's hopes. "I see in the poverty program an opportunity for revivification of the labor movement," he told a union audience in early 1965, "for making it once again the instrument for liberating people in this country who are, by great and good fortune and sometimes great misfortune, born into the working class." Sexton acted on his hopes shortly thereafter, joining several other members of the UAW leadership in accepting high-level positions in the Johnson administration's most creative initiative, the Community Action Program (CAP).[2]

Sexton's enthusiastic embrace of the Great Society as a vehicle for social change lies in marked contrast to current analyses of the relationship between the labor movement and the political culture of post–World War II America. In the late 1930s and early 1940s, Nelson Lichtenstein, Ira Katznelson, Alan Dawley, and others have argued, the labor movement's militant wing, under the umbrella of the Congress of Industrial Organizations (CIO), promoted a social democratic political program similar to that which emerged in sections of western Europe in the postwar era. In particular, CIO spokesmen demanded that they be given a formal role in the management of the economy through some form of democratic economic planning and that national resources be redistributed through a vast expansion of the welfare state.[3]

In the immediate postwar era, however, the CIO unions abandoned their plans for a "social democratic breakthrough" in American politics. Led by UAW president Walter Reuther, the CIO's anticommunist faction seized control of the organization in 1947 and 1948. In a series of brutal political maneuvers over the next few years, they aligned the CIO with the emerging Cold War consensus, purged its communist members, and rejected third-party politics in favor of a permanent place within the Democratic Party. Once safely within the Democratic fold, Reuther and his allies abandoned the CIO's demands for a say in corporate decision making and a significant expansion of the welfare state. Instead, they accepted the much narrower goal of winning ever-larger wage settlements for their members through a collective bargaining process carefully circumscribed by the federal government. By the late 1940s, the unions of the CIO, once the "vanguard in America," had become a special interest group.[4]

Labor's demobilization had a profound effect on national liberal politics, according to the current interpretation. Without a powerful labor movement pushing them to the left, postwar policy makers were free to pursue a mild reformism at home and an aggressive anticommunism abroad. The result was a policy mix that left corporate power unchecked, the welfare state underdeveloped in comparison to western Europe, and national resources drained by the incessant demands of the military-industrial complex. The labor movement's acquiescence in, indeed support of, this narrow program in turn undermined the Democratic Party's political power. Convinced that it had solved the "labor question" that had bedeviled the nation throughout the first half of the century, the party slowly and painfully refocused its efforts to solving the problem of racial inequality. That effort culminated in Lyndon Johnson's Great Society. By the mid-1960s, Katznelson contends, organized labor had become "almost totally disinterested" in substantive changes in the political

economy. Consequently, the Great Society's planners were able to es-
chew class-based policies for piecemeal reform designed to address
the "intertwined questions of race and inequality." That constricted
policy program, Katznelson concludes, ripped the Democratic Party's
core constituencies apart and opened the door for the conservative
triumphs of the 1980s.[5]

In this essay, I offer a very different analysis of labor's postwar political activism. I will do so through an examination of the response
of the nation's largest industrial union, the United Automobile
Workers, to 1960s liberal reform, and particularly to the Great Society. The UAW leadership, I argue, played a pivotal part in forging
the political alliance that paved the way for the war on poverty, and
it was deeply involved in the policy matrix that shaped the Great Society's most experimental programs. UAW officials built these connections not because they accepted the premises of postwar
liberalism but rather because they saw in the Great Society the
chance to push federal policy toward the social democratic agenda
that the current interpretation says organized labor abandoned in
the late 1940s. The effort failed. The reason for that failure, though,
cannot be traced simply to labor's lack of vision, to its willingness to
act as a special interest group within a pluralist state. The UAW
leadership, at least, wanted organized labor to be much more.

When Walter Reuther and his allies took control of the UAW in
1946, they seemed the very embodiment of what C. Wright Mills
would later call the "new men of power": labor leaders fully integrated into the existing politico-economic system; managers, rather
than champions, of working-class discontent; in both style and substance far cries from the union militants of the 1930s. In fact, the 39-
year-old Reuther and his closest advisors were very much products
of that turbulent decade, and particularly of a coterie of socialists
and liberals who in the 1930s articulated a vision of state power that
the Reutherites made their own. Combining Debsian socialism, the
technocracy of Thorstein Veblen, and the liberal statism of the late
New Deal, Reuther and his advisors argued that the "inordinate productivity" of modern technology gave Americans the power to create
a full-employment economy of unparalleled abundance. That goal
would not be achieved, however, until basic production decisions
were taken out of the hands of corporate managers and placed under
public control. For the most part, the Reutherites did not advocate

public ownership of industry. They insisted, rather, that the federal government could control corporate decision making through a series of industry-level planning boards, membership of which was to be evenly divided between representatives of business, government, and labor. Such a planned economy, Reuther claimed, would foster an "economic democracy" that would ensure the survival of political democracy.[6]

The UAW's social democrats developed their agenda in the key institutions of 1930s socialism: the Student League for Industrial Democracy, Brookwood Labor College, the Socialist Party (SP) caucus within the early CIO. Like many other socialists, the Reuther bloc shifted from the SP to the Democratic Party late in the decade. They did so for practical reasons. Whatever its shortcomings, the New Deal had won the allegiance of the UAW rank and file. The Reutherites believed it was impossible, therefore, to build an alternative working-class party. ". . . there was an enormous feeling for Roosevelt, an enormous feeling," Sexton recalled years later. "A great many workers in this country at that time had a real class feeling about the Democratic Party . . ."[7]

Reuther and his allies were not naive. They realized that the Democratic Party was not a class party, that some of its most powerful figures were in fact conservative. They were convinced, however, that the party could be transformed into a social democratic party if sufficient pressure were brought to bear on it. The UAW certainly could not do the job alone. As Stephen Amberg argues elsewhere in this book, the UAW's social democrats therefore committed themselves to building a cross-class, biracial reform coalition, embedded within the Democratic Party and powerful enough to change it. As the Reutherites envisioned it, the coalition would rest on three groups: the industrial unions, African-Americans, and middle-class liberals within the federal government, church groups, and the academy. The UAW would construct the coalition by promoting the immediate reforms that each of its partners favored: the African-American demand for civil rights, the liberal commitment to economic growth and anticommunism. At the same time, the UAW leadership would continually insist that immediate reforms would have no real meaning unless the political economy was fundamentally altered. By fighting for specific goals, one of Reuther's key political advisors explained, "a mass base [will] be established from which forays into more difficult areas can be easily launched."[8]

The UAW leadership pursued this strategy throughout the late 1940s, 1950s, and early 1960s. The union vigorously supported the NAACP's legal attack on Jim Crow in the early 1950s, embraced the Southern Christian Leadership Conference's (SCLC) direct action campaigns late in the decade, and offered financial support to both the Congress on Racial Equality and the Student Non-Violent Coordinating Committee in the early 1960s. Similarly, the UAW backed a host of liberal pressure groups, from Americans for Democratic Action to SANE. The union also established close ties with the liberal wings of American Protestantism and Judaism; it repeatedly reached out to liberal academics; and, in the early 1960s, it served as the primary financial backer for the fledgling Students for a Democratic Society (SDS).[9]

As they supported this array of groups and causes, UAW spokesmen offered a series of proposals designed to democratize economic decision making and to expand the welfare state. In 1949, for example, Reuther called for public control of the housing industry; in 1950 he urged the Truman administration to create a tripartite board to manage the economy for the duration of the Korean war; in the mid-1950s he proposed that technological change be supervised by a national regulatory agency; and in the early 1960s he repeatedly demanded that the Kennedy administration embrace national economic planning.[10]

No matter how hard it tried, however, the UAW leadership could not overcome the political and structural forces pulling the Democratic Party away from even piecemeal reform. The south's one-party political and racial caste systems, coupled with the congressional seniority system, assured southern Democrats disproportionate power on Capitol Hill, power they used to block even the most mild reformism from the late 1930s on. The southerners' ability to deliver a solid Democratic vote in national elections convinced party leaders that it was better to appease than to confront that power. The result was a party more concerned with maintaining consensus than with presenting a coherent reform program. Throughout the 1950s and early 1960s, consequently, the Democratic Party leadership blocked the UAW's initiatives and brushed aside its proposals. "Those UAW people," Senate Majority Leader Lyndon Johnson complained in a private moment in the mid-1950s, were nothing more than "bomb throwers," his derisive name for activists who did not understand the limits of political power.[11]

Then, in the spring and summer of 1963, the Democratic Party's carefully constructed consensus suddenly shattered. First in the streets of Birmingham, Alabama, then in Washington, D.C., thousands of African-Americans directly confronted Jim Crow, in the process pushing to the center of public life the inflammatory issue of racial inequality. Their actions galvanized liberal and radical activists across the country. Campus radicals rushed to the south, anxious to participate in the movement. Liberal clerics pledged their assistance. And congressional liberals promised to support sweeping civil rights legislation. Through their extraordinary acts of moral courage, in other words, the southern civil rights activists had solidified the coalition that the UAW had spent two decades trying to build.[12]

The UAW leadership likewise embraced the movement. The union contributed over $100,000 to the Southern Christian Leadership Conference in the course of 1963. Walter Reuther served as cosponsor of the August March on Washington and was the only white labor leader to speak at the culminating rally. And UAW lobbyists devoted their full attention to supporting civil rights legislation on Capitol Hill. Even as they put the union's considerable resources behind the cause, though, the UAW pushed the emerging civil rights coalition to extend its attack, to move beyond the assault on racial inequality to confront the more basic question of economic injustice.[13]

Specifically, UAW leaders had become convinced that the civil rights struggle had to be linked to a wide-ranging attack on poverty. The idea was not original to the UAW, of course. Reuther's aide Jack Conway was probably aware that Robert Kennedy's staff was discussing the possibility of a federal initiative against poverty. And UAW economist Nat Weinberg had been deeply moved by Michael Harrington's 1962 book, *The Other America*. In January 1963, three months before the Birmingham campaign, Weinberg and Brendan Sexton, a friend of Harrington's through LID, sent Reuther an urgent memo asking him to "spearhead the fight for a better life for America's dispossessed and disinherited." Reuther immediately embraced the idea, telling a staff meeting in February 1963 that he was determined to lead a "concerted assault" on poverty, the centerpiece of which had to be the creation of a full-employment economy. Time and again during the spring and summer, UAW spokesmen hammered away at the theme. Civil rights "is only a beginning and a means," Weinberg wrote shortly after the Birmingham campaign.

"The real end is basic social reform." Walter Reuther's brother, Victor, made the same point in a 1963 essay. "The coalition of Negroes, many churches, a large segment of the labor movement, and the liberals must channel its full energy into the fight for full employment," he wrote. "For without jobs, even the essential protection of a strong civil rights law will prove to be, for millions of Negroes, little more than ashes in the mouth."[14]

As fall faded into winter, the UAW's exhortations seemed to be making very little difference. Of all the civil rights coalition members, only the Brotherhood of Sleeping Car Porters and the tiny Students for a Democratic Society had tied civil rights and economic change in a concrete way. The UAW had strongly encouraged those efforts, underwriting SDS's experimental Economic Research and Action Project, in which college radicals lived in and attempted to organize northern ghettos. For the most part, though, civil rights activism remained focused on racial injustice. Then, on November 22, John Kennedy was assassinated, and suddenly everything changed.[15]

Lyndon Johnson's stunning accession to the presidency left the UAW leadership shocked and concerned. Johnson had been one of the architects of consensus politics, after all, a master of congressional procedure who had used his skills to block progressive legislation throughout the 1950s. For his part, LBJ knew that his administration would quickly become mired in distrust and acrimony unless he allayed the fears of his party's liberal wing. In the weeks after Kennedy's assassination, he turned his considerable talents to the task, wooing liberal and labor support with a barrage of personal and policy initiatives designed to place the president ahead of the civil rights coalition.[16]

Reuther was one of the first to receive the fabled "Johnson treatment." Late in the afternoon of November 23, LBJ phoned the UAW president and pleaded for his help in the trying days ahead. "My friend, I need your help and support more than ever," Reuther recalled the president saying. Johnson called Reuther several times over the next several weeks, always asking for Reuther's suggestions. "Everybody was pretty set up about the fact that the new president wanted advice from Walter and wanted his help," Reuther confidant Joseph Rauh recalled. "We all thought that was great." More importantly, from the UAW's point of view, Johnson took the idea of a federal attack on poverty—still in the planning stages in the last days of the Kennedy White House—and made it the center-piece of his administration. In his January 1964 State of the Union message, LBJ declared an "unconditional war on poverty," the primary weapon of which would be a sweeping effort by federal authorities to provide "better schools and better health and better homes and better training . . . to help more Americans . . . escape from squalor and misery and unemployment. . . ."[17]

As the administration unveiled the details of the war in early 1964, it became increasingly clear that it would not meet all of the UAW's hopes. As Ira Katznelson says, the war on poverty broke from the policies of postwar liberalism only in its scope, not in its shape. Cobbled together from a host of long-pending programs and proposals, the poverty program offered no challenge to corporate power and made no attempt to reshuffle existing class relationships. Its welfare programs did not address class inequities but rather redistributed income from the middle and working classes to the poor. And the programs were no more coherent in their purpose or coverage than the patchwork of agencies created in the New Deal.[18]

The UAW leadership recognized these shortcomings. The administration's antipoverty programs, Reuther told the House Committee considering the White House's package in April 1964, "while they are good, are not adequate, nor will they be successful in achieving their purposes, except as we begin to look at the broader problems [of the American economy]." Reuther then offered the same social democratic analysis he had been making since the 1940s. "Poverty," he said, "is a reflection of our failure to achieve a more rational, more responsible, more equitable distribution of the abundance that is within our grasp. . . ." Resources were skewed, Reuther continued, because "those in our economy who possess a large measure of freedom to appropriate their fair share . . . have been abusing that freedom, particularly the major corporations that dominate whole industries." It followed, therefore, that poverty would only be eliminated by combining welfare and other public spending measures with the democratic control of industry. "A democratic planning agency will provide the mechanism for a rational approach to national problems," Reuther concluded. "Democratic planning would speed enormously the solution of our nation's pervasive problem of poverty."[19]

Despite their reservations, the UAW leadership rightly saw the administration's antipoverty program as a significant step away from the politics of consensus. The union's leaders thus threw the UAW's full weight behind the war on poverty, determined to move it beyond its initial formulation and toward more far reaching change. "I feel very hopeful about the system," Sexton wrote as the poverty struggle took shape. "The thing looks malleable, and fast. I wouldn't say that happy days are here again but I will say that it looks possible to . . . move . . . toward collective goals, political and spiritual." The UAW leadership was determined not to let the moment pass.[20]

As any number of scholars have noted, the war on poverty had imbedded in it one component that had the potential to redistribute political power: the Community Action Program (CAP). CAP required communities to create poverty boards to administer federal antipoverty efforts and to develop new initiatives. Each community could shape is board as it saw fit, with one proviso: boards were to insure the "maximum feasible participation" of the poor themselves in their deliberations. In theory, then, CAP gave heretofore largely disenfranchised groups a formal place within national and local power structures, precisely the formulation that the UAW had long advocated, albeit in social welfare rather than economic programs. It is hardly surprising, therefore, that in 1964 the UAW turned its full attention to CAP, working to make its performance match its promise.[21]

The White House gave the UAW its greatest opportunity to influence CAP. In March 1964 Johnson asked Reuther's longtime administrative assistant, Jack Conway, to serve as CAP's director. "Intrigued" by the still undefined concept, Conway accepted the appointment. He remained director for the next year and a half, during which time he tried to shape CAP in the UAW's image. Conway wanted local community action organizations to follow the UAW model of formalized power sharing through tripartite boards. "I developed a three cornered stool concept," he recalled, "which was that the best community action organization had very strong representation from local government, from private agencies, and from the people. . . . If you could figure out how to get this kind of a three cornered stool, that was the best, that's what we strove for."[22]

Reuther dovetailed the UAW's response to the war on poverty with Conway's CAP. In March 1964, Reuther sketched out a proposal for a Citizens Crusade Against Poverty (CCAP), through which, he hoped, the organizations that had constituted the previous years' civil rights coalition could be formally integrated into the poverty fight. CCAP would act as a liaison between the administration, coalition members, and the poor. Working through CCAP, coalition members would join with the local poverty boards to implement existing programs and propose new policies; CCAP would work with administration officials to transform grass-roots proposals into fully funded programs; and the Crusade would train the representatives of the poor who sat on community boards. The result would be a "tripartite partnership" among CCAP, the federal government, and the poor themselves.[23]

Funded by a million-dollar grant from the UAW, CCAP was intimately linked to the administration's domestic policy matrix. CCAP's training program for the poor, for instance, received the bulk of its funding from the Ford Foundation, which had also underwritten the juvenile delinquency programs that had served as CAP's forerunners. When the Community Action Program wanted to establish its own training program, Conway hired Brendan Sexton to head the effort. Similarly, when Reuther chose CCAP's first executive director in early 1965, he hired Richard Boone, who had been one of the driving forces behind the Community Action Program.[24]

Reuther also increasingly identified with Johnson on personal terms. "[John Kennedy] and I were on the same wavelength," Reuther told a reporter. "I think I'm equally close to Lyndon Johnson, but I approach him differently. He was poor. I too know poverty. Lyndon Johnson and I came from the same family background." LBJ did his best to encourage Reuther's feelings, carefully stroking his ego throughout 1964. "Thank you, my friend, for being at my side," LBJ wrote Reuther after a Democratic fund-raiser. "I can always count on you and for that kind of unswerving friendship I am mighty grateful." LBJ did not simply flatter Reuther, though. He also welcomed his input on policy questions. Between November 1963 and November 1964, Johnson spoke privately to Reuther at least a dozen times. Walter Reuther, Hubert Humphrey later insisted, "was consulted as often as any man outside the government." After years of struggle and defeat, the UAW leadership had finally made it to the center of power.[25]

UAW leaders understood that access to the administration's policy-making mechanisms would not by itself assure a change in the nation's political economy. In late 1964 and early 1965, however, the entire structure of American political life seemed to shift to the left. And the UAW seemed perfectly positioned to lead the social democratic breakthrough it had long dreamed of. The movement to the left was undergirded by the Democrats' triumph in the 1964 presidential election. Lyndon Johnson's sweeping victory over Barry Goldwater broke the southern stranglehold on the Democratic Party. LBJ's landslide proved that a Democratic presidential candidate did not need to carry the deep south to win election, and the Democrats' sweep of the northern congressional races gave the party's center-liberal bloc the numeric strength to override the southern bloc on Capitol Hill. The Dixiecrats suffered another blow early the next year, when the SCLC forced the administration to back a voting rights bill that would finally enfranchise southern African-Americans. "Instead of Dixiecrats coming out of the deep south . . . to block social legislation," Reuther insisted as the voting rights bill neared passage, "you're going to have some of the most progressive congressmen coming out of the deep south. This is going to make a tremendous difference in the whole relationship of forces in the political arena of American society."[26]

As the power of the Dixiecrats waned, some of the key sectors of the civil rights coalition extended their demands beyond calls for racial equality to social democratic change. Its national reputation growing, SDS linked up in early 1964 with the remnants of the old socialist left and growing progressive forces in academia to draft a broad critique of the American political economy. The result was a widely publicized manifesto, "The Triple Revolution," calling for a "new consensus" committed to democratic economic planning. Late that year, Martin Luther King likewise endorsed social democracy. Though he had long had doubts about the efficacy of capitalism, King had studiously avoided any overt support for substantive economic change during the SCLC's campaigns of 1963 and 1964. During his Nobel Prize tour of Sweden in December 1964, however, King told reporters that he considered Scandinavia's economic structure to be a model for the United States, a view that he increasingly made part of his agenda the following year. At its convention in late 1965, the most conservative member of the civil rights coalition, the AFL-CIO, also went on record in support of democratic economic planning, endorsing a Reuther-drafted resolution calling for a national planning agency.[27]

For Reuther and his staff, it was a moment of exultation. "We are in the midst of a great revolutionary change of forces . . . in American society," Reuther told the UAW's executive board in March 1965.

"This change is of such dimensions, I think, that the historians will really put it in the category of a major social revolution." The UAW leadership knew that the revolution was far from complete—social democracy still remained an ideal, not a reality—but the coalition's activists were clearly trying to lay the basis for a significant change in the American political economy. Alone among the coalition members, the UAW, firmly integrated into the administration's inner circle, was best positioned to build on that basis. In 1965, Reuther tried to do just that, extending the community action concept in a new and bold direction, the reconstruction of urban America.[28]

In mid-May 1965, Reuther sent LBJ a four-page memorandum proposing "an urban TVA to stop erosion of cities and people." Specifically, the UAW president suggested that the federal government demonstrate its ability "to create architecturally beautiful and socially meaningful communities" by rehabilitating and redesigning inner-city neighborhoods in six select cities. Reuther's plan called for the federal government to do more than repair old homes and build new structures; the demonstration neighborhoods would be transformed into "research laboratories for the war against poverty" by becoming sites for new schools, old age centers, social service outlets, and open spaces for community interaction. In keeping with the spirit of CCAP, neighborhood renewal plans were to be drawn up by local nonprofit corporations, which would bring together city officials, local businessmen, labor leaders, community elites, and neighborhood residents.[29]

In part, Reuther saw his demonstration cities plan as a frontal assault on what he believed to be the fulcrum of racial tension in the north, housing. He did not see the proposal simply as an end in itself, however. He also believed that it could serve as a test of social democratic experimentation in national policy. "National goals must, in the future," he explained, "be set by the people of the nation. And the means by which we plan to achieve them must spring from the people's mandate. The key to this whole problem of rebuilding American's great urban centers is for us to demonstrate the practical ability to make public planning for people compatible with private planning for profit. The demonstration cities program . . . is a new and significant step forward."[30]

Reuther presented his demonstration concept to Johnson in an off-the-record White House meeting in May 1965, suggesting that if the president were interested, he should establish a special task force to explore the idea more fully. Within a month the White House had created an eight-man task force that brought together progressive policy elites from academia, business, labor, civil right, and the public sector. The group thus represented the technocratic constituencies that the UAW hoped to see on future planning boards. By the time the task force first met in October 1965, the president had dramatically widened its responsibilities. Not only was it to draft legislation creating the demonstration cities program, it was also to create an organizational structure for the newly created Department of Housing and Urban Development (HUD). In essence, then, Johnson had given the task force a mandate to define the administration's urban policy.[31]

With Reuther in charge of the drafting process, the demonstration cities concept emerged from the task force with only minor alterations. As the task force deliberations proceeded throughout the rest of 1965, however, Reuther developed an even broader goal. Arguing that HUD needed to be more than a bricks-and-mortar agency, he suggested that the administration transfer the community action program from its current agency to the new department. White House insiders insisted that the UAW president had more than institutional reorganization in mind when he offered the proposal. At least some aides wanted Reuther to be named HUD's first secretary, and he let it be known that he would accept the position if offered. If he were able to engineer CAP's transfer, therefore, he could become the de facto head of the war on poverty in the new year.[32]

Reuther's maneuver did not work. Top administration officials blocked CAP's transfer, and Johnson named Robert Weaver, not Reuther, HUD's first secretary. That Reuther could even have considered such a coup possible, though, and, more importantly, that he had been able to make a proposal as innovative as Model Cities a central part of the national agenda, indicates the extent to which the UAW had become a part of the administration's policy-making machinery. Reuther clearly saw himself in those terms, writing to LBJ in October that he was proud to be "a devoted member of your working crew." Reuther's willingness to work with the adminstration was undoubtedly a matter of ego. But it was also a matter of program. In a little more than two years, Lyndon Johnson had presided over a vast expansion of American political life, an expansion that in late 1965 seemed to be moving toward the type of social democratic reform that had informed Walter Reuther's politics since the late 1930s. The UAW had every reason to join the Great Society.[33]

In the end, the Great Society did not fulfill the UAW's expectations. The war on poverty was devastated, in large part, by the Johnson administration's deepening involvement in Vietnam, which drained federal resources from domestic spending and split apart the liberal community. Perhaps more fundamentally, the UAW and its allies never managed to break Johnson's commitment to carefully calibrated piecemeal reform. The resulting gap between the war on poverty's promise and its performance left many African-Americans frustrated with and suspicious of the administration's efforts. By 1966 and 1967, that frustration had turned into hostility, nowhere more tragically than in the UAW's home base, Detroit. Victor Reuther had proved correct. By 1967 the promise of the Great Society had become, for many African-Americans, little more than ashes.[34]

At the same time, the Johnson administration never moved beyond its concern for the underclass to confront the problems of the working class as a whole. Convinced that the Great Society was costing them money while offering them no benefits, many white workers turned against the president and his programs. The backlash swept through the UAW with particular force. Between 1964 and 1966, the Democrats' share of the white UAW rank-and-file vote dropped by approximately 15 percent, and in at least one state in 1966—California—UAW rank-and-filers gave the Republican candidate for governor, Ronald Reagan, a majority of their vote. The backlash would only intensify over the next few years, taking on, as it did so, a profoundly racist caste.[35]

The UAW thus was caught within the massive disillusionment and profound social conflict that rent national politics in 1967 and 1968. For very different reasons, African-Americans, white workers, liberals, and the New Left all came to see the UAW, as they saw the Johnson administration, as a prop for the status quo. That perception effectively destroyed the Johnson administration and effectively ended the New Deal order, replacing it with a Republican ascendancy that reached the apex of its power in the 1980s.[36]

In the final analysis, then, the UAW's relationship to the Great Society is a study of labor's failure: the UAW's inability to redefine the nation's policy-making structures; its inability to maintain a cross-class, biracial coalition committed to continued reform; its inability to fashion a more democratic political economy in postwar America. The current interpretation of labor's place in the postwar political order does not fully explain that failure, however. Rather than dismissing unions as disinterested in fundamental reform, scholars need to ground labor's failure in the complex interaction between labor's goals and the context within which they were pursued, between what labor wanted and what it could achieve. The story of labor's place in the postwar order, in other words, is not just the story of a promise betrayed, but also of struggles fought—and lost.

———————————— NOTES ————————————

1. Oral History Interview with Brendan Sexton, November 6, 1978, Box 10, Brendan Sexton Collection, Archives of Labor and Urban Affairs (hereafter referred to as ALUA), Wayne State University, Detroit, Mich.; Alan Haber to Brendan Sexton, Aug. 31, 1961, Box 60, Mildred Jeffrey Collection, ALUA.

2. Sexton address to the Detroit Labor Conference to Mobilize Against Poverty, April 24, 1965, Box 49, Jeffery collection; Sexton book notes, 1965, Box 7, Sexton Collection; Sexton to Walter Reuther, May 7, 1965, Box 378, Walter P. Reuther Collection (hereafter referred to as WPR), ALUA.

3. Most of the literature on 1930s social democracy focuses on shop-floor empowerment. Only in the last few years have historians begun to examine organized labor's political program as a reflection of social democracy. See Nelson Lichtenstein, "From Corporatism to Collective Bargaining: Organized Labor and the Eclipse of Social Democracy in the United States," in Steve Fraser and Gary Gerstle, ed., *The Rise and Fall of the New Deal Order, 1930–1980* (Princeton: Princeton University Press, 1989), 122–52, and, more importantly, Lichtenstein, *The Most Dangerous Man in Detroit: Walter Reuther and the Fate of American Labor* (New York: Basic Books, 1995), chapters 4–11; Ira Katznelson, "Was the Great Society a Lost Opportunity?" in Fraser and Gerstle, *New Deal Order*, 190; Gary Gerstle, *Working Class Americanism: The Politics of Labor in a Textile City* (Cambridge: Cambridge University Press, 1989), chapter 5. Steve Fraser, *Labor Will Rule: Sidney Hillman and the Rise of American Labor* (New York: The Free Press, 1991), is an extraordinary study of the origins and ambiguities of organized labor's social democratic agenda.

4. Nelson Lichtenstein, *Labor's War at Home: The CIO in World War II* (Cambridge: Cambridge University Press, 1982), chapter 12; Lichtenstein, "Conflict Over Workers' Control: The Automobile Industry in World War II," in Michael Frisch and Daniel Walkowitz, ed., *Working Class America: Essays on Labor, Community, and American Society* (Urbana: Univer-

sity of Illinois Press, 1983), 284–311; Lichtenstein, "UAW Bargaining Strategy and Shop Floor Conflict, 1946–1970," *Industrial Relations* 24 (1985), 360–81; Lichtenstein, "Life at the Rouge: A Cycle of Workers' Control," in Robert Asher and Charles Stephenson, ed., *Life and Labor: Dimensions of American Working Class History* (Albany: State University of New York Press, 1986), 237–48; Lichtenstein, *Most Dangerous Man*, chapters 12–14; Ronald Schatz, "Philip Murray and the Subordination of the Industrial Unions to the United States Government," in Melvin Dubofsky and Warren Van Tine, ed., *Labor Leaders in America* (Urbana: University of Illinois Press, 1987), 239–56; Lichtenstein, "Walter Reuther and the Rise of Labor-Liberalism," in Dubofsky and Van Tine, *Labor Leaders*, 291–301; Gerstle, *Working Class Americanism*, chapter 10; Alan Dawley, "Workers, Capital, and the State in the Twentieth Century," in J. Carroll Moody and Alice Kessler-Harris, ed., *Perspectives on American Labor History: The Problem of Synthesis* (DeKalb: Northern Illinois University Press, 1990), 166–79; Katznelson, "Lost Opportunity," 190–91; Mike Davis, *Prisoners of the American Dream* (London: Verso Press, 1986), 52–101. The literature on the purge of the CIO's communist members is voluminious. For an excellent survey, see Robert Zieger, "Toward the History of the CIO: A Bibliographic Report," *Labor History* 26 (1985), 491–500, and Zieger, "The CIO: A Bibliographic Update and Archival Guide," *Labor History* 31 (1990), 413–24. The best study of the institutional framework of collective bargaining is Christopher Tomlins, *The State and the Unions: Labor Relations, Law, and the Organized Labor Movement in America, 1880–1960* (Cambridge: Cambridge University Press, 1985).

5. Lichtenstein, "Social Democracy," 140–45; Lichtenstein, *Most Dangerous Man*, 299–445; Davis, *Prisoners*, 82–101; Dawley, "Workers, Capital, and the State," 173–78; Katznelson, "Lost Opportunity," 190–92, 195.

6. C. Wright Mills, *The New Men of Power: American's Labor Leaders* (New York: Harcourt Brace, 1948); Alan Brinkley, "The New Deal and the Idea of the State," in Fraser and Gerstle, *New Deal Order*, 87–94; Fraser, *Labor Will Rule*; Nick Salvatore, *Eugene V. Debs: Citizen and Socialist* (Urbana: University of Illinois Press, 1982); Thorstein Veblen, *The Engineer and the Price System* (New York: B. W. Huebsch, 1921). For various examples of Reuther's agenda, see Walter Reuther, "The Challenge of Peace," American Labor Conference on International Affairs, *Pamphlet*, 1945, Box 3, UAW Special Projects Department Collection, ALUA; UAW press releases, October 6, 1946, and December 7, 1946, Box 8, UAW Fair Practices Department Collection, ALUA; Reuther to L. B. Drach, October 19, 1945, Box 24, WPR; Reuther radio script, n.d., Box 540, WPR; Roy and Fania to Walter, Mae, and Linda Reuther, October 31, 1944, Box 79, Victor Reuther Collection, ALUA.

7. Irving Howe and B. J. Widick, *The UAW and Walter Reuther* (New York: Random House, 1949), chapters 9 and 12; Emmanuel Geltman and Irving Howe, "The Tradition of Reutherism: An Interview with Brendan Sexton," *Dissent* 19 (Winter 1972), 57. See Lizabeth Cohen, *Making a New Deal: Industrial Workers in Chicago* (Cambridge: Cambridge University Press, 1990), 267–89, for a discussion of working-class allegiance to the Democratic Party.

8. Stephen Amberg, "The CIO Political Strategy in Historical Perspective: Creating a High-Road Economy in the Postwar Era," above; Walter Reuther address to Americans for Democratic Action, February 22, 1948, Box 4, UAW Fair Practices Department Collection; Victor Reuther, "Look Forward Labor," *Common Sense* 14 (December 1945), 8–9; Walter Reuther address to NAACP, June 28, 1946, Box 4, UAW Fair Practices Department Collection; Walter Reuther statement for UAW convention, n.d. [1946], Box 89, WPR; Brendan Sexton transcript, n.d. (1965–1966), Box 7, Sexton Collection. The UAW's strategy followed a classic social democratic pattern explored most fully in Gosta Esping-Andersen, *Politics Against Markets: The Social Democratic Path to Power* (Princeton: Princeton University Press, 1985), and Adam Przewoski, *Capitalism and Social Democracy* (Cambridge: Cambridge University Press, 1985).

9. I examine these relationships in detail in *The UAW and the Heyday of American Liberalism, 1945–1968* (Ithaca: Cornell University Press, 1995).

10. Walter Reuther, "Homes For People, Jobs For Prosperity, Planes for Peace," 1949, Box 59, WPR; U.S. Congress, Senate Committee on Banking and Currency,, *Hearings*, 82d Congress, 1st sess. (Washington, D.C.: Government Printing Office, 1951), 2186; U.S. Congress, Joint Committee on the Economic Report, *Hearings*, 84th Congress, 1st sess. (Washington,D.C.: Government Printing Office, 1955), 97–149; Nat Weinberg, "Practical Approaches to the Problems Raised By Automation," May 15, 1956, Box 54, UAW Washington Office Collection, Paul Sifton and Samuel Jacobs Files, ALUA; U.S. Congress, Senate Committee on the Judiciary, *Hearings*, 85th Congress, 2d sess. (Washington, D.C.: Government Printing Office, 1958), 2179–2203; Nat Weinberg to Walter Reuther, June 3, 1961, Box 2, UAW Special Projects Department Collection; Walter Reuther statement to Joint Economic Committee, February 7, 1962, Box 4, UAW Special Projects Department Collection; Reuther address to the Center for the Study of Democratic Institutions, January 22, 1963, Box 4, UAW Special Projects Department Collection.

11. Richard Bensel, *Sectionalism and American Political Development, 1880–1980* (Madison: University of Wisconsin Press, 1984), 222–43;

Robert Garson, *The Democratic Party and the Politics of Sectionalism, 1941–1948* (Baton Rouge: Louisiana State University Press, 1974), particularly chapter 5; John Frederick Martin, *Civil Rights and the Crisis of Liberalism: The Democratic Party, 1945–1976* (Boulder, Colo.: Westview Press, 1976); transcript of phone conversation between Adlai Stevenson and Lyndon Johnson, January 10, 1953, Box 1, Notes and Transcipts from Johnson Conversations, Lyndon B. Johnson Presidential Library (hereafter referred to as LBJL), University of Texas, Austin, Tex.

12. The literature on the civil rights movement of the early 1960s is voluminious. Among the best studies are Clayborne Carson, *In Struggle: SNCC and the Black Awakening of the 1960s* (Cambridge, Mass.: Harvard University Press, 1981), 9–95; David Garrow, *Bearing the Cross: Martin Luther King, Jr., and the Southern Christian Leadership Conference* (New York: William Morrow, 1986), 127–355; and Adam Fairclough, *To Redeem the Soul of America: The Southern Christian Leadership Conference and Martin Luther King, Jr.* (Athens: University of Georgia Press, 1987), 57–191. On white liberal support for the movement, see James Findlay, "Religion and Politics in the Sixties: The Churches and the Civil Rights Act of 1964," *Journal of American History* 77 (June 1990), 66–75; Steve Gillon, *Politics and Vision: The ADA and American Liberalism, 1947–1985* (New York: Oxford University Press, 1987), 148–49.

13. Emil Mazey to Walter Reuther and James Carey, May 10, 1963, and Joseph Rauh to Walter Reuther, May 13, 1963, Box 117, WPR; Arnold Aronson to cooperating organizations, July 25, 1963, Box 1, Series D, Leadership Conference on Civil Rights Collection (hereafter referred to as LCCR), Library of Congress, Washington, D.C.; minutes of LCCR meetings, July 24, 1963, and July 31, 1963, Box 1, Series D, LCCR; series of memos from UAW lobbyists, July–August 1963, Box 1, Series G, LCCR; Victor Reuther to Martin Luther King, Jr., Box 20, Martin Luther King, Jr. Collection, Martin Luther King, Jr., Center for Non-Violent Social Change, Atlanta, Ga.; Frank Wallick to Victor Reuther, July 30, 1963, no box number, UAW Citizenship-Legislative Department Collection [unprocessed collection]; Walter Reuther address to the March on Washington, August 28, 1963, Box 4, UAW Special Projects Department Collection.

14. Brendan Sexton and Nat Weinberg to Walter Reuther, January 21, 1963, Box 19, Nat Weinberg Collection, ALUA; Weinberg to Walter Reuther, January 25, 1963, Box 19, Weinberg Collection; Otha to Nat Weinberg, Irving Bluestone, Brendan Sexton, and Roy Reuther; Weinberg to Walter Reuther, July 3, 1963, both in UAW Citizenship-Legislative Department Collection [no box number]; Victor Reuther article for National Council of Churches, December 30, 1963, Box 19, Weinberg Collection.

15. On ERAP, see Irving Bluestone to Carroll Hutton, August 9, 1963; Irving Bluestone to Walter Reuther, January 6, 1964; Bluestone to Paul Schrade, February 11, 1964, all in Box 523, WPR.

16. On the UAW leadership's concern over LBJ's assuming the presidency, see Oral History Interview of Jack Conway, April 10, 1972, John F. Kennedy Presidential Library, Boston, Mass. On LBJ's commitment to the liberal agenda, see Doris Kearns, *Lyndon Johnson and the American Dream* (New York: Harper and Row, 1976), 199, and Michael R. Beschloss, ed., *Taking Charge: The Johnson White House Tapes, 1963–1964* (New York: Simon and Schuster, 1997), 25, 83–84. This is not to suggest that Johnson embraced civil rights for purely political reasons. LBJ was genuinely concerned for civil rights, but he expressed that concern within the political context which formed the centerpiece of his life. See T. Harry Williams, "Huey, Lyndon, and Southern Radicalism," *Journal of American History* 60 (September 1973), 267–93.

17. Walter Reuther note to file, December 3, 1963, Box 368, WPR; Oral History Interview with Joseph L. Rauh, July 30, 1969, LBJL; Walter Reuther to Lyndon Johnson, November 23, 1963; Walter Reuther to Lyndon Johnson, December 3, 1963; and Walter Reuther to Lyndon Johnson, January [4], 1964, all in Box 368, WPR. In the last memo, Reuther urged Johnson to commit his administration to a wide-ranging effort to create "an economy of opportunity," to include a "massive national effort to provide a better life for America's submerged third. . . ."

18. Katznelson, "Lost Opportunity," 195–205. Also see Thomas F. Jackson, "The State, the Movement, and the Urban Poor: The War on Poverty and Political Mobilization in the 1960s," in Michael Katz, ed., *The "Underclass Debate": Views From History* (Princton: Princeton University Press, 1993), 411–16.

19. U.S. Congress, House Committee on Education and Labor, *Hearings*, 88th Congress, 2d sess. (Washington, D.C.: Government Printing Office, 1964), 422–69.

20. Walter Reuther to Lyndon Johnson, March 19, 1964, Box 378, WPR; Walter Reuther, "Freedom's Time of Testing," *Saturday Review*, August 29, 1964; Sexton book notes, 1965, Box 7, Brendan Sexton Collection.

21. On CAP, see James Sudquist, *Politics and Policy: The Eisenhower, Kennedy, and Johnson Years* (Washington, D.C.: Brookings Institution, 1968), 137–50; Lillian Rubin, "Maximum Feasible Participation: The Origins, Implications, and Present Status," *Annals of the American Academy of Political and Social Science* 385 (September 1969), 14–29; Daniel Patrick Moynihan, *Maximum Feasible Misunderstanding: Community Action in the*

War on Poverty (New York: Free Press, 1969); Alan Mautsow, *The Unravelling of America: A History of Liberalism in the 1960s* (New York: Harper and Row, 1984), 117–88, 244–52; Jackson, "The State, the Movement, the Poor," 418–20.

22. Oral History Interview with Jack Conway, August 13, 1980.

23. Minutes of the Special Session of the UAW International Executive Board, March 18–26, 1964, Box 80, Region 6 Collection, ALUA; Constitution of the Citizens Crusade Against Poverty, n.d., Box 1, Citizens Crusade Against Poverty Collection (hereafter referred to as CCAP), Walter Reuther Files, ALUA; Walter Reuther to Martin Luther King, Jr., April 17, 1964, and Richard Boone to Officers and Vice-Chairmen of CCAP, March 11, 1966, both in Box 6, Martin Luther King, Jr., Collection; Walter Reuther to Lyndon Johnson, June 26, 1964, Box 368, WPR.

24. Minutes of the regular session of the International Executive Board, May 5–7, 1964, Box 23, Region 9A Collection, ALHUA; Johnson to Reuther, July 23, 1964, "Reuther" File, White House Central Files (hereafter referred to as WHCF), name File; Johnson to Vizzard, Patton, and Reuther, November 2, 1964, "Reuther" File, WHCF, Name File; Brendan Sexton proposal for training program, April 1, 1965, Box 3, CCAP; Sexton to Walter Reuther, May 7, 1965, Box 378, WPR; Irving Bluestone to Walter Reuther, August 26, 1965, Box 1, CCAP.

25. Lyndon Johnson Daily Diary Cards, November 1963–November 1964, LBJL; note of interview with Humbert Humphrey, c. May 15, 1970, Box 2, Frank Cormier and William Eaton Collection, ALUA; "How Tough Is Walter Reuther," *Look*, August 10, 1965; Johnson to Reuther, July 29, 1964, "Reuther" File, WHCF, Name File.

26. For election returns, see Theodore White, *The Making of the President 1964* (New York: Atheneum, 1965), 405–406. The standard account of the Selma campaign is David Garrow, *Protest at Selma: Martin Luther King, Jr., and the Voting Rights Act of 1965* (New Haven: Yale University Press, 1978). Reuther's quote is from the minutes of the regular session of the UAW International Executive Board, March 23–26, 1965, Box 23, Region 9A Collection. The UAW rank and file voted overwhelmingly for LBJ. In all, 85 percent of UAW members who voted cast their ballots for Johnson. See Oliver Quayle and Company, "A Study in Depth of the Rank and File of the United Automobile Workers (AFL-CIO)," 6: 198–200, Box 59, Vice-President Leonard Woodcock Collection, ALUA.

27. Tom Hayden, *Reunion: A Memoir* (New York: Random House, 1988), 125; Donald Agger, *et al.*, "The Triple Revolution," *Liberation* 9 (April 1964), 9–15; Bayard Rustin, "From Protest to Coalition Politics," in Marvin

Gettleman and David Mermelstein, ed., *The Great Society Reader: The Failure of American Liberalism* (New York: Random House, 1967), 263–76; Garrow, *Bearing the Cross*, 364, 427; Adam Fairclough, "Was Martin Luther King a Marxist?" *History Workshop* 15 (Spring 1983), 117–25; Proceedings of the Sixth Constitutional Convention of the AFL-CIO, 1965 (Washington, D.C.: American Federation of Labor-Congress of Industrial Organizations, 1965), 296–304; Michael Harrington, *Socialism* (New York: Saturday Review Press, 1970), 264–65.

28. Minutes of the Regular Session of the International Executive Board, March 23–26, 1964, Box 23, Region 9A Collection.

29. Reuther to Johnson, May 13, 1965, Box 406, WPR. The idea of demonstration cities was not original to Reuther, nor did he draft the memo he sent to Johnson. Detroit Mayor Jerome Cavanagh first proposed the concept to the White House when he served as a member of the president's 1964 task force on cities, although he perceived the concept in somewhat different terms than those which Reuther presented. See Oral History Inteview with Jerome Cavanagh, March 22, 1971, LBJL. It seems likely, though I have no documentation to prove it, that Reuther developed his concept in cooperation with Cavanagh and Detroit city planner Charles Blessing. Reuther's memo was drafted by Oskar Stonarov, an architect and Reuther confidant. The Johnson administration accepted the idea as Reuther's and consistently referred to it as such.

30. Minutes of the regular session of the UAW International Executive Board, January 10–13, 1966, Box 24, Region 9A Collection; Reuther statement to the Senate Committee on Government Relations, December 5, 1966, Box 4, UAW Special Projects Department Collection.

31. Reuther handwritten notes, May 20, 1965, and June 23, 1965, Box 369, WPR; Lyndon Johnson, *The Vantage Point: Perspectives on the Presidency, 1963–1969* (New York: Holt, Rinehart, and Winston, 1971), 329; Joseph Califano to Lyndon Johnson, September 16, 1965, Box 9, WHCF Ex BE4/Automobiles; Califano to Johnson, n.d., Box 1, Special Files, Legislative Background—Model Cities, LBJL; summary of task force meeting, October 15, 1965, Box 1, Special Files, Model Cities; minutes of the regular session of the UAW International Executive Board, January 10–13, 1966, Box 24, Region 9A Collection; Califano to Johnson, October 9, 1965, Box 5, WHCF Ex HS 3. The task force included Reuther; urban planner Robert Wood of MIT; Harvard Law Professor Charles Haar; Kermit Gordon, former director of the Bureau of the Budget; William Rafsky, former development coordinator for the city of Philadelphia; Industrialist Edgar Kaiser; Benjamin Heineman, chairman of the Chicago and Northwestern Railway; and the National Urban League's Whitney Young.

32. Harry McPherson to Jack Valenti, December 22, 1965, Box 5, WHCF HS 3; Oskar Stonorov to Walter Reuther, November 15, 1965, Box 407, WPR; draft report of the Task Force on Urban Problems, December 1965, Box 407, WPR; McPherson to Johnson, December 9, 1965, Box 1, Ex LG; *Los Angeles Times*, December 1965; McPherson to Johnson, December 13, 1965, Box 252, Ex FG 170.

33. Final draft of Demonstration Cities proposal, December 8, 1965, Box 407, WPR; outline of Joseph Califano presentation to Johnson, December 1965, Box 1, Special Files—Model Cities; January 24, 1966, draft of Demonstration Cities bill and Johnson message to Congress on American cities, January 26, 1966, both in Box 2, Special Files, Model Cities; McPherson to Johnson, December 9, 1965, and McPherson to Califano, December 22, 1965, both in Box 1, WHCF, Ex LG; Reuther to Johnson, October 18, 1965, Box 368, WPR.

34. Matusow, *Unravelling of America*, provides a fine overview of the dissolution of liberal reform in the mid-1960s. Sidney Fine, *Violence in the Model City: The Cavanagh Administration, Race Relations, and the Detroit Riot of 1967* (Ann Arbor: University of Michigan Press, 1989), is the definitive account of the Detroit riot.

35. Quayle survey, Box 59, Woodcock Collection. Historians have increasingly demonstrated that white workers grew disillusioned with liberalism prior to the mid-1960s. See Bruce Nelson, "Autoworkers, Electoral Politics, and the Covergence of Race and Class: Detroit, 1937–1945," in this volume, and Thomas J. Sugrue, *The Origins of the Urban Crisis: Race and Inequality in Postwar Detroit* (Princeton: Princeton University Press, 1996), especially chapters 8 and 9. It is important to note, however, that white workers' disillusionment focused almost exclusively on the local level until the 1960s.

36. Boyle, *The UAW and the Heyday of American Liberalism*, recounts the UAW's position within liberal politics in the mid-1960s.

Gary M. Fink

9

Labor Law Revision and the End of the Postwar Labor Accord

Gone are the employer's goon squads and the billyclubs; today's union busters wear business suits and carry attaché cases. Sharp lawyers and Madison Avenue propagandists have replaced the straightforward concern with brass knuckles with carefully calculated devices designed to destroy, without leaving any visible bruises, the desire of workers to organize.

AFL-CIO Executive Council
February 1977

The U. S. Senate took its sixth and final cloture vote on June 22, seeking to stop a filibuster on S. 2467, the Labor Law Revision Bill of 1978. After securing fifty-eight of the sixty votes needed to end debate, leaders of the cloture effort saw their frail coalition begin to disintegrate. Majority Leader Robert Byrd then recommitted the bill to the Senate Human Resources Committee, thus ending the most ambitious effort since the New Deal to strengthen American workers' eroded collective bargaining rights under the National Labor Relations Act. Labor and its allies in the Senate had made substantial concessions to win over wavering senators, and the administration used its considerable arsenal of patronage, trade-offs, and constituency favors, all to no avail.

It was a disastrous defeat for organized labor that had worked hard to elect sympathetic senators and representatives to the Congress and a friendly Democrat to the White House. More to the point, the Democratic Party firmly controlled the House and had a near filibuster-proof majority in the Senate. So what happened? Although contemporary analysts found numerous reasons for the defeat, they concentrated on the labor movement's declining power and influence along with the seeming inability of the Carter administration to push significant reform legislation through Congress. The case could be made without great difficulty.[1]

The labor movement's power and influence had reached high tide shortly after World War II but steadily declined thereafter. With a remarkable absence of success, the labor lobby had tried since 1948 to repeal Section 14b of the Taft-Hartley Act that allowed individual states to enact legislation prohibiting the closed or union shop, preferential hiring, and maintenance of membership agreements between employers and unions. Similar frustration accompanied the efforts to enact a federal common situs picketing law overturning an adverse 1951 Supreme Court decision: in *National Labor Relations Board v. Denver Building and Construction Trades Council*, the Court prohibited striking building-trades unions from picketing other contractors and subcontractors on the same construction site.[2]

Now, to carry its freight on labor law reform, organized labor found itself dependent on a former governor from a right-to-work state who prided himself on being a moderate-conservative Washington outsider. Perhaps inevitably, the two erstwhile allies ultimately blamed each other for the defeat. But frustration, more than reasoned reflection, inspired such recriminations. In reality, labor and the administration had combined forces to wage a relatively effective campaign for this controversial legislation, but one that simply failed to overcome the tide of American industrial relations history running so strongly against it.

Recently, Melvyn Dubofsky associated the failure of the reform effort during the Carter administration with "the death of industrial pluralism and the New Deal System." Christopher Tomlins takes the argument even further, exposing organized labor's delicate legal status even during the halcyon days of the New Deal. The class-conflict model inherent in collective bargaining simply violated too directly the concept of individualism and property rights so deeply imbedded in the American psyche. The fate of the 1978 labor law reform effort provides no cause to challenge either of these analyses.[3]

Indeed, even if reform legislation had passed, it probably would have changed little. As Kevin Boyle concludes in this volume, the failure of organized labor, or more specifically, Walter Reuther and the UAW, "to fashion a more democratic political economy in postwar America" left corporate dominance largely unchecked. Thus labor law reform, weakened as it was in the congressional process, still would have had to undergo the same judicial and agency review that so effectively had gutted the legislative intent of the NLRA. The following review of labor law reform's storied history during the Carter administration further testifies to the labor movement's declining political fortunes, its problematic alliance with the Democratic Party, and something of the character of the Carter administration.

Labor leaders had anticipated good things during the election year of 1976. Given the fallout of the Watergate affair and Gerald Ford's unpopular pardon of Richard Nixon, it promised to be a good year for Democrats, and the party's most visible candidates—Hubert Humphrey, Walter Mondale, Stuart Udall, Edward Kennedy, Henry Jackson—all had excellent labor-liberal credentials. The only dark cloud on labor's distant horizon took the form of two southern governors, the bumptious George Wallace of Alabama and Georgia's less well known former governor, Jimmy Carter. As the campaign season progressed the complexion of the "southern threat" changed as party liberals rallied behind Carter to defeat Wallace in the critical Florida presidential primary. That victory, along with his strong showing in earlier primaries, raised the former Georgia governor to front-runner status in the campaign. Yet, while clearly preferable to Wallace, Carter inspired little enthusiasm among most labor leaders. Nevertheless, after a final unsuccessful effort to undermine the Carter candidacy in the Pennsylvania primary, labor recognized the inevitable and made its peace with the new Democratic nominee.[4]

Although Carter wanted and needed labor support during the autumn campaign, he clearly felt no special obligation to the movement and cavalierly dispatched some of its most basic legislative objectives, including the aforementioned common-situs picketing bill and the repeal of Section 14b of the Taft-Hartley Act. He did promise to sign these measures into law if passed and gave labor law reform a cool, somewhat equivocal endorsement. It was not much, but it was better than the alternative. Labor had shepherded the picketing bill though the Congress earlier, only to have Gerald Ford veto it, and by 1976, 14b had become more a symbolic litmus test than a realistic legislative objective. On the more positive side, Carter pleased labor with his selection of Senator Walter Mondale, a Hubert Humphrey protege, as his vice presidential running mate and with his endorsement of national health insurance, one of organized labor's most cherished goals.[5]

Conflict and discord punctuated the early days of the Carter presidency. Organized labor and the new Democratic administration disagreed over such matters as the appointment of a secretary of labor, deficit spending and the threat of inflation, tax policies, public service employment, and changes in the minimum wage rate. Clearly, labor's traditional legislative agenda had relatively little support in the Congress or among the "new" Democrats now occupying the White House. Actually, even before Carter officially took the oath of office, organized labor publicly disassociated itself with the administration. In a tone reminiscent of his attacks on Nixon and Ford, AFL-CIO president George Meany accused Carter of breaking campaign promises, and a few days later, Secretary-Treasurer Lane Kirkland announced that henceforth the labor federation would maintain an independent posture during the Carter presidency.[6]

Unless common ground could be found, the labor movement seemed likely to lose much of its influence in an administration it had helped to elect. Conversely, the administration confronted the distinct possibility of losing the support of one of the Democratic Party's most important constituency groups. Ultimately, labor law reform provided an issue around which these improbable allies could coalesce. Although differences emerged regarding details, both labor and the administration agreed on the principle of reform. The labor movement had been seeking an adjustment in federal labor-relations law since the passage of the Taft-Hartley Act in 1947. By the mid-1970s, adverse agency rules and regulations and evolving judicial precedent had elevated labor law revision to the top of organized labor's legislative priority list.[7]

For a fiscally conservative president who worried much about inflation and balanced budgets, labor law reform seemed an ideal issue with which to pacify his labor allies; it had no significant budgetary implications and seemed unlikely to be inflationary. Moreover, from Carter's perspective labor law revision was a public interest issue rather than a special interest concern such as situs picketing legislation that only affected a relatively small and select group of workers. The opportunity to engage in good-faith collective bargaining was, after all, a right that had been conferred on all workers whether or not they chose to exercise it. Labor law revision would simply reaffirm that right.[8]

Labor law reform, then, became the critical issue that held together the fragile alliance between organized labor and the Carter administration. Had it passed, labor no doubt would have felt compelled to support the president in 1980. This certainly would have foreclosed Edward Kennedy's challenge in the primaries and could have significantly altered the political landscape in the 1980 election (although not likely the result). The failure of labor law reform had the opposite effect, further estranging the administration from its most likely allies in the labor movement and facilitating a debilitating challenge in the Democratic primaries that not only undermined the incumbent president but also emasculated his party.

Critics later charged that Carter and his White House staff lacked commitment to labor law reform and, as a result, failed to conduct the type of campaign necessary to secure its passage. In other words, reform was possible, but the administration botched it. In retrospect, this analysis is, at best, only partially true. To be sure, Carter and his staff warmed only slowly to labor law reform, but by the time the U. S. Senate took its critical votes on the measure, the administration was totally committed to the bill. Indeed, it spent liberally from the small fund of political capital available to it to pass the measure. By the summer of 1978, the White House staff had come to see labor law revision as the domestic equivalent of the Panama Canal treaties, the administration's uppermost foreign policy objective. It envisioned these two measures as the "bookends" that would enclose the range of foreign and domestic achievements that Carter could take to the electorate in 1980. Thus, labor law reform had become almost as important to Carter as it was to organized labor.

But meaningful labor law reform had not been an easy sell either to the president or to the Congress. Although, as noted earlier, Carter had ambiguously committed himself to reform during the fall campaign, it clearly was not high on his list of presidentially identified priorities for the Ninety-Fifth Congress. Like the Panama Canal treaties, labor law revision would arouse intense opposition that could jeopardize the passage of other desired legislation. The labor movement, however, was prepared to go forward with this measure with or without administration support, so Carter could not stall the measure indefinitely.

Secretary of Labor Ray Marshall championed labor law reform within the administration and served as the White House's principal liaison with organized labor. The Texas economist believed the revision effort should accomplish three broad objectives: to strengthen the remedies available to the National Labor Relations Board (NLRB) to enforce existing labor laws; to improve the operations of the NLRB to make it a more efficient, equitable, and predictable regulatory agency; and to strengthen the collective bargaining rights of American workers.[9]

During the spring of 1977, Marshall carried on extensive negotiations with the AFL-CIO in an effort to reach an agreement acceptable both to labor and the administration. After having failed to get a common-situs picketing bill through the House—the same bill passed earlier but was vetoed by Gerald Ford—labor wanted and clearly needed administration support of the labor law revision measure. After weeks of hard bargaining, AFL-CIO representatives compromised with the administration on numerous points, including the axing of three of its more controversial proposals: a provision to repeal 14b; a procedure that in some cases would have allowed certification of a union as a bargaining agent without an election; and a stipulation that would have required employers taking over a business to honor an existing union contract. In submitting Marshall's compromise draft to the president, Stuart Eizenstat, Carter's domestic policy chief, tried to impress upon Carter the significance of the bill to labor. "It is difficult to overestimate the importance of this matter in terms of our future relationship with organized labor," Eizenstat wrote. "Because of budget constraints and fiscal considerations, we will be unable to satisfy their desires in many areas requiring expenditure of government funds. This is an issue without adverse budget considerations, which the unions very much want. I think it can help cement our relations for a good while."[10]

Hamilton Jordan, one of Carter's closest friends and advisors, agreed and urged strong administration support of the bill. He believed such advocacy would promote more cordial relations with the labor movement and "encourage a reasonable approach on [other] issues." This politically sensitive presidential advisor noted that labor law reform had particularly strong support from such "progressive" unions as the United Auto Workers (UAW), the Machinists, and the Communications Workers. "These unions represent our real base of support in labor," he said, and "it is important that we honor their priorities." Jordan also believed that a unified campaign for labor law reform could convince the UAW to reaffiliate with the AFL-CIO.

This goal, he concluded, "is in our best interest, because it will bring fresh, progressive and reasonable ideas into an organization (the AFL-CIO) which is now stale and obstreperous."[11]

Yet Carter continued to vacillate. Rejecting the advice of Eizenstat, Mondale, and Marshall, he refused to classify the bill as an administration measure, preferring instead to send Congress a message "endorsing the concepts and principles" of labor law reform without getting involved in specifics. In reality, of course, the administration was—and for some time had been—deeply involved in developing a measure it could support. The Marshall draft worked out with the AFL-CIO was circulated among the inner core of White House advisors and prompted a mixed reaction. Bert Lance, director of the Office of Management and Budget (OMB) and one of the president's oldest and most trusted advisors, objected to almost every substantive provision in the bill. Juanita Krebs, Commerce, and Charles Schultze, Council of Economic Advisors (CEA), were less antagonistic but still had reservations. Krebs, for example, objected to a striker job-replacement guarantee that might "disturb the delicate balance between management and labor rights in the collective bargaining process." Schultze worried about the economic consequences of an increased number of strikes with higher wage settlements. Predictably, Vice President Mondale and Ray Marshall strongly endorsed the bill, and Stuart Eizenstat generally agreed with them.[12]

By the time the bill reached Carter's desk, substantial accord had been reached on most of the complex measure's numerous provisions. In an effort to strengthen and facilitate the enforcement of federal labor law, the administration agreed to increase the NLRB from five to seven members, to allow the decrees of administrative law judges to be affirmed by two-member rather than three-member panels of the NLRB, to reduce the time lag between filing petitions and the holding of representation elections, to debar employers who willfully violated labor law from participating in federal contracts for three years, and to provide for reinstatement and double back pay for employees unlawfully discharged for union activities.

Several points of contention remained, however, including an equal time provision permitting union organizers to address employees on company time if the employer did so. Another disputed clause would have permitted striking workers bargaining over an initial contract to return to their old jobs even if it meant the discharge of replacement workers. Disagreements also existed over the organization of plant guards and the issuance of mandatory injunctions for unlawful dismissal and refusal to bargain.[13]

The president's concern with the latter problems were more tactical than principled. He feared, for example, that the property rights implications of the equal-time provision would be used as the theme of a postcard campaign that ultimately could jeopardize passage of the entire bill. Carter eventually supported the compromises worked out by Marshall on all of these matters but the job-guarantee provision for striking workers, which he wanted further time to study and eventually discarded. Although he approved the compromises worked out on the other issues, Carter continued to hedge, refusing to include these provisions in his presidential message on the subject. Instead, it was decided that during his testimony on the bill, Ray Marshall would disclose the president's support. Carter also rejected a suggestion that he meet with Senators Jacob Javits and Harrison Williams and Representative Frank Thompson Jr., the bill's sponsors, to draw attention to the issue and to acknowledge the efforts of congressional leaders who would be responsible for guiding the bill through the legislative labyrinth. Clearly, the president still sought to distance himself from the labor law reform, a reticence that fed the suspicions of labor leaders who already doubted the former Georgia governor's commitment to their cause. Thus Carter's actions compromised much of the goodwill that his advisors had hoped to build by supporting this measure, and, as they had predicted, did so without gaining credibility from labor's adversaries.[14]

On July 18 Labor Secretary Marshall released the president's labor law reform message and briefed the press at a White House news conference on the "concepts and principles" of reform the administration supported. Shortly thereafter, Frank Thompson introduced H.R. 8410, the Labor Law Reform Act of 1978, and Harrison Williams introduced a companion bill, S. 2467. AFL-CIO spokespersons immediately endorsed the bill, praising the administration's work on it and privately conveying the federation's gratitude to the administration for its backing.[15]

Because employer groups such as the Business Roundtable and the National Chamber of Commerce had been consulted and changes in the original draft legislation had been made in response to their concerns, Stuart Eizenstat assumed that business interests would be less strident in their opposition to the bill than might otherwise be expected. "While the business community will certainly oppose the bill," he told the president, "they view it as much more acceptable than earlier versions and will therefore be less vociferous in condemning the administration for its position." The administration's domestic policy chief clearly misjudged the venomous character of these groups, which, after securing concessions from the administration, used all the resources at their command to kill the legislation.[16]

Before the end of the summer, supporters of the reform legislation had launched a vigorous campaign to secure its passage. Seven former secretaries of labor gave the bill their unqualified endorsement, and a broad-based coalition called Justice on the Job had been organized to support the administration's labor law reform effort. Hubert Humphrey agreed to chair the organization. Success quickly rewarded that effort as HR 8410 sailed through the House on October 6 by a vote of 257 to 163. Chastened by their earlier defeat on situs picketing, labor lobbyists had taken no chances. They discussed their concerns about specific provisions of the bill with individual House members, generated appropriate information for them, and made compromises when necessary. In the end, labor spokespersons pretty much got the bill they wanted.[17]

The decisive nature of the vote in the House for labor law reform shocked business groups that had become somewhat complacent after the earlier, relatively easy defeat of situs picketing legislation. The National Association of Manufacturers, along with the Chamber of Commerce, the Business Roundtable, and various right-wing conservative groups, such as the National Right to Work Committee, quickly mobilized their forces against the bill. Labor responded in kind but lacked the kind of resources available to business interests. The stage was thus set for the battle that would be waged in the U.S. Senate when the Congress reconvened in January 1978.

Although Walter Mondale told the delegates to the AFL-CIO's twelfth biennial convention, meeting shortly after House action on the bill, that the Carter administration had "no higher priority next year than the passage of labor law reform in the Senate," an administration decision to take up the Panama Canal treaties first dashed labor's hopes that labor law reform would be considered early in the new session. In seeking to explain that decision, legal scholars Thomas Ferguson and Joel Rogers reminded readers of *The Nation* that Carter was a card-carrying member of the free-trade-oriented Trilateral Commission. They speculated that the president had elevated the controversial Panama Canal treaties ahead of labor law reform on his congressional agenda because of the influence within the Democratic Party of the "phalanx of big banks and multinationals who feared the impact a rejection of the treaties might have on their Latin American investments."[18]

Business forces certainly appreciated the extra time to mobilized their troops. "Time is in our favor," concluded G. John Tysee, labor relations attorney for the Chamber of Commerce. "Delay has dissipated the momentum caused by the easy victory of similar House legislation in October," he said, and "given the Chamber additional time to mobilize grass-roots opposition." Whatever the reason for taking up the Panama Canal treaties first, effective labor law reform probably died with that decision. After the bruising Senate battle to ratify the treaties had ended, several proponents of revision legislation in that body asked Frank Moore, Carter's legislative liaison, to put off labor law reform because of "the political flak" they had already taken on Panama. Moreover, it was feared, correctly as it turned out, that Republican Senate Minority Leader Howard Baker would "become an active opponent in order to 'redeem' himself among Republicans who were unhappy about his support of the Panama Canal Treaties."[19]

Reform supporters confronted other problems as well. The death of Hubert Humphrey in early January 1978 removed from the Congress one of the most eloquent champions and effective leaders of the reform effort. Then an early winter coal strike had generated significant public animosity toward organized labor. Finally, and unexpectedly, labor law reform generated almost as much emotional heat as the Panama Canal treaties. Actually, many senators reported receiving twice the mail on labor law reform that they did on Panama, and presidential mail on the subject ran almost ten to one against it.[20]

Nonetheless, a solid majority of senators appeared to favor the bill. The crucial question was whether the proponents had the necessary sixty votes to end an anti-labor filibuster. Ever cautious, Majority Leader Robert Byrd hesitated to bring the measure to the floor until he was sure he had the votes to invoke cloture. Victor Kamber, director of the AFL-CIO Task Force on Labor Law Reform, representatives of the Department of Labor, and vote counters in Alan Cranston's Senate office all believed they had at least sixty-three votes for cloture. Along with Senator Byrd, however, Frank Moore and his staff were less optimistic. They counted fifty-two solid votes on the first roll call and six additional votes on subsequent ballots.

The final vote would have to be garnered from among three "very shaky" senators who felt they already had been politically damaged by their Panama vote and, for the time being at least, wanted to avoid another unpopular vote. At the same time that Democratic leaders courted potential cloture votes, Republican Senators Orrin Hatch, Richard Lugar, John Tower, and Jesse Helms effectively organized the conservative effort "to talk the bill to death."[21]

Opponents focused their attack on three particularly sensitive issues that could easily be exploited for maximum partisan impact: the bill's supposedly injurious effect on small business; the short time period for the conduct of elections, which, it was argued, failed to provide employers adequate time to make their case against unionization; and the equal access provision's potentially adverse effect on an employer's property right. Nik Edes of the U.S. Department of Labor's Office of Legislation and Intergovernmental Relations provided the White House staff an ominous description of the legislative climate awaiting the bill. This reform has become, he said, "one of the most emotional issues to reach the Senate in years. The debate will be strident and bitter and it is going to require the best efforts of the Administration to help win a victory."[22]

Although still unsure about the cloture vote, Byrd announced that he would call up S. 2467 on May 15. Meanwhile, the president, who earlier had distanced himself from the legislation, now increased his efforts on its behalf. To rally support for labor law reform, he invited eighty-nine labor leaders, reformers, lawmakers, and reporters to a highly visible "Law Reform Breakfast" on May 9, where he told the bill's supporters: "You will have a strong, consistent partner in the White House." Indeed, as the decisive vote in the Senate loomed, the administration now increasingly characterized labor law reform as one of its major legislative objectives.[23]

Shortly after the Senate began consideration of the bill, the president made an unprecedented appearance before the Illinois state legislature to urge approval of the Equal Rights Amendment. During a ranging question and answer session following his brief formal address, Carter received several questions about labor law reform. The questioners expressed particular concern about the debarment of businesses (or the "blacklisting of businesses" as critical legislators phrased it) that violated federal law. The president responded by strongly reaffirming his support of the measure, including the debarment provision, which he argued was entirely reasonable. "There is some need for a threat of punishment to any person in this country who violates a law," he said, "and if business violates the laws of the United States, there has to be some threat of consequences adverse to that business." The usual punishment for such behavior, Carter reminded his audience, "is imprisonment and/or heavy fines."[24]

As the debate in the Senate heated up, the AFL-CIO intensified its effort to publicize the unethical and illegal practices of unscrupulous employers. The centerpiece of their campaign was a May 17 Labor Law Reform Rally held at Lafayette Park across the street from the White House and the Chamber of Commerce. Ray Marshall addressed the rally and was joined on the podium by such luminaries as Theodore Bikel, president of Actor's Equity, and Larry Brown, Kermit Alexander, and Ken Reeves of the National Football League. In the afternoon, a "Victim's Vigil" featured individuals who had been harmed by the injustices practiced by companies such as J. P. Stevens, telling their stories to a sympathetic throng of reform exponents. The next day, Victor Kamber led the "victims" and other union supporters on a march to the Capitol where they lobbied on behalf of the bill. The "vigil" was labor's response to a Chamber of Commerce effort to bring small-business men and women from key states to Washington to lobby their senators against the bill.[25]

The extent to which such rallies effectively counteracted the massive negative publicity generated by business groups is difficult to determine and perhaps immaterial, for the real decision on labor reform remained lodged in the hands of a relatively small group of senators who would determine the fate of labor law reform by voting for or against cloture. These swing senators had considerable leverage, and they used it to the fullest. Senator Ted Stevens, for example, wanted to hold up Senate consideration of an Alaskan wilderness bill strongly favored by environmentalists. Others wanted to be identified as the authors of key compromise amendments that would provide them a rationale for supporting cloture and the bill. Most got what they wanted. Meanwhile, as Labor Secretary Marshall had predicted, Senators Hatch, Lugar, Helms, and company avoided germane issues in their attacks on the bill and instead "concentrated on 'union bosses,' 'labor racketeering,' 'inflation,' 'destroying small business,' and other matters which go to the heart of our national policy of fostering industrial democracy."[26]

Majority Leader Byrd delayed the first cloture vote until June 7 to give proponents additional time to organize their forces. Still, only forty-two senators backed the first cloture effort, shocking reform advocates inside and outside the administration. Several senators who had promised to support cloture were absent, while others pledged to change their vote on some subsequent ballot. But the message was ominous; too many senators believed they had more to lose than to gain by supporting labor law reform. Even if they managed to invoke cloture, moreover, the administration's key legislative lobbyists worried that they might not have enough votes to pass S. 2467. Several senators had agreed to back cloture but said they could not risk a favorable vote on the legislation itself. Labor's friends in the Senate would also have to figure out how to break a post-cloture "filibuster by amendment," a tactic that had been developed by Senator James Allen of Alabama during the Panama Canal treaties debate. Orrin Hatch reportedly had over 500 amendments ready to introduce in the event that the filibuster was broken.[27]

On the second ballot, seven additional senators supported cloture, four of whom had been absent on the first vote and the other three as a result of Democratic senators who switched their votes. Still considerably short of the requisite number of votes needed to end debate, Senator Bryd, with the support of the bill's sponsors, offered a package of amendments that substantially weakened four of the bill's more important but controversial provisions. Fifty-four senators then voted for cloture on the third tally and on the subsequent vote four Republican senators joined the majority, bringing the count to fifty-eight. Another senator, probably Lawton Chiles of Florida, agreed to vote for cloture if the bill's supporters came up with the sixtieth vote. The search for that last vote ultimately centered on three southern Democrats, John Sparkman (Ala.), Dale Bumpers (Ark.), and Russell Long (La.), and a conservative midwestern senator, Edward Zorinsky (Neb.). But the administration and its labor allies never found that final vote, and after the fifth ballot, support for the measure began to disintegrate. At this point, Senator Byrd recommitted the bill to the Human Resources Committee where it died.[28]

Symbolically, the defeat marked the final demise of the postwar accord that had inhered in key industries since World War II. Beyond the industrial sector of relatively dense unionization, little tolerance for organized labor existed, and by the 1970s, even the labor movement's core constituency had begun to crumble. In the face of technological change, deregulation in communications and transportation, and intensified international competition, American industry became more cost conscious. In an increasingly internation-alized and competitive market economy, higher labor costs could no longer be passed along to consumers. To maintain profits, costs had to be reduced. Rather than making the necessary investment to boost productivity, American business attacked organized labor where it existed and resolved to maintain a union free environment elsewhere.[29]

These business stratagems set the context for the labor law revi-sion debate of 1978. Labor law reform cut against the corporate grain; anything that might empower labor in its effort to resist man-agement's cost-saving or profit-maximizing initiatives could not be tolerated. Thus, American business aligned itself with various right-wing reactionary groups to mount a massive campaign against it. Reacting to the accelerated decline of comity in industrial relations, Douglas Fraser dramatically announced his resignation from John Dunlop's prestigious Labor Management Group, the last and most visible manifestation of corporate liberalism and the postwar indus-trial accord. In his letter of resignation, the UAW leader, citing the "dishonest and ugly multimillion-dollar campaign" against the labor law reform bill, accused business leaders of waging "a one-sided class war against labor." Meanwhile, the AFL-CIO's Lane Kirkland advocated repeal of the National Labor Relations Act, concluding it not only had become meaningless to labor but an additional weapon in the hands of corporate America. Industrial pluralism, to the ex-tent that it had ever existed, indeed had died.[30]

ACKNOWLEDGMENT

The author wishes to thank Merl E. Reed, Robert H. Zieger, and Robert Asher for reading and commenting on earlier drafts of this essay.

───────────────────── NOTES ─────────────────────

1. For a provocative account of labor's declining political influence, see Michael Goldfield, *The Decline of Organized Labor in the United States*

(Chicago: University of Chicago Press, 1987). Two accounts that specifically relate labor's decline to labor law and the state are Melvyn Dubofsky, *The State and Labor in Modern America* (Chapel Hill: University of North Carolina Press, 1994), esp. chapter 8, and Joel Rogers, "In the Shadow of the Law: Institutional Aspects of Postwar U.S. Union Decline," in Christopher L. Tomlins and Andrew J. King, eds., *Labor Law in America: Historical and Critical Essays* (Baltimore: The Johns Hopkins University Press, 1992), 283–302. Industrial relations experts also envisioned a diminished role for organized labor. See, for example, Thomas A. Kochan, Harry Katz, and Robert McKersie, *The Transformation of American Industrial Relations* (New York: Basic Books, 1986); Charles C. Hecksher, *The New Unionism: Employee Involvement in the Changing Corporations* (New York: Basic Books, 1988); and Michael J. Piore and Charles J. Sabel, *The Second Industrial Divide: Possibilities for Prosperity* (New York: Basic Books, 1984).

2. The current interest in reform is reflected by the large turnout of union leaders, attorneys, legal scholars, and labor educators for a recent labor law conference co-sponsored by the AFL-CIO and Cornell University. See *Labor Education News*, UCLA Institute of Industrial Relations 3 (Winter 1994), 9–10. After years of relative obscurity, the history of labor law in recent years has attracted so much attention that practitioners in the field have taken to referring to the "new" and "old" labor law histories. For a discussion of the differences, see Wythe Holt, "The New American Labor Law History," *Labor History* 30 (Spring 1989): 275–93. See also, Karl Klare, "Labor Law as Ideology: Toward a New Historiography of Collective Bargaining Law," *Industrial Relations Law Journal* 4 (1981): 450–82. Along with such classics as Irving Bernstein, *The New Deal Collective Bargaining Policy* (Berkeley: University of California Press, 1950) and Harry A. Millis and Emily Clark Brown, *From the Wagner Act to Taft-Hartley: A Study of National Labor Policy and Labor Relations* (Chicago: University of Chicago Press, 1950), see James A. Gross, *The Making of the National Labor Relations Board: A Study in Economics, Politics, and Laws* (Albany, N.Y.: State University of New York Press, 1974), and *The Reshaping of the National Labor Relations Board: National Labor Policy in Transition* (Albany, N.Y.: State University of New York Press, 1981); Christopher L. Tomlins, *Law, Labor, and Ideology in the Early American Republic* (Cambridge: Cambridge University Press, 1993) and *The State and the Unions: Labor Relations, Law, and the Organized Labor Movement in America, 1880–1960* (Cambridge: Cambridge University Press, 1985); Tomlins and King, *Labor Law in America*; and William E. Forbath, *Law and the Shaping of the American Labor Movement* (Cambridge: Harvard University Press, 1991). For an account of recent efforts to reform labor law, see Martin Halpern, "Arkansas and the Defeat of Labor Law Reform in 1978 and 1994," unpublished paper read at the 1997 conference at the Jimmy Carter Library.

3. Tomlins, *The State and the Unions*; Dubofsky, *The State and Labor in Modern America*, and "Jimmy Carter and the End of the Politics of Productivity," forthcoming in Gary M. Fink and Hugh D. Graham, ed., *The Carter Presidency: Policy Choices in the Post New Deal Era* (Lawrence: University Press of Kansas, 1998). For a discussion of the industrial pluralist system and the centrality of labor to the liberal Democratic coalition, see David Plotke, *Building a Democratic Political Order: Reshaping American Liberalism in the 1930s and 1940s* (New York: Cambridge University Press, 1996), esp. chapters 4–8, and Karen Orren, "Union Politics and Postwar Liberalism in the United States," *Studies in American Political Development* 1 (1986): 215–52, and "Organized Labor and the Invention of Modern Liberalism in the United States," *Studies in American Political Development* 2 (1987): 317–64.

4. Patrick Anderson, *Electing Jimmy Carter: The Campaign of 1976* (Baton Rouge: Louisiana State University Press, 1994), provides an interesting account from an insider's perspective. See also Jules Witcover, *Marathon: The Pursuit of the Presidency* (New York: Viking Press, 1977); James Wooten, *Dasher: The Roots and the Rising of Jimmy Carter* (New York: Summit Books, 1978); Betty Glad, *Jimmy Carter: In Search of the Great White House* (W. W. Norton and Co., 1980); and Kandy Stroud, *How Jimmy Won: The Victory Campaign from Plains to the White House* (New York: William Morrow and Co., Inc., 1977). For a discussion of organized labor's role in the 1976 elections, see Gary M. Fink, "Fragile Alliance: Jimmy Carter and the American Labor Movement," and Taylor Dark, "Organized Labor and the Carter Administration: The Origins of Conflict," in Herbert D. Rosenbaum and Alexej Ugrinsky, ed., *Keeping Faith: The Presidency and Domestic Policies of Jimmy Carter* (Westport, Conn.: Greenwood Press, 1994), 783–803, 761–82.

5. Fink, "Fragile Alliance," 784–89, and "George Meany, Jimmy Carter, and the Failure of Democratic Party Constituency Politics," unpublished paper read at the 1994 annual meeting of the Organization of American Historians, Atlanta, Ga., April 14, 1994.

6. See Stephen Amberg's essay in this volume, pp. 241. For a critical study of Carter's presidency, see Burton I. Kaufman, *The Presidency of James Earl Carter, Jr.* (Lawrence: University Press of Kansas, 1993). Two recently published biographies also contain interesting analyses of Carter and his administration: Kenneth E. Morris, *Jimmy Carter: American Moralist* (Athens: University of Georgia Press, 1996), and Peter G. Bourne, *Jimmy Carter: A Comprehensive Biography from Plains to Postpresidency* (New York: Scribner, 1997).

7. For a general discussion of the state of labor law in 1978, see William B. Gould IV, *A Primer on American Labor Law*, 3d ed. (Cambridge: MIT Press, 1993), esp. chapter 7.

8. Most writers on Carter acknowledge his disdain for special interest groups, but Edwin C. Hargrove puts it at the core of his analysis in *Jimmy Carter as President: Leadership and the Politics of the Public Good* (Baton Rouge: Louisiana State University Press, 1988). Charles O. Jones adopts a similar emphasis in *The Trusteeship Presidency: Jimmy Carter and the United States Congress* (Baton Rouge: Louisiana State University Press, 1988).

9. "Press Briefing by F. Ray Marshall, Secretary of Labor, and Carin Ann Clauss, Solicitor, Office of the Secretary of Labor," July 18, 1977, Landon Butler Papers, Box 112, Folder Labor Law, 1979 [1], Jimmy Carter Library.

10. Stuart Eizenstat to Carter, June 30, 1977, Folder 7/13/77 [1], Box 37, Staff Secretary File, Jimmy Carter Library.

11. Hamilton Jordan to Carter, n.d. [approx. July 1, 1977], Folder Labor Law, 1977 [1], Box 112, Landon Butler Papers.

12. Jerry J. Jasinowski to Eizenstat, July 8, 1977, and Eizenstat to Bill Johnston, July 11, 1977, Folder 7/13/77 [1], Box 37; Bert Lance to Carter, n.d., Charles Schultze to Carter, June 30, 1977, and Walter Mondale to Carter, June 30, 1977, Folder 7/1/77 [1], Box 35, Staff Secretary File.

13. Eizenstat and Johnston to Carter, July 11, 1977, Folder 7/13/77 [1], Box 37, Staff Secretary File.

14. Ibid.

15. Eizenstat to Carter, July 17, 1977, Folder 7/18/77 [2], Box 37; Eizenstat to Carter, August 1, 1977, Folder 8/1/77 [2], Box 41, Staff Secretary File; "Press Briefing by F. Ray Marshall, Secretary of Labor, and Carin Ann Clauss, Solicitor, Office of the Secretary of Labor," July 18, 1977, Folder Labor Law, 1979 [1], Box 112, Landon Butler Papers; *New York Times*, July 19, 1977; *AFL-CIO News*, July 23, 1977.

16. Eizenstat to Carter, August 1, 1977, Folder 8/1/77 [2], Box 41, Staff Secretary File.

17. *AFL-CIO News*, September 10, 17, October 8, 1977; *Congressional Quarterly*, October 8, 1977, 2123, 2124.

18. "Labor Law Reform and Its Enemies," *The Nation*, January 6–13, 1979.

19. *Congressional Quarterly*, February 11, 1978, 330, 331, and May 6, 1978, 1097, 1098; Frank Moore to Carter, April 8, 1978, Folder 4/10/78 [2], Box 79, Staff Secretary File; Nik Edes to Landon Butler, Laurie Lucey, and Bill Johnston, May 5, 1978, Box 113, Landon Butler Papers. See also *AFL-CIO News*, December 17, 1977.

20. Moore to Carter, April 8, 1978, Folder 4/10/78 [2], Box 79; Moore to Carter, April 22, 1978, Folder 4/24/78 [2], Box 82, Staff Secretary File; Hugh Carter to Carter, January 13, 1978, Folder 2/24/78, Box 74, Jimmy Carter Library.

21. Moore to Carter, April 22, 1978, Folder 4/24/78 [2], Box 82; Moore to Carter, April 30, 1978, Folder 5/1/78 [No. 1], Box 83, Staff Secretary Files; Nik Edes to Landon Butler, Laurie Lucey, and Bill Johnston, May 5, 1978, Box 113, Landon Butler Papers.

22. Nik Edes to Landon Butler, et al, May 5, 1978, Folder 4/27/78–10/5/78, Box 113, Butler Papers.

23. Butler to Carter, May 9, 1978, Folder 5/9/78, Box 84, Staff Secretary File; *AFL-CIO News*, May 6, 13, 1978.

24. *AFL-CIO News*, June 3, 1978.

25. AFL-CIO Press Release, May 15, 1978, Vertical File, Labor Law Reform Folder, George Meany Memorial Archives, Washington, D.C. Ray Marshall had earlier urged the president to hold a "meeting with victims" at the White House to publicize his support of reform. In this case, Stuart Eizenstat advised against such a meeting, arguing that this ploy would not change any critical votes in the Senate and "from a national standpoint the less visible you are on this divisive issue, the better." Eizenstat to Carter, May 11, 1978, Folder 5/9/78, Box 84, Staff Secretary File.

26. Marshall to Carter, May 19, 1978, Folder 5/20/78, Box 85, Staff Secretary File.

27. Frank Moore and Bob Thomson to Carter, June 8, 1978, Folder 6/8/78, Box 92, and Frank Moore and Bob Thomson to Carter, June 9, 1978, Folder 6/9/78, Box 92, Staff Secretary File.

28. Moore and Thomson to Carter, June 9, 19, 1978, Folders 6/9/78 and 6/20/78, and Eizenstat and Johnston to Carter and Moore to Carter, June 19, 1978, Folder 6/20/78, Box 87, Staff Secretary File; *Congressional Quarterly*, June 17, 24, 1978, 1519, 1520, 1599; *Congressional Quarterly Almanac 1978*, 284–87.

29. For an elaboration of this argument, see Rogers, "In the Shadow of the Law," 283–302.

30. Dubofsky, *The State and Labor in Modern America*, 227; *Washington Post*, July 20, 1978; *New York Times*, July 20, 1978. The Labor Management Group was formed during the Nixon administration and continued thereafter on a semi-official basis under the leadership of John Dunlop. Along with the leadership of the AFL-CIO, United Automobile Workers, and the International Brotherhood of Teamsters, it included officials from such companies as General Electric, General Motors Corporation, Du Pont, Sears Roebuck, Mobil Oil, Bechtel, and First National City Bank of New York. For a discussion of business's political activism, see David Vogel, *Fluctuating Fortunes: The Political Power of Business in America* (New York: Basic Books, 1989).

Contributors

Stephen Amberg received the Ph.D. in political science from the Massachusetts Institute of Technology in 1987. He is an associate professor in the Division of Social and Policy Sciences at the University of Texas at San Antonio. He is the author of *The Union Inspiration in American Politics* (Philadelphia: Temple University Press, 1994) and of articles and reviews in social science, history, and labor studies journals.

Robert Asher is professor of history at the University of Connecticut. He is general editor of the series in American Labor History published by the State University of New York Press. He is the author of *Concepts in American History* (New York: HarperCollins, 1996) and co-editor of *Autowork* (Albany, N.Y.: SUNY Press, 1995).

Kevin Boyle is an associate professor of history at the University of Massachusetts, Amherst. He is the author of *The UAW and the Heyday of American Liberalism, 1945–1968* (Ithaca: Cornell University Press, 1995) and co-author, with Victoria Getis, of *Muddy Boots and Ragged Aprons: Images of Working-Class Detroit, 1900–1930* (Detroit: Wayne State University Press, 1997).

Gary M. Fink is professor of history at Georgia State University. His most recent books include *The Fulton Bag and Cotton Mill Strike, 1914–1915* (Ithaca: ILR Press, 1993) and *Race, Class, and Community in Southern Labor History* (Tuscaloosa, Ala: University of Alabama Press, 1994). His co-edited book, *The Carter Presidency: Policy Choices in the Post New Deal Era*, will be released in 1998.

Gilbert J. Gall is an associate professor of labor studies and industrial relations at Penn State University. He is the author of *The Politics of Right to Work* (Westport, Conn.: Greenwood, 1988) and has published articles in such journals as *The Historian*, *Labor Studies Journal*, and *Labor History*. He has just completed a full-length biography of CIO general counsel Lee Pressman.

Julie Greene received her Ph.D. from Yale University. She is currently assistant professor of history at the University of Colorado at Boulder, where her teaching focuses on U.S. labor and political history. She is the author of *Pure and Simple Unionism: The American Federation of Labor and Political Mobilization, 1881 to 1917* (New York: Cambridge University Press, 1998).

Bruce Nelson teaches history at Dartmouth College. He is the author of *Workers on the Waterfront: Seamen, Longshoremen, and Unionism in the 1930s* (Urbana: University of Illinois Press, 1988). He is completing a book on organized labor and the struggle for black equality in the United States.

Richard Oestreicher is an associate professor of history at the University of Pittsburgh. He is the author of *Solidarity and Fragmentation: Working People and Class Consciousness in Detroit, 1875–1900* (Urbana: University of Illinois Press, 1986) and "Urban Working-Class Poltical Behavior and Theories of American Electoral Politics, 1870–1940," *Journal of American History* 74 (1988). He is nearing completion of a social history of American working people from 1790 to 1850.

Peter Rachleff is professor and chairperson of the History Department at Macalester College, where he has taught since 1982. He is the author of *Black Labor in Richmond, Virginia, 1865–1890* (Urbana: University of Illinois Press, 1989) and *Hard-Pressed in the Heartland: The Hormel Strike and the Future of the American Labor Movement* (Boston: South End Press, 1993), as well as essays on the Knights of Labor, Croatian immigrants, and packinghouse workers. His essay in this volume is drawn from a larger work in progress, tentatively titled, "Organizing From Wall to Wall: The Independent Union of All Workers, 1933–1937."

Index

Adams, Kacy, 86
Adamson Act (1916), 84–85, 87, 92, 99 n. 32
affirmative action, 29, 174, 181, 182, 183
African-Americans, 5, 10, 28, 40, 89, 183, 196, 204, 220, 222, 230; discrimination against, 27, 181, 196, 204–05; migration to north, 42, 145; right-to-work movements and, 195, 204–06, 207, 208–09, 210, 212; voting patterns of, 28, 38, 40–41, 146, 227, 195, 196, 210; workers, 21, 73, 81, 93, 123, 141, 143, 144, 181, 182, 205, 212. *See also* affirmative action; civil rights; civil rights movement; racial conflict
Albert Lea Employees Labor Association, 112
Alexander, Kermit, 250
Allen, James, 251
Amalgamated Association of Iron, Steel, and Tin Workers, 52, 56. *See also* iron- and steelworkers
American Agricultural Movement, 209

American Alliance for Labor and Democracy, 93–94
American Association for Labor Legislation, 78, 82
American Federation of Labor (AFL): anti-statism of, 6, 72, 75, 76, 77, 80, 82, 92, 93, 149 n.13; conflict with CIO, 7, 107, 111–12, 114, 124–27, 144; conservatism of, 73, 127; Democratic Party and, 72, 73, 74–76, 88, 90, 91, 92, 93, 94, 95, 170; discriminatory practices of, 73, 85; labor law and, 74, 75, 77–78, 85; Labor's League for Political Education, 164; membership in, 94, 146; Minnesota Farmer-Labor Party and, 104; 1937 Detroit municipal elections and, 122, 124; UAW and, 9, 207, 244–45. *See also* CIO; Detroit and Wayne County Federation of Labor; UAW
American Federation of Labor-Congress of Industrial Organizations (AFL-CIO): Committee on Political Education (COPE), 164, 171, 174, 176–77, 179; Democratic

261

Party and, 165, 172, 174, 176–77, 183, 184, 241–42, 244; divisions within, 9, 164, 183; economic planning and, 227; free trade and, 184; in Indiana, 198; Industrial Union Department (IUD), 174, 200–01; labor law reform and, 10, 200–01, 207, 244, 245, 246, 247, 248, 250, 252; leadership of, 1, 11, 212; merger, 171, 180, 181; in Ohio, 203–04; organizing campaigns, 11; post-1955 politics and, 1, 11, 164, 172, 174, 176–77, 180, 199, 241, 242. *See also* civil rights; UAW
American revolution, 54, 57
Americans for Democratic Action (ADA), 221, 170, 174
anarchism and anarchists, 2
artisan republicanism, 2, 5, 54–55, 65
artisans, 25, 53–54, 55, 59
Automotive Industrial Workers Association (AIWA), 131, 132, 141

Baker, Charles, 203–04
Baker, Howard, 248
balance of payments, 180
banking and financial reform, 37
Barkan, Al, 183
Barth, Joe, 60
Benson, Alan, 90
Benson, Elmer, 113, 114–15
Bernstein, Irving, 145
Bikel, Theodore, 250
Boone, Richard, 226
Brandeis, Louis, 83
Brody, David, 7
Brookwood Labor College, 220
Brophy, John, 121, 139, 140
Brotherhood of Locomotive Firemen and Engineers, 88

Brotherhood of Sleeping Car Porters, 223
Brown, Joe, 137, 139
Brown, Larry, 250
Bryan, William Jennings, 71, 74–75, 77, 90
Bumpers, Dale, 251
Burdelow, A., 64
Burleigh, Edward, 59–60
Burr Agency, 203
Business Roundtable, 246, 247
Byrd, Robert, 239, 248, 249, 250–51

Canak, William, 197
Capra, Frank, 39
Carnegie Corporation, 56
Carter, Jimmy, 9, 10, 239–40, 241, 242–47, 249–50, 251; wage-price policy of, 181
Catton, Bruce, 167
Chiles, Lawton, 251
Christian American Association, 197
Chrysler Corporation, 168; Dodge Main Plant (Hamtramck, Mich.), 132
Citizens' Crusade Against Poverty (CCAP), 225–26, 228
civil rights, 9–10, 123, 173–74, 182, 183, 203, 227; AFL-CIO and, 181, 182, 183, 185; CIO and, 181, 185; Democratic Party and, 3, 26–28, 29, 40, 84, 89, 171–172, 182, 183, 218, 222; fifteenth amendment (1870), 30; integration of skilled trades, 180, 181, 182; UAW and, 129–30, 143, 146, 181, 220, 221–23. *See also* African-Americans; civil rights movement; racial conflict; UAW
Civil Rights Act (1964), 181, 182

civil rights movement, 40, 172, 173, 181, 221–22, 227. *See also* African-Americans; civil rights; racial conflict

Civil War, 54, 56

class conflict, 19, 25, 26, 34, 37, 38, 44, 111, 132, 135–36, 168–69, 185, 201, 252; electoral rules and, 31, 32; producerism and, 51, 57–58, 59, 62, 64. *See also* working class

Clayton Antitrust Act (1914), 77, 85

Clinton, Bill, 1, 41, 159, 160

closed (union) shop, 240

Cold War, 3

collective bargaining: bureaucratization of New Deal system, 26, 169, 173; decline of New Deal system, 25, 43, 159–60, 162, 174, 183, 184, 186, 212, 240, 251–52; Independent Union of All Workers and, 110, 111; limits of New Deal system, 26, 163, 185; New Deal system, 3, 8, 26, 27, 36, 37, 160, 161, 162–63, 164, 166, 167, 170, 172, 173, 180–81, 182, 185, 186, 189 n.21, 218, 239, 242–43. *See also* closed shop; common situs picketing; Democratic Party; labor law; open shop; Republican Party

Commission on Industrial Relations (CIR), 78–81, 82, 85, 86, 94

Commission on the Future of Worker-Management Relations, 159–60

Committee on Industrial Relations, 81–82

common situs picketing, 240, 241, 244, 247

Communication Workers of America (CWA), 244

communism and communists, 2, 107, 108, 109, 111, 114, 137; anti-communism, 141, 171, 173, 218, 220

Communist Party of the United States (CPUSA), 95, 104, 107, 109, 112, 113, 128, 138, 141. *See also* CIO; Minnesota Farmer-Labor Party

Communist Party Opposition (CPO), 138

Community Action Program (CAP), 217, 225, 226, 229

Conference on Economic Progress, 174

congress. *See* U.S. Congress

Congress of Industrial Organizations (CIO), 65; Communist Party and, 95, 112, 113, 114; conflict with AFL, 7, 107, 111–12, 114, 124–27, 144, 167, 184, 185; Democratic Party and, 3, 8–9, 26, 95, 121–22, 160–61, 169–73, 184–85, 218; in Indiana, 198; interpretations of, 169, 217–18; membership in, 42, 146; Minnesota Farmer-Labor Party and, 104; 1937 Detroit municipal elections and, 121, 123, 124–27, 133, 134; 1945 Detroit municipal elections and, 146; Political Action Committee (PAC), 164; organizing campaigns of, 114, 134, 172; role in 1930s politics, 95, 121–22, 160–61; role in 1940–1950s politics, 8–10, 160–61, 169–70, 172, 185; social democracy and, 166–67. *See also* AFL, civil rights

Congress on Racial Equality (CORE), 221

Conway, Jack, 222, 225

corporations: de-regulation of, 183; government policy toward, 28–29, 35, 36, 37, 163, 166–67, 183, 184, 185, 224; successful versus unsuccessful, 4, 35. *See also* de-industrialization; labor law, business influence on
Coughlin, Rev. Charles, 38, 127, 131, 132, 141, 151 n.24
Cranston, Alan, 248
crime, 41, 42, 43

Davis, Ben I., 62
Davis, John W., 38
Davis, Mike, 127
Dawley, Alan, 218
Debs, Eugene, 2, 62, 85
de-industrialization, 23; industries' movement to south, 173
Democratic Farmer-Labor Party (DFL), 103, 115. *See also* Minnesota Farmer-Labor Party
Democratic Party, 19, 29, 34, 35, 36, 165, 174, 176; business and, 88, 89–90, 165, 185; Catholics and, 34, 38, 42; Coalition for a Democratic Majority, 183; decline in 1970s–1990s, 1, 26, 27, 29, 40–43, 174, 177; ethnic groups and, 38–39, 41–42; labor unions in the 1930s and 1940s and, 3, 6–9, 22, 26, 27, 35, 37, 95, 121, 144, 160, 161, 166, 184–85; labor unions in the post-World War II era and, 3–4, 8–9, 10–11, 26, 27, 162, 164, 166, 167, 169–70, 171–173, 174, 180, 183, 184–186, 198, 218–19, 221, 239–42, 243, 244; labor unions in the progressive era and, 2–3, 6, 71–78, 82, 83–93, 94, 95; labor law reform and, 3, 6, 8, 37–39,

73–74, 75, 83, 84, 87–88, 92, 94, 167, 171, 177, 181, 240–41, 247, 249; liberal wing of, 7, 26, 28, 37, 42, 170, 171, 174, 176, 227; "New Politics" wing of, 183; southern wing of, 26, 27, 34, 38, 39, 40, 41, 171–72, 185, 221, 227. *See also* AFL; civil rights; racial conflict; UAW
demonstrations and rallies, 87, 123, 131, 222
Detroit and Wayne County Federation of Labor (DFL), 124, 125, 126
Detroit Building Council, 124
Doll, Tracy, 128, 136, 142
domestic workers, 21, 27
Douglas, Paul, 27, 28
downsizing, 23
Draper, Alan, 176–177
Dubofsky, Melvyn, 240
Dunne, Ray, 108

Eastman, Max, 91–92
Eaton, Thomas, 54
economic expansion: post-1930s, 19, 173, 174, 180; slowing in 1970s–1990s, 19, 23–24, 183
economic globalization, 3, 20, 28–29, 159, 161, 174, 184, 186, 251–52
economic planning, 8–9, 37, 166, 183, 220, 221, 224, 227. *See also* AFL-CIO; social democracy; Reuther, Walter, ideology of
Edes, Nik, 249
education, 24
eight-hour day, 75, 78, 83, 84, 85, 87, 92
Eisenhower, Dwight, 39, 198, 199
Eizenstat, Stuart, 244, 245
elections, congressional: 1906 elections, 74; 1908 elections, 74; 1912

elections, 31; 1950 elections, 28; 1958 elections, 198; 1960s and 1970s elections, 173; 1994 elections, 1, 43
elections, gubernatorial: 1930–36 Minnesota elections, 103, 115; 1938 Minnesota election, 104, 105
elections, municipal, 32; 1937 Detroit elections, 7–8, 122–45; 1943 Detroit elections, 28; 1945 Detroit elections, 28, 146–47
elections, presidential: 1896 election, 71, 92, 106; 1900 election, 91; 1904 election, 61; 1908 election, 74–76, 83; 1912 election, 31, 61–62, 83, 91; 1916 election, 6, 71, 82, 83–92, 95, 106; 1920 election, 94; 1924 election, 94–95; 1924–1936 elections, 39; 1932 election, 36; 1932–1948 elections, 19; 1936 election, 38, 92, 95, 104, 107, 121, 132, 133; 1948 election, 39, 44 n.1, 172; 1952 election, 172; 1956 election, 172, 198; 1960 election, 42, 173, 180; 1964 election, 40, 177, 227; 1968 election, 41, 181; post-1968 elections, 19, 41, 43; 1972 election, 40; 1976 election, 241; 1980 election, 44 n.1, 243; 1988 election, 44 n.1; 1992 election, 41, 43
electoral system: coalitions within, 4, 25, 30, 31, 32–33, 38, 72, 161; rules of, 4, 20, 30–33, 43, 161–62, 163–64, 165, 170; U.S. system versus parliamentary system, 30–31, 33
Ellis, Frank, 106, 107–08, 109, 110, 111, 112, 113
employment: policies on, 163, 180, 183, 190 n.33, 223

Equal Employment Opportunity Commission (EEOC), 182
Equal Rights Amendment (ERA), 249
Erlich, Mark, 211
ethnic groups, 5, 41–42, 93, 122–23, 132; German-Americans, 91, 93, 127; Irish-Americans, 40, 93, 127; Jewish-Americans, 38; nativism; 33–34, 38, 63, 131–32, 141; Polish-Americans, 40, 123, 132, 138, 142–43, 147; southern and eastern European-Americans, 38; white Anglo-Saxon Protestants, 33, 143. *See also* working class, divisions within
Ettor, Joseph, 86
Ewald, Robert, 124

Farm Bureau Federation, 197
farmer-labor alliance, 71, 80, 90, 103, 105, 196, 207–08, 209–10. *See also* Minnesota Farmer-Labor Party
farmers, 21, 25, 27, 59, 115, 196, 208; tenant, 37, 81, 89
Federal Housing Authority (FHA), 27
Federal Reserve System, 164
Fellner, Kim, 210
Ferguson, Thomas, 247
Fischer, Ben, 129, 134
Fitzpatrick, John, 81
Flynn, Elizabeth Gurley, 86
Folan, Eddie, 109–10
Forbath, William, 74
Ford Foundation, 226
Ford Motor Company, 143–44; River Rouge Plant (Dearborn, Mich.), 144
Ford, Gerald, 181, 241, 244
Fordism, 163

Foster, William Z., 79
Frankensteen, Richard, 124, 127, 128, 130–32, 135, 136, 137, 140, 142, 146, 147
Fraser, Douglas, 252
Fraser, Steve, 127
Friedlander, Peter, 132
Furuseth, Andrew, 77

G.I. Bill (1944), 23
Gallagher, Daniel, 139
Garretson, Austin, 78
gay rights, 41
General Federation of Women's Clubs, 82
General Motors Corporation, 65, 123, 135, 137, 163, 168; Ternstedt plant (Detroit, Mich.), 138
Germer, Adolph, 136, 138
Godfredson, Svend, 109, 112, 114
Goldman, Emma, 86
Goldwater, Barry, 40, 199, 227
Gompers, Samuel, 2, 6, 72, 73, 74, 75, 76, 77, 78, 80, 81, 82, 83, 85, 89, 92, 93, 95, 99 n.32
Graham, Frank, 28
Great Depression, 35, 36, 37, 44, 160, 161
Great Society, 26, 27, 224, 225, 230; UAW and, 10, 217–19, 224–231. *See also* Johnson, Lyndon
Green, William, 124
Greer, L. Matt ("Hugo the Third," "Jack Frost"), 58, 60, 61, 64
Griffiths, W. J., 57

Hall, Ed, 137
Harriman, Florence, 79
Harrington, Michael, 222
Harvey, William, 86
Hatch, Orrin, 249, 250, 251
health care reform, 19–20, 21, 78; Medicare/Medicaid, 177

Helms, Jesse, 249, 250
Hencks, "Old Dad," 57
Hill, Herbert, 172
Hispanic Americans, 41, 42, 81, 181
Hoenig, Joseph, 60
Holloway, John, 29
Homestead, Penn.: voters in, 38–39
Hoover, Herbert, 36
Hopkins, Harry, 134
Hormel Corporation, 103, 104, 105; Austin, Minn., plant, 108, 109, 110, 112, 113
House, Edward, 89
Howe, Frederic, 81
Hughes, Charles Evans, 87, 88, 90, 91
Hughes, Langston, 39
human relations programs, 167, 168–69
Humphrey, Hubert, 41, 103, 115, 170, 226, 241, 242, 247, 248

Illinois Conference of Small Business, 199
immigration, 41; restrictions on, 81, 85
Industrial Workers of the World (IWW), 62, 79, 85, 94, 104, 107–08, 109
industry councils, 166–67, 220. *See also* social democracy; workers' participation in management
inflation, 180
Ingersol, Robert, 62
Independent Union of All Workers (IUAW), 7, 104, 106, 107, 108, 109, 110–14; collective bargaining and, 110, 111; community activism of, 110–11; decline of, 111–14; locals of, 110; 1937 Albert Lea sit-down strikes and, 112–13; political action of, 110, 111
initiative and referendum, 52, 60

International Association of Machinists (IAM), 73, 244
International Brotherhood of Electrical Workers (IBEW), 205, 212
International Brotherhood of Teamsters, 9, 103, 113, 114, 184, 207; Local 574 (Minneapolis, Minn.), 107, 108, 109, 114
International Gas, Coke, and Chemical Workers Union, 114
International Typographical Union, 126
International Union of Oil, Chemical, and Atomic Workers, 114
iron- and steelworkers, 5–6, 52–53, 67 n.3, 114; background of, 56; craft versus industrial unionization of, 63; distrust of party politics, 60–61, 65; producerism and, 52, 53, 57–65. *See also* Amalgamated Association of Iron, Steel, and Tin Workers; United Steelworkers of America

J. P. Stevens Company, 250
Jackson, Henry, 241
Javits, Jacob, 246
Jeffries, Edward, 28, 146–47
Jensen, Andrew, 63
Johnson, Lyndon, 10, 26, 39, 40, 177, 180–81, 217, 221, 223–24, 225, 226, 227, 228, 229, 230, 235 n.16. *See also* Great Society; Kennedy-Johnson wage-price policy
Jones, Mary ("Mother"), 91
Jordan, Hamilton, 244
Justice on the Job, 247

Kamber, Victor, 248, 250
Katznelson, Ira, 26, 218, 219, 224
Keating-Owen Child Labor Act (1916), 83, 88

Kennedy, Edward, 241, 243
Kennedy, John, 39, 42, 173, 180–81, 221, 223, 226
Kennedy, Robert, 222
Kennedy-Johnson wage-price policy, 180–181
Kennerly, J. A., 64
Keynesian economics, 37, 66, 163, 180, 220
Keyserling, Leon, 37
King, Rev. Martin Luther, Jr., 208–09, 227
Kirkland, Lane, 242, 252
Knights of Labor, 2
Knudsen, William, 135
Kohler, Herbert V., 200
Kohli, Peter, 62
Korean War, 221
Kovacic, Matt, 109–10
Krebs, Juanita, 245
Krugman, Paul, 24
Kryczki, Leo, 123–24
Ku Klux Klan, 129, 141, 143

labor law: business influence on, 10, 26, 73–74, 87, 167, 197, 199, 200, 203, 246–47, 248, 250, 251, 252; courts and, 74, 94, 186, 240; reform of, 10, 20, 80, 83, 183, 199, 207, 211, 239–52; state governments and, 9, 103, 163, 195–98, 199, 203–10; unions' influence on, 10, 74, 75, 77–78, 177, 196–97, 200–212, 240–41, 242, 243, 244, 247. *See also* AFL; AFL-CIO; closed shop; collective bargaining; common situs picketing; Democratic Party; open shop; Republican Party; U.S. Congress
Labor Law Revision Bill (1978), 239–52
labor-liberal alliance, 220; in progressive era, 6, 72–73, 76, 82, 83,

86, 90, 92, 93; in 1930s, 6–8, 37, 42; in 1940s–1950s, 8–10, 170–71, 201–04; in 1960s–1970s, 9, 10–11, 174, 177, 180, 181, 183, 196, 223–31, 240, 242–43; interpretions of, 1, 2–11, 217–19, 230–31. *See also* Democratic Party; liberalism and liberals; middle class

Labor-Management Conference, 167

Labor-Management Relations Act. *See* Taft-Hartley Act

Labor-Management Group, 252, 257 n.30

labor party, 4, 31, 32, 33, 75, 111, 170; proposals for, 124

Labor's Non-Partisan League, 122

LaFollette, Robert, 94–95

LaFollette Seamen's Act, 77

Lance, Bert, 245

League for Industrial Democracy, 122, 217

Lamoureux, P., 63

Latimer, Ira, 199–200

Lehman, Herbert, 200

Leiserson, William, 37

Lennon, John, 76, 78, 81, 88

LeSueur, Arthur, 86

Lewis, John L., 65–66, 121, 136, 138, 166, 167

liberalism and liberals, 2, 3, 4, 9–10, 26, 27, 28, 35, 37, 76, 80, 82, 89, 92, 170–71, 172, 174, 177, 178, 196, 200, 220, 227, 230, 241. *See also* Democratic Party, liberal wing of; labor-liberal alliance; middle class

Liberty League, 38

Lichtenstein, Nelson, 7, 217–18

Liggett, Walter, 105–06, 111

Lilly, Richard C., 105, 117 n.8

Lincoln, Abraham, 55

Long, Russell, 251

Lovestone, Jay, 138

Lubell, Samuel, 40

Lugar, Richard, 249, 250

Manley, Basil, 79–80, 82

Marot, Helen, 81

Marshall, Ray, 243–44, 245, 246, 250

Martel, Francis Xavier (Frank), 124, 126, 127, 133

Martin, Homer, 124, 133, 136, 137–40, 142, 145, 151 n.24, 153 n.38

McAdoo, William, 89

McGovern, John, 60–61

McGovern, Michael, 64

Meany, George, 174, 183, 200, 242

meat packers, 107, 108. *See also* United Packinghouse Workers of America

media: and elections, 32–33

Meier, August, 146

middle class, 8, 20, 32, 37, 134, 142, 144, 147, 182; liberals, 196, 220

Miller, Berkeley, 197

Milliken, Roger, 199

minimum wage legislation, 22

Minnesota Farmer-Labor Party (FLP), 7, 103–04, 105, 106–07, 114–15; Communist Party and, 112; Democratic Party and, 103, 105, 107, 115; Independent Union of All Workers and, 110, 111; 1937 Albert Lea sit-down strikes and, 113; Republican Party and, 105. *See also* CIO; Democratic Farmer-Labor Party

Mitchell, James P., 199

Model Cities Act (1966), 228–29, 237 nn.29, 31

Mondale, Walter, 241, 242, 245, 247

Montgomery, David, 54

Mooney, Tom, 79
Moore, Frank, 248
Mortimer, Wyndham, 137, 139, 140, 144
municipal ownership, 78, 79, 82, 129
Murphy, Frank, 128, 132, 142, 144, 149 n.13, 151 n.24
Murphy, Joseph, 64
Murray, Philip, 185
Muse, Vance, 197
Myre, Helmer, 112, 113

National Association for the Advancement of Colored People (NAACP), 28, 145, 146, 221
National Association of Colored Women, 82
National Association of Manufacturers (NAM), 74, 167, 168, 197, 247
National Child Labor Committee, 82
National Consumers' League, 82
National Council for Industrial Peace (NCIP), 200, 205
National Defense Advisory Commission, 166
National Farmers' Union, 209
National Housing Act (1949), 27
National Industrial Recovery Act (1933): section 7(a), 36
National Labor Relations Act (1935), 20, 21, 22, 27, 37, 167, 168, 239, 241, 252
National Labor Relations Board (NLRB), 20, 26, 27, 37, 168, 171, 244, 245
National Labor Relations Board v. Denver Building and Construction Trades Council (1951), 240
National Planning Association, 174
National Right to Work Committee (NRTWC), 199–200, 247

National Urban League, 174
National War Labor Board (NWLB), 62, 94
Nestor, Agnes, 81, 88
New Deal order (1932–80): agendas of, 5, 21–23, 25, 37, 38, 44, 49 n.40, 219; criticism of, 3, 7, 10–11, 20–21, 25–27, 28, 37, 130, 144; interest group politics of, 36, 164, 171; New Deal coalition, 1, 3, 5, 11, 25, 26–27, 28, 35, 36, 38, 39, 40, 41, 42–43, 121–22, 123, 133, 147, 182, 183, 219, 230. *See also* collective bargaining; Democratic Party; Roosevelt, Franklin; working class, voting patterns of
new left, 169, 230. *See also* Students for a Democratic Society
Nilson, Carl, 108, 109, 110
Nixon, Richard, 41, 173, 241; wage freeze and, 181
North Dakota Non-Partisan League, 105–06
Nowak, Stanley, 138, 142

O'Brien, Patrick Henry, 121, 126, 128, 129, 130, 135, 142
O'Connell, James, 76, 78, 81
O'Connell, Tom, 114
Ohioans for Right to Work (ORTW), 203, 204
Oliver, Eli, 122, 135
Olson, Floyd, 104–06, 112
O'Neill, William, 204
open shop, 74, 82, 94. *See also* collective bargaining; labor law; right-to-work movements
Order of Railroad Telegraphers, 88

Packinghouse Workers Organizing Committee. *See* United Packinghouse Workers of America

Panama Canal treaties (1978), 243, 247–48, 249, 251

Palmer, A. Mitchell, 94

Pepper, Claude, 28

Perkin, Harold, 51–52

Perot, H. Ross, 43

Phillips, Kevin, 23, 41

Pickert, Heinrich, 129

Pinchot, Amos, 81

Pinkston, Theodore, 205–06, 212

Plotke, David, 28

political economy, 35, 37, 173, 186; Democratic Party and, 49 n.40, 165, 184; interpretations of, 20–21, 25, 28–29, 159–62, 217–18; Republican Party and, 184

producerism, 4, 5, 66, 86–87, 166, 185–86; artisan republicanism and, 57, 61, 62; Christian socialism and, 57–58; consumerism and, 65–66; decline of, 65–66; definition of, 51–52; origins of, 53–56; single tax and, 59–60; unionization and, 63

Progressive ("Bull Moose") Party, 77

Quinn, Pat, 132

racial conflict, 4, 20, 33, 40–42, 44, 182, 185, 230; Democratic Party and, 26–28, 40–43, 174, 183, 218–19; in 1930s Detroit, 123, 129–30, 141; in 1940s Detroit, 8, 145–47. *See also* African-Americans; Ku Klux Klan; white workers

Radic, Stjepan, 109

radicalism and radicals, 5, 7, 27, 86, 114; anti-radicalism and red-baiting, 32, 37, 64, 94, 113, 127, 131, 133, 146

railroad brotherhoods, 83–84, 85, 86, 87, 88

Randolph, A. Philip, 208

Rauh, Joseph, 223

Reading, Richard W., 126, 133, 135, 142, 143

Reagan, Ronald, 184, 230

redistribution of wealth, 3, 19, 21–24, 25, 37, 43, 45 n.6, 55, 80, 86, 183, 224; multiple wage earner families and, 24, 43; young families and, 24

Reeves, Ken, 250

Republican Party, 19, 29, 34, 36, 39, 40, 74, 75, 90, 94, 165, 176, 177; business and, 165, 184, 185; labor law reform and, 167, 248, 249, 250–51; labor unions and, 2–3, 75–76, 87, 198; nativism and, 34, 38, 42; progressive wing, 82, 171, 198; resurgence in 1970s–1990s, 1, 3, 20, 29, 40–43, 44, 174, 177, 180, 212; in sunbelt states, 42

Reuther, Roy, 137

Reuther, Victor, 136, 139, 223, 230

Reuther, Walter: civil rights and, 222, 227; ideology of, 66, 185, 201–03, 219–20, 223–24, 228–29; 1937 Detroit municipal elections and, 124, 128, 130, 141, 142, 143; post-World War II politics and, 174, 180, 181–82, 201–03, 218, 221, 225–31, 241; right-to-work movements and, 198–203, 208; UAW factionalism and, 137, 139, 146

right-to-work movements, 9, 196, 197–98, 199; in 1957 Indiana, 198; in 1958 Ohio, 195, 197–98, 203–07, 212; in 1978 Missouri, 195–96, 207–10; unions' opposition to, 196, 198, 200–12; voters' response to, 196, 204, 206–07,

210. *See also* labor law; open
shop; Reuther, Walter
Rising, Fred Charles, 57–58
riots, 40; 1943 Detroit riot, 146;
1967 Detroit riot, 230
Robeson, Paul, 28, 39
Rockefeller, John D., Jr., 79
Rogers, Joel, 247
Roosevelt, Eleanor, 200
Roosevelt, Franklin Delano, 36, 38,
39, 93, 121, 122, 133, 134, 144,
220. *See also* New Deal order
"Roosevelt Recession," 144–45
Roosevelt, Theodore, 34, 83, 84, 87
Rudwick, Elliot, 146
Ruggles, William, 197

SANE (National Committee for a
Sane Nuclear Policy), 221
Schlesinger, Arthur, Jr., 7
Schoemann, Peter, 182
Schultze, Charles, 245
Scrom, R. D., 59
Seidman, Joel, 122, 141
Serviceman's Readjustment Act.
See G.I. Bill
Sexton, Brendan, 217, 220, 222,
225, 226
Sherman Antitrust Act (1890),
73–74, 77
Skidmore, Thomas, 54–55
Skocpol, Theda, 71
Skoglund, Carl, 108
Skowronek, Stephen, 71
Sloop, Marvin, 209–10
Smith, Al, 38
Smith, John, 135
social democracy, 10, 25, 26, 28,
166–67, 171, 177, 180, 182, 218,
219–20, 221, 225, 226–29,
230–31; western European mod-
els of, 19, 21, 25, 31, 159–60, 161,
166, 185, 201–02, 218. *See also*

CIO; economic planning; industry
councils; workers' participation in
management
Social Security entitlements, 21–22,
37, 38
socialism and socialists, 2, 4, 5, 52,
57–58, 59, 60, 64, 65, 73, 80, 83,
84, 85, 86, 89, 91, 92, 107, 108,
111, 137, 219, 227
Socialist Party (SP), 31, 33, 61, 62,
73, 77, 90, 91–92, 109, 112,
123–24, 128, 129, 130, 134, 220
Socialist Workers Party (SWP), 104,
107, 112, 113
Southern Christian Leadership
Conference (SCLC), 221, 222,
227
Sparkman, John, 251
Springsteen, Bruce, 20
Stassen, Harold, 115
state-building, 71–72, 78, 80, 82, 83
States' Rights Party, 172
Steelworkers' Organizing Committee. *See* United Steelworkers of
America
Steiner, Ermil, 209
Stevens, Ted, 250
Stevenson, Adlai, 172
Strachan, Alan, 128, 134, 136, 140,
144
strikes, 32, 73–74, 82, 110, 125,
162; 1892 Homestead strike, 5,
56; 1904 St. Joseph, Missouri,
meatpacking strike, 108; 1911
Lawrence textile strike, 79; 1914
Ludlow massacre, 79; 1933
Hormel strike, 105; 1934 Min-
neapolis truckers' strike, 105;
1936–1937 sit-down strikes, 65,
112, 123, 132, 134, 135–36, 137;
1945–46 strike wave, 167; 1978
coal strike, 248
Studebaker Corporation, 168

Student League for Industrial Democracy (SLID), 220
Student Non-Violent Coordinating Committee (SNCC), 221
Students for a Democratic Society (SDS), 221, 223, 227
suburbanization, 41–42
Sugar, Maurice, 128, 130, 135, 141, 142, 143
Sultan, Paul, 207
Sutherland, George, 78
syndicalism and syndicalists, 107, 108, 111, 125

Taft, William Howard, 61, 78, 94
Taft-Hartley Act (1947), 10, 167–68, 171, 172, 177, 240, 241, 242, 244; Case Bill and, 167
tax policy, 41, 45 n.6, 46 n.9; in cities, 42; reform of, 80; single tax, 52, 69 n.23, 79
technological change, 20, 28–29, 65, 161, 173, 180, 219, 221
Thal, Ed, 124, 126
Thomas, R. J., 128, 140, 142
Thompson, E. P., 51
Thompson, Frank, Jr., 246
timber workers, 113
Tomlins, Christopher, 240
Tower, John, 249
Townley, A. C., 105
Trade Union Leadership Council (TULC), 181
Travis, Bob, 137
Trotskyism and Trotskyists, 107, 108, 109, 111, 112, 113, 114
Truman, Harry, 39, 167, 171, 209, 221
Tysee, G. John, 248

Udall, Stuart, 241
unemployment, 159; policies on, 21, 37, 38, 80, 129

Union Party, 38
United Automobile Workers (UAW): Chrysler Corporation and, 168; civil rights and, 28, 146, 181, 220, 221, 222–23, 225–28; conflicts with AFL and AFL-CIO, 124–27, 134, 207, 244–45; contractual gains of, 169; Democratic Party and, 220, 221, 226, 244; factionalism within, 136–40, 144, 145, 146, 184; Ford Motor Company and, 143–44; General Motors and, 65, 123, 135, 137, 168; Great Society and, 217–19, 224–31, 241; Independent Union of All Workers and, 113; in Indiana, 198; Local 3 (Hamtramck, Mich.), 128, 132; Local 6 (Detroit, Mich.), 128; Local 155 (Detroit, Mich.), 125, 143; Local 156 (Flint, Mich.), 125; Local 157 (Detroit, Mich.), 143; Local 174 (Detroit, Mich.), 128, 143; members' voting patterns, 135, 140–44, 220, 230, 236 n.26; 1937 Detroit municipal elections and, 7–8, 122–45; 1943 Detroit municipal elections and, 82; 1945 Detroit municipal elections and, 28, 146–47; organizing drives, 125, 135, 138; Political Action Committee (PAC) of, 128, 140; skilled workers in, 143; Studebaker and, 168
United Labor Committee (ULC), 207, 209, 210
United Mine Workers (UMW), 73, 85, 86, 184, 207; District 50, 114
United Organized Labor Committee of Ohio (UOLO), 203–04
United Packinghouse Workers of America, 103, 109, 113. *See also* meat packers

U.S. Chamber of Commerce, 197,
246, 247, 248, 250; local
branches, 112, 113, 197
U.S. Congress, 31–32, 39, 40, 165,
174, 178, 179, 181, 183; investigations by, 9, 82, 198; labor law
reform and, 30, 181, 243, 246,
247, 248–51; liberal Democrats
in, 177
U.S. constitution, 30–31
U.S. Department of Housing and
Urban Development (HUD), 229
U.S. Department of Labor, 76, 248,
249
U.S. Supreme Court, 32, 36, 74, 77,
83, 165, 186, 240
United Steelworkers of America
(USWA), 112, 113, 169, 184, 217.
See also iron- and steelworkers
urban renewal. *See* Model Cities
Act

Veblen, Thorstein, 219
Vietnam War, 41, 230
Voorhees, Joe, 108–09
Voting Rights Act (1965), 181, 227

Wagner, Robert, 37
Wagner Act. *See* National Labor Re-
lations Act
Walden, A. J., 132
Walker, John, 91–92, 93
Wallace, George, 241
Walsh, Frank, 6, 72–73, 78–82, 83,
84, 85–87, 88, 89, 91, 92, 93, 94,
95
Walsh, Joe, 200
War on Poverty. *See* Great Society
Ward, Charley, 105, 117 n.8
Weaver, Robert, 229
Weightman, Philip, 195, 204,
205–06, 212
Weinberg, Nat, 222

welfare state, 1, 3, 10, 20, 21, 27,
28, 37, 38, 159, 171, 174, 199,
200, 201, 218, 224, 225; racializ-
ing of, 41
West, George, 86
White, John, 81
white workers, 81, 95, 208; mid-
western-born, 140; racial conflict
and, 40–41, 42, 145–47, 129, 141,
182, 230; southern-born, 123,
132, 137, 140; voting patterns of,
28, 146–47, 177
Wilentz, Sean, 54
Williams, Harrison, 246
Wilson, William B., 76, 88
Wilson, Woodrow, 6, 71, 72, 76, 77,
78, 82, 83–85, 86, 87, 88, 89, 90,
91, 93, 94
Winstanley, Gerrard, 53
Wise, Rabbi Stephen, 90
women, 143, 174; workers, 73, 80,
89, 93, 111, 181; voting patterns
of, 88
women's movement, 3, 29, 41, 173,
183; nineteenth amendment
(1920) and, 30
Women's Trade Union League
(WTUL), 83, 88
Wood, Gordon, 54
workers' participation in management, 8, 27, 160, 162, 163,
166–67, 184, 185, 186, 218,
219–20. *See also* industry councils; social democracy
working class: consciousness of, 2,
7–8, 51, 64–65, 66, 122, 134,
160–61, 166, 169, 172, 185, 220;
conservatism of, 2, 141; consumerism and, 3, 37, 65–66,
172, 173; divisions within, 4,
5–6, 8, 34, 49 n.36, 52, 63, 65,
66, 81, 93, 115, 122–23, 127,
172–73; higher education and,

24; skilled segment of, 5–6, 23, 53, 55, 63, 73, 81, 95, 180, 181, 182, 196; unity of, 35, 39, 44, 93, 107, 122, 123–24, 185–86, 211–12; unskilled segment of, 5, 63, 73; voting patterns of, 19, 31–32, 38, 39, 44 n.1, 72, 87, 89, 91, 115, 164, 165, 170, 174–76, 184, 196, 198, 206–07, 210, 211–12
workmen's compensation, 83

World War I, 62–63, 88, 90, 91, 93–94
World War II, 22, 145, 161, 166, 167; and postwar conversion, 167

Yohe, William F., 59

Zaremba, John, 130
Zorinsky, Edward, 251
Zuk, Mary, 142, 154 n.50

DATE DUE
